Practical Linux System Administration

A Guide to Installation, Configuration, and Management

Kenneth Hess

Beijing · Boston · Farnham · Sebastopol · Tokyo

Practical Linux System Administration

by Kenneth Hess

Published by O'Reilly Media, Inc., 1005 Gravenstein Highway North, Sebastopol, CA 95472.

O'Reilly books may be purchased for educational, business, or sales promotional use. Online editions are also available for most titles (*https://oreilly.com*). For more information, contact our corporate/institutional sales department: 800-998-9938 or *corporate@oreilly.com*.

Acquisitions Editor: John Devins	**Indexer:** Ellen Troutman-Zaig
Development Editor: Jeff Bleiel	**Interior Designer:** David Futato
Production Editor: Gregory Hyman	**Cover Designer:** Karen Montgomery
Copyeditor: Justin Billing	**Illustrator:** Kate Dullea
Proofreader: Tim Stewart	

April 2023:   First Edition

Revision History for the First Edition

2023-04-18:   First Release

See *https://oreilly.com/catalog/errata.csp?isbn=9781098109035* for release details.

978-1-098-10903-5

[LSI]

Table of Contents

Preface

I love to teach. Some of my earliest memories are of teaching other kids to do something—play chess, paint, or build forts for action figures. I taught other students in high school and college. Teaching is something I do naturally. When I write articles, whitepapers, or books, I adopt the role of a teacher. I place the reader in a classroom and teach them tasks or concepts, such as changing permissions on a file or adding a new user to a system. This is how my mind works. This book, like almost everything I write, is a manifestation of that almost innate desire to teach, pass on some knowledge, and plant a seed of curiosity that grows, blossoms, and spreads to others. I hope you find inspiration in this book that leads you to do the same.

Who Should Read This Book

This book is for anyone who wants to explore Linux for the first time as a system administrator or for someone who wants to transition to such a role for work or as a serious hobby. It's also meant for those preparing to take certification exams requiring some Linux knowledge.

Why I Wrote This Book

I wrote this book to fill existing knowledge gaps for system administrators. I would have purchased this book for myself early in my career and kept it at my desk for reference. Sure, there's plenty of technical information in the book, as you might expect, but there's also career guidance and some coverage of the nontechnical aspects of being a system administrator.

Navigating This Book

This book is organized as follows:

- Chapter 1 introduces you to Linux via installation and initial setup.
- Chapter 2 explores the command-line interface, essential to working with Linux as a system administrator.
- Chapter 3 demonstrates how to customize the user experience and introduces you to the global system configuration files.
- Chapter 4 focuses on user management.
- Chapter 5 is an overview of Linux networking.
- Chapter 6 is a how-to for software management.
- Chapter 7 deals with storage concepts.
- Chapter 8 is a discussion of maintaining system health.
- Chapter 9 provides you with some tools for monitoring your system.
- Chapter 10 explores scripting and automation.
- Chapter 11 covers Windows interoperability using the Samba suite.
- Chapter 12 teaches some practical troubleshooting techniques.
- Chapter 13 helps you secure your system.
- Chapter 14 summarizes educational opportunities you should explore to keep yourself up-to-date and sharpen your skills.
- Chapter 15 is advice to help you keep your career moving forward.

Conventions Used in This Book

The following typographical conventions are used in this book:

Italic
> Indicates new terms, URLs, email addresses, filenames, and file extensions.

`Constant width`
> Used for program listings, as well as within paragraphs to refer to program elements such as variable or function names, databases, data types, environment variables, statements, and keywords.

`Constant width italic`
> Shows text that should be replaced with user-supplied values or by values determined by context.

This element signifies a tip or suggestion.

 This element signifies a general note.

 This element indicates a warning or caution.

Using Code Examples

Supplemental material (code examples, exercises, etc.) is available for download at *https://oreil.ly/practical-linux-system-admin-code*.

If you have a technical question or a problem using the code examples, please send email to *bookquestions@oreilly.com*.

This book is here to help you get your job done. In general, if example code is offered with this book, you may use it in your programs and documentation. You do not need to contact us for permission unless you're reproducing a significant portion of the code. For example, writing a program that uses several chunks of code from this book does not require permission. Selling or distributing examples from O'Reilly books does require permission. Answering a question by citing this book and quoting example code does not require permission. Incorporating a significant amount of example code from this book into your product's documentation does require permission.

We appreciate, but generally do not require, attribution. An attribution usually includes the title, author, publisher, and ISBN. For example: "*Practical Linux System Administration* by Kenneth Hess (O'Reilly). Copyright 2023 Hess Media and Consulting, LLC, 978-1-098-10903-5."

If you feel your use of code examples falls outside fair use or the permission given above, feel free to contact us at *permissions@oreilly.com*.

O'Reilly Online Learning

 For more than 40 years, *O'Reilly Media* has provided technology and business training, knowledge, and insight to help companies succeed.

Our unique network of experts and innovators share their knowledge and expertise through books, articles, and our online learning platform. O'Reilly's online learning platform gives you on-demand access to live training courses, in-depth learning paths, interactive coding environments, and a vast collection of text and video from O'Reilly and 200+ other publishers. For more information, visit *https://oreilly.com*.

How to Contact Us

Please address comments and questions concerning this book to the publisher:

O'Reilly Media, Inc.
1005 Gravenstein Highway North
Sebastopol, CA 95472
800-998-9938 (in the United States or Canada)
707-829-0515 (international or local)
707-829-0104 (fax)

We have a web page for this book, where we list errata, examples, and any additional information. You can access this page at *https://oreil.ly/practical-linux-system-admin*.

Email *bookquestions@oreilly.com* to comment or ask technical questions about this book.

For news and information about our books and courses, visit *https://oreilly.com*.

Find us on LinkedIn: *https://linkedin.com/company/oreilly-media*

Follow us on Twitter: *https://twitter.com/oreillymedia*

Watch us on YouTube: *https://www.youtube.com/oreillymedia*

Acknowledgments

Being a Linux system administrator requires sacrifices from you and your family. I've often stated that a sysadmin's whole family works for a company. This might be true for any job you have, but it seems especially relevant for system administrators. Linux system administration is a great career choice, but take time for yourself, your spouse, and your children. Remember that you don't live to work; you work to live. You can't get missed moments back—the milestones, events, and celebrations that create an existence that will be remembered fondly.

Thank you to my wife, Melissa, who always supports my creative pursuits.

I'd also like to thank the following people who helped make this book possible:

- John Devins, O'Reilly acquisitions editor
- Jeff Bleiel, O'Reilly development editor
- Gregory Hyman, O'Reilly production editor
- Technical reviewers Daniel Barrett and Adam McPartlan

## CHAPTER 1

Getting Started with Linux

Linux system administration means different things to different people. Administration, for this book, means the daily actions that a Linux system administrator (sysadmin) must take to manage and support users, maintain system health, implement best practices for security, install software, and perform housekeeping tasks. This chapter covers Linux installation, initial setup, and system exploration using simple shell commands.

You'll spend a significant portion of your time at the command line, also known as the command-line interface (CLI). Linux system administrators rarely install or use GUIs on their supported server systems. This chapter introduces you to the CLI and some simple commands to navigate the filesystem, locate important files, and familiarize yourself with the Linux CLI.

Installing Linux

One of the first things every Linux system administrator learns is how to install Linux. There's no single *correct* way to install Linux, but a few guidelines and suggestions will make your life easier as your users' needs change.

While this section won't go into detailed step-by-step instructions on installing Linux, the basic steps are outlined here. For most junior-level sysadmins, system installation generally occurs via automated means such as Kickstart or another enterprise-level delivery system.

Preparing Your System for Linux

If this is your first time installing Linux, I suggest that you install it into a virtual machine (VM). That way, you don't have to dedicate an entire piece of hardware to a learning system and you won't potentially render your system inoperable by attempting to install Linux in parallel to your current system, creating a multiboot computer. (Setting up multibooting is a more advanced concept and is beyond the scope of this book.)

If you don't already have it installed, a good place to start with virtualization is to download and install the latest version of VirtualBox (*https://oreil.ly/X4dKu*). Virtual-Box is an application that allows your current computer to act as a VM host system where you may install virtual guests, such as Linux, into a separate, functioning computer system. VirtualBox runs on various host operating systems (OSs) and supports various guest operating systems, including Linux. The host OS and guest OS can be different from one another. Your computer (host OS) can be a Windows, Mac, or Linux-based system but have guest Linux systems installed on it as VirtualBox VMs.

Downloading and Installing Linux

Next, you'll need to select a Linux distribution (distro) to install so that you can practice issuing commands, changing configurations, rebooting, installing software, creating users, and so on. I suggest you select a Linux distro based on the one your current employer uses. If your company doesn't use Linux yet or you're not employed in a system administrator role, then select from one of the following popular distributions:

Debian (https://oreil.ly/hxbxl)
Debian is a top-level distribution from which many other distributions are derived. Debian is community-supported, open source, and free.

OpenSUSE (https://oreil.ly/hsBY4)
OpenSUSE is a community-supported, top-level distribution with many faithful followers worldwide. Its commercial version, SUSE Linux Enterprise, has widespread adoption.

Red Hat Enterprise Linux (https://oreil.ly/0nvvM)
Red Hat is a commercially supported Linux distro that enjoys worldwide enterprise adoption and is now owned by IBM.

Ubuntu (https://oreil.ly/zoK4o)
Ubuntu is very popular and has both (Debian-derived) community and commercially supported distributions. Ubuntu also offers ready-made VirtualBox (and other) VMs to help you get a quick start.

The downloaded ISO file is a bootable Linux image. You don't have to do anything to it if you use it to create a VM. A VM will boot from the ISO image and begin the installation process. After configuring your VM in VirtualBox, select Settings from the Oracle VM VirtualBox Manager, as shown in Figure 1-1.

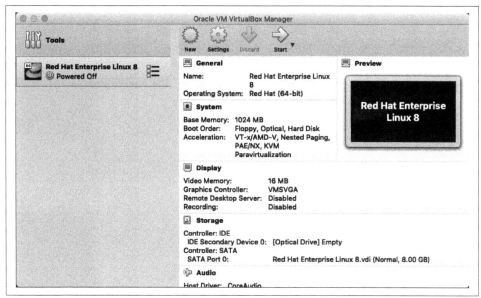

Figure 1-1. The Oracle VM VirtualBox Manager application and a configured virtual machine

Then, select Storage, as shown in Figure 1-2.

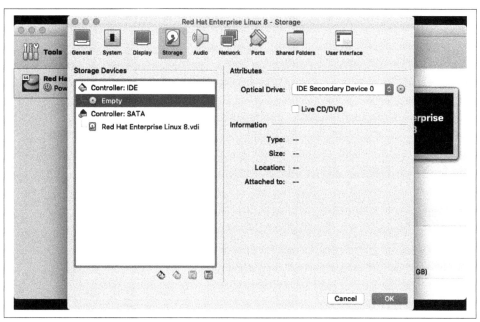

Figure 1-2. Virtual machine settings with Storage settings selected

Select the empty optical disk drive under the IDE controller in the Storage Devices pane and then select the optical disk icon in the Attributes pane to browse for your ISO image file. Figure 1-3 shows several ISO files available in this menu.

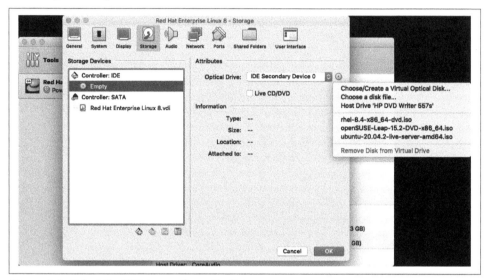

Figure 1-3. Select the ISO image from the list

Once you've selected your ISO image, click OK to proceed. When you start your VM, it will boot from this ISO image to begin installation onto your VM's virtual disk.

When your system boots, you can accept the default settings. If you have experience installing Linux, you can change the default settings to suit your needs. Create a user account when prompted to do so. If your distribution prompts you to give the root account a password, do so. You must remember this password because, without it, you'll have to reinstall your Linux VM or try to recover it. Installing Linux can take several minutes, and a reboot is required at the end of the installation process.

Getting to Know Your New Linux System

After installation, the first thing you need to do is log in using the username and password that you created during installation. You're placed into your home directory inside a shell (or operating environment) upon login. Your home directory (/home) is a subdirectory of the / directory. The Linux filesystem is a hierarchical filesystem, similar to Microsoft Windows. At the top level, there is the root directory, which is represented by the / symbol. Windows uses a drive letter, such as C:, for the root directory. On Windows, you can have many drive letters with their own root levels, such as C:, D:, E:, and so on. In Linux, there is only one root directory, /. All other directories are subdirectories of the root directory. The following directory tree illustrates the Linux root directory and its subdirectories:

```
/
|- bin
|- dev
|- etc
|- home
|- lib
|- media
|- mnt
|- opt
|- proc
|- root
|- run
|- sbin
|- srv
|- sys
|- tmp
|- usr
└ var
```

Note that there are only directories under the / (root) filesystem and no individual files, although some Linux distributions have a few symbolically linked files in /. All files are kept in directories. You'll explore many of these subdirectories throughout the rest of the book. Table 1-1 provides a brief overview of the files and information in each directory.

Table 1-1. The Linux filesystem

Directory	Description
/	The root filesystem only contains other directories but no individual files.
/bin	The binaries directory contains executable files. Points to /usr/bin.
/dev	The device directory contains device files to address peripherals.
/etc	Contains system configuration files for users and services.
/home	Users' home directories.
/lib	System libraries files. Points to /usr/lib.
/media	Directory for mounting media such as USB drives or DVD disks.
/mnt	The mount directory for mounting remote filesystems.
/opt	Directory in which third-party software is installed.
/proc	A virtual filesystem that tracks system processes.
/root	The root user's home directory.
/run	Variable and volatile runtime data.
/sbin	System binary (executable) files.
/srv	Might contain data from system services.
/sys	Contains kernel information.
/tmp	Directory for storing session information and temporary files.

Directory	Description
/usr	Programs and libraries for users and user-related programs.
/var	Variable files such as logs, spools, and queues.

System files are protected from user modification. Only the root (administrative) user can modify system configuration files and settings. Users generally have write access only to their own home directories, the */tmp* directory, and shared directories specifically created and modified by the administrator.

In the next section, you learn how to interact with your new Linux system at the command line.

Learning the CLI

The *command-line interface,* or CLI, is how most system administrators interact with their Linux systems because server systems don't typically have a graphical interface. In Microsoft Windows terminology, a CLI-only system, such as a Linux server, would be equivalent to a Windows Server Core system where you only have access to command-line utilities.

As the name suggests, you interact with the Linux system using commands that you enter with a keyboard or *standard input* (stdin). The source from stdin can also be file redirection, programs, and other sources, but in the context of this book, stdin refers to keyboard input unless otherwise noted. Many commands are informational and display data about the system or system activities to the screen or *standard output* (stdout). Sometimes you'll receive an error from the system known as standard error (stderr). You'll see the full and abbreviated versions of these terms used interchangeably throughout this text and in other Linux-related documentation that you'll find elsewhere.

You must learn a few commands to interact successfully with the filesystem. By "learn," I mean commit to memory rather than looking them up online. There are only a few commands like this, and there are a few options that you should also commit to memory so that your interaction with the system becomes natural and efficient. Don't worry about harming the system with any command I cover—I'll warn you when a command should be used carefully.

There are a few things you need to know before jumping into issuing commands. The first is that Linux doesn't use file extensions. This means that the file *filename.exe* has no more meaning to Linux than the file *Financial_Report.txt* or *Résumé.doc.* They are all files and might not be executable or text files. In Linux, you can name a file almost anything you want to (there are a few limitations), but use whitespace in filenames with caution because doing so requires you to use quotation marks around the filename.

The second thing to know about Linux is that filenames are case-sensitive. In other words, *filename.txt* and *filename.TXT* are two different files. I will prove this later in the chapter. For now, take my word for it. The third thing to know is that a file's permission determines whether you can execute the file, edit the file, or even look at the file's contents. Fourth, every Linux location is uniquely named by its path from the root (/) directory. For example, if you mention the password file in Linux, it's shown as */etc/passwd*. This is known as the *absolute* path and is the standard convention for speaking about or referring to files on the system. Fifth, Linux assumes you know what you want to do and that you've spelled everything correctly when you issue a command, so be careful, because some actions are irreversible.

Finally, Linux (like Unix, or more generally "*nix" systems) is not "chatty" like the Windows operating systems are. Linux systems, for example, don't prompt you with an "Are you sure?" message when you remove (delete) files. Again, the Linux system assumes you want to execute the command you issue if you correctly spell all parts of the command. Spelling counts at the Linux command line.

Navigating the Linux filesystem means exploring the various system directories, learning to return to your home directory, and listing directory contents differently. If you're a Windows user and you've worked at the Command Prompt (cmd) or PowerShell prompt (PS) on that platform, then the Linux command line will be familiar to you.

The short list of commands in the following sections will acquaint you with the Linux filesystem, files, and the contents of your home directory.

pwd

The pwd (print working directory) command displays where you are on the filesystem. If you type the pwd command now, followed by the Enter key, the command responds with /home/*your_login_name*. Always ensure that you press the Enter key after each command so that you can receive a response:

```
$ pwd
/home/student1
```

The $ is your shell prompt that shows you're logged into the system as a user. You'll use this command more later in the chapter.

cd

The cd (change directory, or current directory) command places you into a new directory, returns you to your home directory, and moves you to a higher level or a subdirectory. The cd command is analogous to the Windows cd command:

```
$ cd /etc
$ pwd
/etc
```

Simply entering cd returns you to your home directory regardless of where you are on the filesystem, as demonstrated here:

```
$ pwd
/etc
$ cd
$ pwd
/home/student1
```

When you cd to a directory, use its absolute path:

```
$ cd /usr/bin
```

You can cd to a subdirectory without the absolute path if you're currently in the parent directory:

```
$ cd
$ pwd
/home/student1
$ cd /usr
$ cd bin
$ pwd
/usr/bin
```

The cd command is one that you'll use every time that you connect to a Linux system.

ls

The ls (list) command displays a list of files and directories within the location you specify. If you don't specify a location, ls displays the list of files and directories in your current directory:

```
$ cd
$ pwd
$ /home/student1
$ ls
```

You have no visible files in your home directory yet because you haven't created any and none exist by default. However, you can list files from other directories by specifying the absolute path to the directory list you wish to see. There are too many files to list here in the /usr/bin directory, so I've truncated it to these few:

```
$ ls /usr/bin
a2x          getcifsacl       p11-kit           snmpping
a2x.py       getconf          pack200           snmpps
ac           getent           package-cleanup   snmpset
...
```

There are files in your home directory, but they're hidden because of the way they're named. Files that begin with a period (.) are hidden from a regular ls command. To see these files, you must use a command option to allow you to see all files:

```
$ ls -a
.  ..  .bash_history  .bash_logout  .bash_profile  .bashrc  .gnupg  .zshrc
```

Your listing might vary slightly from this, but understand that all directories and files whose names begin with a period are hidden from standard file lists using the ls command with no options. You can cd into hidden directories or list files within them:

```
$ ls .gnupg
private-keys-v1.d  pubring.kbx
```

The ls command is one you'll use every time you log into your Linux system and is certainly one that you want to commit to memory. I will use the ls command throughout this book and introduce you to many more options for it along the way. Now that you've learned the basics of filesystem navigation, it's time to cover rebooting and shutting down your system.

Starting, Rebooting, and Shutting Down a Linux System

The most basic tasks facing any Linux sysadmin are starting, restarting, and shutting down a system. If you have computer experience, you know that powering off a system without issuing a shutdown command is bad. It's bad because doing so can, for example, corrupt open files, leave open files in an "open" state, disrupt running services, and cause problems with database transaction logs, possibly resulting in data loss.

Proper knowledge of how to start, restart, and shut down a system is of great value to sysadmins.

Starting a System

For physical systems, you press the power button and release it to start a system. This begins the power-on self-test (POST) and boot process. Watching the console during boot is important because the system notifies you and logs any issues as it starts up. Watch the screen for any errors or anomalies along the way. (The worst message you can experience on boot is a "kernel panic," which will be covered later in the book.) Hopefully, all is well with your system, and the process ends with a login prompt.

The startup process is quite short but can identify systemic problems such as memory, disk, filesystem, and network issues. I'll cover troubleshooting in a later chapter, but be aware now that you should watch the boot process carefully, noting any problems for later investigation.

Restarting a System

Restarting or rebooting a system is a standard sysadmin practice. Although you might read or hear the contrary, there's nothing wrong with rebooting your system. You should do so regularly for all of the reasons stated in the previous section. Restarting a system clears memory, refreshes connections, and ensures the system is healthy. A good reboot can cure certain nagging problems, such as an application that drains your system's memory, but only temporarily.

Any issues resolved with a reboot should be investigated more thoroughly after the system is up and stable. Restarting a system allows you to troubleshoot before application problems, logging problems, or network problems place the system back into a state when it requires another reboot.

Shutting Down a System

Shutting down means issuing a command that gently and appropriately closes all programs and eventually powers off the system. This gentle shutdown also warns shell users that the system is going down so that everyone can save their work and log off.

System shutdown should be reserved for hardware maintenance, relocation, or decommissioning. Some enterprise policies require that systems go through a full shutdown once a year to identify hardware issues that might not manifest themselves except through a complete system failure. Technicians and sysadmins usually take this opportunity to perform hardware maintenance or hardware checks at the same time.

Summary

This first chapter got you up and running with a live Linux system, covered some Linux basics, explored a few essential commands, and instructed you on the how and why of system startup, rebooting, and shutdown. In Chapter 2, you'll learn more about using the CLI and how to use commands to create, remove, and modify files. You will also learn about Linux permissions, how to set and interpret them, and how to set a global default permission for users.

Working with Permissions and Privileged Accounts

For sysadmins, the CLI is home. Typing at the keyboard is standard fare. You'll need to become comfortable with the command line, its idiosyncrasies, and its shortcuts— yes, there are command-line shortcuts. There's a lot to learn about Linux at the command line. There are dozens of commands, each with dozens of options. Sure, you'll only use a handful of commands and a limited number of options for each command, but you need to know how to find the options you need and how to use them when you need to.

The true power of the CLI is in its ease of use. The CLI was the first interface that users and programmers had with which to address their operating environments. The fact that the CLI is still in use some 50 years later is a testament to its power and usefulness to the sysadmin and user alike. This chapter teaches you to work at the command line as a regular user and as a root user. You also learn to set and modify file permissions and the effects that those permissions have on files.

Working as a Regular User

There are two user types on a Linux system: regular users and a root, or administrator, user. Regular users each receive their own home directory and somewhat limited system use. The root user also has a home directory (*/root*). Regular users have almost unlimited power in their own home directories to create, modify, remove, and manipulate files but have almost no power outside of that single location. Many system commands are available to regular users. In contrast, other commands are restricted to those granted limited root user access through the sudo command or direct access to the root user account.

The general and most security-conscious rule is that you should always work as a regular user unless some task requires privileged (root user) access, which is covered in the next section.

Working as the Root User

The root user is the all-powerful account on any Linux system. The root user can create, edit, move, or remove any file on the system. The root user can reboot, change runlevels, and shut down the system. There are three methods of becoming the root user:

- Logging in as the root user
- Using the su (substitute user) command
- Using the sudo command

Logging in as Root

On some Linux distributions, you can directly log in as the root user on a system via SSH across the network or interactively at the console. Some Linux distributions prevent SSH root logins by default, while others leave it up to the administrators to decide. It's not recommended to SSH to a system and login as root. The primary reason is that if you allow across-the-network root access to a system, then it's possible that malicious actors can attempt to brute force a root login. You don't want this to happen. Later in the book, I'll show you how to prevent SSH root logins, if not already disabled, on your distribution.

You shouldn't directly log in as root at the console because doing so prevents system logging from recording who has logged in and become root. Recording who uses the root user account is important because when something goes wrong, you want to know which administrator performed the actions. This record-keeping's purpose is not to lay blame. Still, it is necessary to meet some regulatory requirements and to correct the actions of a system administrator who needs a teachable moment or some advanced training. The next two options we discuss are better, safer ways to become the root user.

Using the su Command

One of the appropriate methods of becoming the root user is to use the su (substitute user) command. The caveat with using su is that the user must know the root user password. If administrative users know the root password, it's difficult to prevent those same administrators from directly logging in as root. Using the su command to become root is acceptable, but only if the root password changes after each use. In larger enterprises, security groups maintain root passwords, and system administrators can check out the root password temporarily to perform maintenance.

The root user may su to any other user account on the system without knowing the user's password. This power allows administrators to log in as, or become, any user for troubleshooting purposes because it's often difficult for users to accurately describe problems they're experiencing. It also prevents a user from revealing their password to an administrator, which should force the user to change their password.

To su to another account is a simple procedure. Issue the su command and the user account you wish to su to. For this example, I use the full prompt rather than just the $ to demonstrate the user change:

```
[bjones@server1] $ su root
Password:
#
```

The # prompt informs you that you are now logged in as the root user. In this book, the user prompt is $ and the root is #, to distinguish a standard user's prompt from the root user's. Any command you issue now is done with root privilege, which means that you must be careful because there are no restrictions on the account.

The better method of using su is using the su - command because the - means that you also want to take on the root user's full environment rather than just the account privilege. The display is much too long to show here, but if you issue the env command, you'll see the original user's environment variables rather than root's:

```
# env
```

Use the exit command to return to the original user account, as shown here:

```
# exit
[bjones@server1] $
```

And now issue the su command with the - option. You don't have to specify root in this command because the default is root:

```
[bjones@server1] $ su -
Password:
# env
```

The root user's environment variables are now displayed. Using the su - command is the equivalent of logging into the console as the root user. Any user may su to any other user account, which requires one to know the other user's password:

```
[bjones@server1] $ su cdavis
Password:
[cdavis@server1] $
```

Using the sudo Command

The best method to obtain root access is to use the "substitute user do" or "execute a command as another user" (sudo) command. The sudo command allows an appropriately configured user account to issue individual commands as the root user. The sudo command must precede each command issued. On first use, the sudo command requires that the *sudoer* (a user account configured for sudo use) supply their own password, as shown in the following code listing. Knowledge of the root password isn't required.

```
$ sudo env
[sudo] password for bjones:
bjones is not in the sudoers file.  This incident will be reported.
[bjones@server1 ~]$
```

The warning that the user is not in the *sudoers* file means that the user account, bjones, is not configured in the */etc/sudoers* file. In the next section, I demonstrate how to set up a user to be a sudoer.

 The sudo command, the */etc/sudoers* file, and the sudoer user label are interesting because they have their own unique pronunciations. The accepted pronunciation for sudo is "soodoo" and sudoer is "soodooer." Some sysadmins pronounce them as "soodoe" and "soodoe-ers," but no one takes issue with either pronunciation.

Creating a Sudoer

You must have root user access to edit the */etc/sudoers* file and to use the visudo utility, whose only purpose is to edit the */etc/sudoers* file. You shouldn't edit it directly with vi, Emacs, or any other text editor. To edit the */etc/sudoers* file, issue the visudo command as root with no options:

```
# visudo
```

The */etc/sudoers* file is a simple text file describing users, groups, and commands that can work with root or other user privileges. You can create a sudoer with very restrictive permissions (i.e., to run a single command as root) or permissive: run any command as root without entering a password to do so. I prefer to configure a mixture of the two by creating sudoers who can run any command as root but must supply their password.

Hundreds of possible configuration scenarios exist for the */etc/sudoers* file and sudoers. It's out of the scope of this book to explore more than what's given here as examples. In this first example, I demonstrate how I set up my user account to use sudo. My settings require me to enter my password when using sudo:

```
## Allow root to run any commands anywhere
root    ALL=(ALL)       ALL
khess   ALL=(ALL)       ALL
```

I copy the root user's setting and insert my user account in its place. The setting takes effect immediately. Setting up a user account to use sudo without issuing a password is not recommended. Using a password when issuing a command is an attempt to make it more difficult to make mistakes while wielding root privilege. The same can be said of the sudo command itself. The theory is that if an administrator has to issue the sudo command, they will make fewer mistakes as root because it requires them to think specifically about their command action and its results.

Reading and Modifying Permissions

This section teaches you how to read and modify file permissions. You must learn file permissions to set and modify access to files and directories appropriately. Knowing file permissions helps troubleshoot when users can't access a file or directory.

File permissions are simple but central to Linux security. Their simplicity can make them susceptible to neglect and misconfiguration. Frustrated sysadmins sometimes loosen permissions to solve a problem but never return to the issue or reset the permissions to their proper settings.

Read, Write, and Execute

The three Linux file permissions or modes are read (r), write (w), and execute (x):

Read
> View a file or list directory contents.

Write
> Create and modify a file or copy, move, and create files in a directory.

Execute
> Execute/run a file or cd into a directory.

As mentioned in Chapter 1, a file's name does not determine whether it's executable, as is the case for MS Windows (*.exe* files, etc.). A Linux file is executable or not based on its permissions.

Using the rwx designations in permissions is known as *symbolic mode*. The symbolic mode is one of two methods of identifying permissions. The other is the numeric mode, which assigns values to each of the rwx permissions.

Numerical Permission Values

Each of the permission modes has its own assigned numerical value. This shortcut method makes setting permissions easier for sysadmins.

The read permission has a value of 4, write has a value of 2, and execute has a value of 1. Permission values can range from 0 to 7. A zero permission value means no permission. Table 2-1 summarizes this idea.

Table 2-1. Numerical permission values

Permission mode	Numerical value
Read	4
Write	2
Execute	1
None	0

In the next section, you will find out how these permissions work together with group permissions to create a simple but complete file security system.

Group Permissions

Four file permissions apply to a user's group: user, group, others, and all. The "all" group includes user, group, and others. It is a shorthand method of globally assigning permissions to a file or directory. Each group has a shorthand designation as well, as shown in Table 2-2.

Table 2-2. Group permissions

Permission group	Value
User	u
Group	g
Other	o
All	a

Users and sysadmins may set permissions on files for each group individually or all groups simultaneously. Each Linux file and directory is assigned read, write, and execute permissions for each group. The next section ties all of the permissions settings together for you.

Bringing Permissions into Focus

In this subsection, I'll create a simple but complete file security system that shows how all the permissions we've discussed work together. The examples in this section will use the file *file.txt*. If you want to follow along with the example, issue the following command to set up your file:

```
$ touch file.txt
```

This command creates an empty file named *file.txt* for you. Next, issue the `ls` command with the `-l` (long) option to see file permissions:

```
$ ls -l
-rw-rw-r--. 1 khess khess 0 Jun 19 17:35 file.txt
```

Figure 2-1 illustrates the positions and their designations (in bold). The first position is for special file types, such as directories with a d in that position (`dr-xr-xr-w`). Regular files have a - (`-rw-rw-rw-`) to show that they're not directories or other special files. The next nine positions are user, group, and other permissions locations. The first "triad," or three positions, are for the user, the second for group, and the final three are for other users.

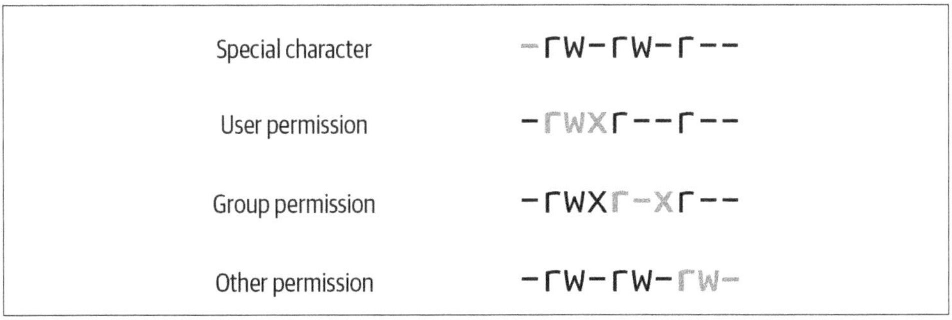

Special character	−ⲅw−ⲅw−ⲅ−−
User permission	−ⲅwxⲅ−−ⲅ−−
Group permission	−ⲅwxⲅ−xⲅ−−
Other permission	−ⲅw−ⲅw−ⲅw−

Figure 2-1. Special character position and user, group, and other permission locations

Figure 2-2 shows the numerical permissions for each listing and then an explicit label for the user (u), group (g), and other (o) triads.

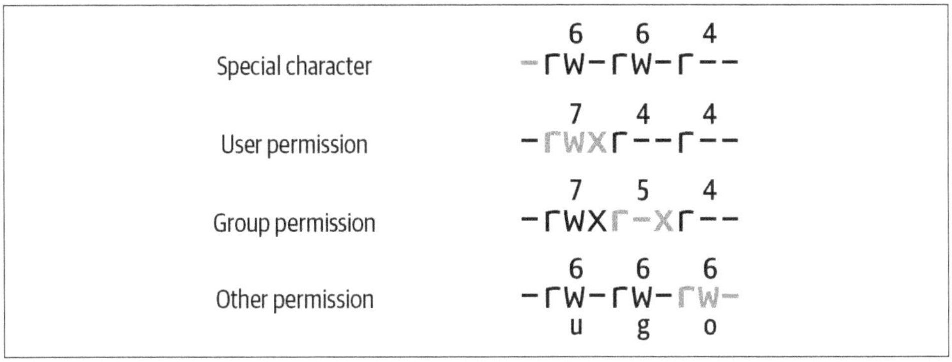

Special character	6 6 4 −ⲅw−ⲅw−ⲅ−−
User permission	7 4 4 −ⲅwxⲅ−−ⲅ−−
Group permission	7 5 4 −ⲅwxⲅ−xⲅ−−
Other permission	6 6 6 −ⲅw−ⲅw−ⲅw− u g o

Figure 2-2. Numerical permission values and user, group, and other (ugo) designations

As shown in Figure 2-2, numerical permissions are additive for each triad to create a permission profile for a file. For example, a file with `-rw-rw-r--` permissions has a numeric permission value of 664. The read permission has a value of 4 added to the value of the write permission, which is 2, which equals 6. All three possible permissions, `rwx`, yield a value of 7.

If a file has permission equal to 750, the rwx representation is `-rwxr-x---`. This means that others outside the designated user and group have no permission for the file.

The *other* group is often referred to as *world*. For example, if permissions for a file are `-rw-rw-r--`, this file is referred to as *world readable* rather than as *other readable*. Permissions for the "other" group are especially sensitive because allowing write or execute permissions to files and directories to others (the world) can be a security risk.

Next, you'll learn how to set and change file permissions using multiple methods.

Changing File Permissions

Setting and changing file permissions or *modes* is a common system administrator task. Each file on the filesystem has permissions that allow or deny access to users, groups, and others. To change file permissions, you use the `chmod` (change mode) command. You can set or modify permissions with the `chmod` command in multiple ways. You don't have to be consistent. You can use `chmod` with either numeric designations or the rwx and ugo designations, but you can't combine the two in the same command. I demonstrate several possibilities and practical examples in the following sections.

Some sysadmins find the symbolic (rwx and ugo) method easier to grasp than the numeric (0, 1, 2, 4) method. You can use either or both methods, because they are equivalent.

Symbolic Mode

Changing permissions using the symbolic mode method is quite simple. Referring to the original *file.txt* file you created in a previous example, view the original permissions with the `ls -l` command:

```
$ ls -l
-rw-rw-r--. 1 khess khess 0 Jun 19 17:35 file.txt
```

The current file permissions aren't adequate. You need to restrict anyone else but yourself from even reading this file. How do you do it? You remove the read permission from others. Removing is equivalent to subtraction because you are subtracting a permission from the current ones given to the file. So, to remove read permission from the file, you subtract read from others using the chmod command:

```
$ chmod o-r file.txt
$ ls -l
-rw-rw----. 1 khess khess 0 Jun 19 17:35 file.txt
```

You have removed read permission from the file for others. Now, no one but you can read (or write to) this file.

When you create a shell script and attempt to execute it with ./file.sh but nothing happens, you should check the file's permissions to see if you've added the execute permission:

```
$ touch file.sh
$ echo "echo Hello" > file.sh
$ ./file.sh
-bash: ./file.sh: Permission denied
```

Permission denied? But I just created the file in my home directory! Checking permissions reveals the problem:

```
$ ls -l
-rw-rw-r--. 1 khess khess 11 Jun 29 19:58 file.sh
```

The file, *file.sh*, is named with a *.sh* extension. Recall that extensions have no effect in Linux and realize that *file.sh* isn't currently executable because it doesn't have the execute permission. You receive the "Permission denied" message when attempting to execute it. To fix the problem, add the execute permission for yourself:

```
$ chmod u+x file.sh
$ ls -l
-rwxrw-r--. 1 khess khess 11 Jun 29 19:58 file.sh
```

Now, *file.sh* is executable:

```
$ ./file.sh
Hello
```

You can add or subtract multiple permissions from a file and even add and subtract permissions within the same command. Here are some examples of each action. The first command removes (deletes—rm file.txt) the file from any previous example.

To add multiple permissions to a file:

```
$ rm file.txt
$ touch file.txt
$ ls -l
-rw-rw-r--. 1 khess khess 0 Jun 29 20:13 file.txt
```

```
$ chmod ug+x,o+w file.txt
-rwxrwxrw-. 1 khess khess 0 Jun 29 20:13 file.txt
```

To subtract multiple permissions from a file:

```
$ ls -l
-rwxrwxrw-. 1 khess khess 0 Jun 29 20:13 file.txt
$ chmod a-x,o-rw file.txt
$ ls -l
-rw-rw----. 1 khess khess 0 Jun 29 20:13 file.txt
```

Now add execute permission for all groups and remove read permission for others:

```
$ rm file.txt
$ touch file.txt
$ ls -l
-rw-rw-r--. 1 khess khess 0 Jun 29 20:13 file.txt
$ chmod a+x,o-r file.txt
$ ls -l
-rwxrwx--x. 1 khess khess 0 Jun 29 20:23 file.txt
```

Be careful to explicitly define which ugo group you want to add or subtract permissions for. Simply supplying a +x or -r defaults to all.

If you don't specify which groups you wish to add permissions or subtract permissions for, the default behavior is for the system to assume the intended group is *all*. This can be dangerous from a security perspective. Never grant permissions to all groups unless that is what you intend to do. In the following example, the execute permission is granted to all groups because you didn't explicitly define which group should receive it:

```
$ rm file.txt
$ touch file.txt
$ ls -l
-rw-rw-r--. 1 khess khess 0 Jun 29 20:34 file.txt
$ chmod +x file.txt
$ ls -l
-rwxrwxr-x. 1 khess khess 0 Jun 29 20:35 file.txt
```

To execute an executable file or script that is not in your path, you must provide the explicit path to the file. If the file is in your current directory, you must tell the shell that it is in your current directory and that you'd like to execute it. Use ./script_name.sh to inform the shell that the file is executable and in your current directory. Here, script_name.sh is the file you wish to execute.

Numeric Mode

For clarity and comparison, the examples in this section are duplicates of the examples in the previous section. But here we use the numeric mode (rather than the symbolic mode) of changing permissions.

Create a new file and check its permissions:

```
$ rm file.txt
$ touch file.txt
$ ls -l
-rw-rw-r--. 1 khess khess 0 Jun 29 21:12 file.txt
```

Remove the read permission from the other group using the numeric method. First, calculate the current permission value of the file and then what you want the new value to be. Currently, the file's permission value is 664. The desired value is 660:

```
$ chmod 660 file.txt
$ ls -l
-rw-rw----. 1 khess khess 0 Jun 29 20:12 file.txt
```

Using the numeric method, there's no adding or subtracting of permissions. You simply reassign a permission value to the file. The code shown next is a repeat of what you did just a page ago and is a symbolic example. You added the execute permission to all and subtracted the read permission from others:

```
$ rm file.txt
$ touch file.txt
$ ls -l
-rw-rw-r--. 1 khess khess 0 Jun 29 20:13 file.txt
$ chmod a+x,o-r file.txt
$ ls -l
-rwxrwx--x. 1 khess khess 0 Jun 29 20:23 file.txt
```

The numeric equivalent is to reassign the value of the original file (664) to the new one (771):

```
$ rm file.txt
$ touch file.txt
$ ls -l
-rw-rw-r--. 1 khess khess 0 Jun 29 20:13 file.txt
$ chmod 771 file.txt
$ ls -l
-rwxrwx--x. 1 khess khess 0 Jun 29 20:23 file.txt
```

Either method of changing permissions is perfectly acceptable; it doesn't matter which method you use. Like most sysadmins, I use both methods interchangeably. It depends more on context and how quickly I want to do something. Changing permissions will become automatic to you with some practice and a few mistakes along the way.

Default Permissions Explained: umask

You might have noticed that when you create a new file, it's created with specific permissions: 664 or -rw-rw-r--. For the root user the default permissions for a new file are 644 or -rw-r--r--. You might now wonder how this happens. A global setting called a umask (user file-creation mask) masks or filters certain permissions from being given to files by default. The execute permission is never given by default, so the umask setting does not explicitly mask it. To find out your user account's default umask value, use the umask command:

```
$ umask
0002
```

You might now wonder why the umask reports four digits; we've only worked with three so far. The first (leftmost) digit is for special permissions such as setuid, setgid, and sticky, which I'll cover in a later chapter. For now, focus only on the rightmost three digits: 002. These three digits correspond to rwx permissions for user, group, and other, respectively. When you create a new file, certain permissions are filtered out. In the case of the 002 umask, the write (w) permission is filtered out, so new files are created as -rw-rw-r--. The 2 is for write permission. When a new file is created, the write permission is masked from the "other" group and therefore isn't given to the new file.

For the root user, the default umask on my system is 0022. The write (w) permission is masked from both group and other. The reason for a umask is security. When a regular user creates a file, you don't want everyone else to be able to write to it—you must explicitly grant this permission. For the root user, the umask prevents the root group and others from writing to files by default. This security feature prevents daemons or programs running as root from writing to certain sensitive files such as the */etc/passwd* file. Everyone may read the file but only the root user may write to it.

You may change your umask value by issuing the umask command and a new value. This temporarily changes the umask during your current login session:

```
$ umask 006
$ touch test.txt
$ ls -l test.txt
-rw-rw----. 1 khess khess 0 Jun 29 22:16 test.txt
```

To make this change permanent, which you may change later, do the following to append the new umask to the end of the *.bashrc* file that resides in your home directory:

```
$ echo umask 006 >> ~/.bashrc
$ source .bashrc
$ umask
0006
```

Every time you log in, your `umask` is set to `006` or `0006` (which are equivalent) and yields a more secure `-rw-rw----` new default file permission.

Summary

In this chapter, you gained more experience working at the command line, learned some new commands, and perhaps more importantly, learned to read and modify file permissions. In Chapter 3, you will learn some file editing basics and how to modify the user's default environment.

Customizing the User Experience

This chapter covers customizing the user experience for yourself and your users. System administrators are often called upon to make minor changes to a user's environment or to the default environment for all users on the system (the latter is known as a global change). As long as any requested alterations and enhancements don't compromise system security or violate corporate policy, there's no harm in making changes that accommodate a user's needs and workflows. Our duty as sysadmins is, after all, to the company first (and then to the user). The user is your customer.

Customizing the default user environment globally changes the environment for everyone on the system. However, you or the user can override some global parameters. You made such an override in Chapter 2 when you added the new umask to your user account. By setting your personal umask preference after the global one was set, you superseded the one set by the system. It's a common practice for users to customize the environments they have control over.

This chapter covers customizing your and your users' environments by editing key files in each user's home directory. As a system administrator, you'll also explore the "global" versions of these environment files that can be changed or added to, enabling you to create a specific experience for your users.

Altering Home Directory Options

In every user's home directory, a few hidden files control most of the user's environment. Since many Linux users use bash, it is the focus of the default and custom user environment discussions in this chapter. (Other shells such as ash, zsh, csh, and ksh are also available to you, and their hidden, user-editable files are similar in name, function, and structure.)

Because some users don't have adequate skills to make the necessary changes, you might have to make them on the users' behalf. The relevant files are as follows:

- *.bashrc*
- *.bash_logout*

Depending on your Linux distribution and previous configuration changes, you might also see files named *.profile*, *.bash_profile*, *.bash_login*, and *.bash_history* in your home directory.

You won't have to make changes to all of them. For example, the *.bash_history* file doesn't require any changes. It's a log of issued commands, and there are no user-configurable items. When you log into a Linux system, the *.bashrc* file executes first, and then the *.bash_profile* executes. The *.bash_logout* file executes upon logout.

 Be careful about which (and how many) programs, scripts, and messages you place in your startup files because if they're corrupt, damaged, or half open, you might find that your login either is delayed or that you're completely unable to log in and will have to be rescued by another sysadmin. Pass this warning on to your users, too.

When you log into a Linux system interactively, a group of files automatically execute to build your user environment, as described in the following sections.

Login Versus Nonlogin Shells

You'll read and hear about two types of interactive shells: login and nonlogin. An interactive login shell is one you SSH to or directly log into by supplying a username and password or SSH key. An interactive nonlogin shell is one for which you call a child shell from your command line:

```
$ bash
$ echo $SHLVL
2
```

The $SHLVL is a variable that tracks your shell level. When you first log into an interactive shell with a username and password or a key, your $SHLVL is 1. Child shells that you call after the first one increment the SHLVL variable. A child shell called in this way is an interactive, nonlogin shell because it is interactive but doesn't involve a new login.

/etc/bashrc

When you interactively log into a Linux system, */etc/bashrc* is the first personalization file to execute. The */etc/bashrc* file also executes on interactive nonlogin shells. The */etc/bashrc* file is a global personalization file that provides your login shell (bash) with functions and aliases. This file should be left as is—meaning that even as a system administrator, you shouldn't edit it.

The information and warning shown here are reprinted from the */etc/bashrc* file. You'll see them if you attempt to edit the file:

```
# System-wide functions and aliases
# Environment stuff goes in /etc/profile

# It's NOT a good idea to change this file unless you know what you
# are doing. It's much better to create a custom.sh shell script in
# /etc/profile.d/ to make custom changes to your environment, as this
# will prevent the need for merging in future updates.
```

The */etc/bashrc* file is analogous to the *.bashrc* file in your home directory. If you need to change functions and aliases, change them there.

/etc/profile

The */etc/profile* file is a system-wide startup file. It provides generic variables, paths, and other settings to all users. A warning in this file, shown in the following code listing, states that you shouldn't edit this file unless you know what you're doing:

```
# System-wide environment and startup programs for login setup
# Functions and aliases go in /etc/bashrc

# It's NOT a good idea to change this file unless you know what you
# are doing. It's much better to create a custom.sh shell script in
# /etc/profile.d/ to make custom changes to your environment, as this
# will prevent the need for merging in future updates.
```

Again, as stated in the warning, it's better to edit the personalization files in the user's home directory or create other global personalization files under */etc/profile.d*.

However, these global settings can be overwritten by the individual personalization startup files located in the home directory. It is the second environment personalization file that executes when you log in to a Linux system. Strangely, it also calls the */etc/bashrc* file so */etc/bashrc* is executed twice.

The */etc/profile* file is analogous to the *.bash_profile* file in your home directory. Change any environment settings there.

.bashrc

The *.bashrc* file is a hidden file in your home directory. It's hidden because you don't want direct access to it when renaming or deleting files with a wildcard. You have full ownership of the file and can edit it at will. This file is for setting and including any functions you might need and setting aliases for commands. After the global personalization files execute, the *.bashrc* file executes. The *.bashrc* file, like its global analog, executes in interactive nonlogin shells. The following is a listing of an unchanged *.bashrc* file. You should augment or change your PATH in this file so that your shell behaves similarly for login and nonlogin instances:

```
# .bashrc

# Source global definitions
if [ -f /etc/bashrc ]; then
    . /etc/bashrc
fi

# User specific environment
if ! [[ "$PATH" =~ "$HOME/.local/bin:$HOME/bin:" ]]
then
    PATH="$HOME/.local/bin:$HOME/bin:$PATH"
fi
export PATH

# Uncomment the following line if you don't like systemctl's auto-paging feature:
# export SYSTEMD_PAGER=

# User specific aliases and functions
```

Aliases are useful shortcuts to commands and their options. For example, if you want a "chatty" version of common commands, create the following aliases in your .bashrc file:

```
alias rm='rm -i'
alias cp='cp -i'
alias mv='mv -i'
```

The -i option means *interactive* and asks you to verify before the command performs its action. You get a verification message when you issue the new aliased rm command. This option is especially handy for destructive commands such as rm because Linux isn't "chatty." For example, it provides no feedback when you remove a file. The -i option provides you with a more Windows command–like experience by prompting you to confirm your actions:

```
$ rm file4.txt
rm: remove regular empty file 'file4.txt'?
```

Aliases are handy if you run the same commands and options frequently. For example, I create a few default aliases on every system I use. My most useful one is for long lists:

```
alias ll='ls -l'
```

You can also create aliases on a per-session basis. This means that you can simply issue the alias command at the command line without saving it to a file, and it remains in effect until you log off or terminate the current shell.

 Many sources recommend placing all customizations in the *.bashrc* file because it's executed for interactive login and nonlogin shells. Making your shell customizations in the *.bashrc* file guarantees shell consistency.

.bash_profile

The last file to execute on an interactive login is the *.bash_profile* file in your home directory:

```
# .bash_profile

# Get the aliases and functions
if [ -f ~/.bashrc ]; then
    . ~/.bashrc
fi

# User specific environment and startup programs
```

You may place customizations in this file that will run in interactive login shells, but they will not be available for interactive, nonlogin shells.

.bash_logout

The *.bash_logout* file executes upon logout. This file is optional. It only exists to allow users to clean up temporary files on exit. One could also use it to log time using the shell or to send a message upon logout.

In the next section, you learn the origins of these shell personalization files and how you can change the defaults for each user.

The /etc/skel Directory

The */etc/skel* directory is a special directory for holding files you want every user to receive in their home directories as you create their user accounts. The files you create in */etc/skel* don't have to be hidden, although the default ones are. These files are copied to the user's home directory during account creation. These are the global copies of the environment personalization files. The list of */etc/skel* default files on Red Hat Enterprise Linux–based systems is shown in the following example:

```
# ls -la /etc/skel
total 28
drwxr-xr-x.   2 root root   76 Jul  4 12:45 .
drwxr-xr-x. 144 root root 8192 Jul  4 11:07 ..
-rw-r--r--.   1 root root   18 Apr 21 10:04 .bash_logout
-rw-r--r--.   1 root root  141 Apr 21 10:04 .bash_profile
-rw-r--r--.   1 root root  376 Apr 21 10:04 .bashrc
-rw-r--r--.   1 root root  658 Mar  3  2020 .zshrc
```

If you create a file in the */etc/skel* directory, it's copied to a new user's home directory during account creation. Existing users won't receive files placed in */etc/skel* after you have created their accounts. You'll have to manually copy those to each user's home directory and change the permissions so that the user has full control of them.

 Linux has a local help system known as manual pages, or *man pages* for short. If you need help for a command, configuration, or system setting, enter man and the keyword to see if the documentation exists for it. For example, for help with the ls command, you'd use $ man ls. You can move through the man pages using vi (Vim) navigation commands.

Customizing the Shell Prompt

Generally, users accept the default prompt presented by the system. Generically, it looks like [username@hostname pwd]$ or, specifically in my case, [khess @server1 ~]$. The tilde (~) represents the user's home directory. For example, in the previous sections discussing personalization scripts, they are often represented as ~/.bashrc and ~/.bash_profile to illustrate that these files are located in the user's home directories.

To set a custom prompt, the shell provides a list of escape characters representing locations, username, time, carriage returns, etc. For example, the default prompt is given by the following code for the prompt environment variable (PS1): PS1="[\u@\h \W]\\$ ". The system sets this default prompt in the */etc/bashrc* file. You may override it with an entry in your *~/.bashrc* file.

Bash allows these prompt strings to be customized by inserting a number of backslash-escaped special characters that are decoded as shown in Table 3-1.

Table 3-1. Backslash-escaped special characters

Special character	Description
\a	An ASCII bell character (07)
\d	The date in "Weekday Month Date" format (e.g., "Tue May 26")
\D{format}	The format is passed to strftime(3) and the result is inserted into the prompt string; an empty format results in a locale-specific time representation. The braces are required.
\e	An ASCII escape character (033)
\h	The hostname up to the first '.'
\H	The hostname
\j	The number of jobs currently managed by the shell
\l	The basename of the shell's terminal device name
\n	Newline
\r	Carriage return
\s	The name of the shell, the basename of $0 (the portion following the final slash)
\t	The current time in 24-hour HH:MM:SS format
\T	The current time in 12-hour HH:MM:SS format
\@	The current time in 12-hour am/pm format
\A	The current time in 24-hour HH:MM format
\u	The username of the current user
\v	The version of bash (e.g., 2.00)
\V	The release of bash, version + patch level (e.g., 2.00.0)
\w	The current working directory, with $HOME abbreviated with a tilde (uses the value of the PROMPT_DIRTRIM variable)
\W	The basename of the current working directory, with $HOME abbreviated with a tilde
\!	The history number of this command
\#	The command number of this command
\$	If the effective UID is 0, a #, otherwise a $
\nnn	The character corresponding to the octal number nnn
\\	A backslash
\[	Begin a sequence of nonprinting characters which could be used to embed a terminal control sequence into the prompt
\]	End a sequence of nonprinting characters

The default prompt is sufficient for most users, but some users and sysadmins prefer something a little different, so they're free to change it. Some clever users have devised codes for colorful and artistic prompts, such as this Christmas-themed prompt:

```
PS1="☺\[\e[33;41m\][\[\e[m\]\[\e[32m\]\u\[\e[m\]\[\e[36m\]@\[\e[m\] \
\[\e[34m\]\h\[\e[m\]\[\e[33;41m\]]\[\e[m\]🌲 "
```

Search online for "fun Linux prompts" and enjoy yourself. After playing with that, you can log out and back in to reset your prompt or enter `PS1="[\u@\h \W]\\$ "` to return to the default.

Summary

In this chapter, you learned how to edit user environments through personalization files and the default location and configuration for adding more files to new accounts. You also learned these files' locations, the order they're loaded, and which ones you should edit for a particular effect. Finally, you had a brief overview of the shell prompt and how to alter it.

In Chapter 4, you'll get an overview of user management from user account creation to managing users through groups to how to grant access to resources.

Managing Users

As a system administrator, you'll spend a significant portion of your time managing users. You'll also spend time troubleshooting user problems that aren't account- or permissions-related, such as connectivity problems, broken applications, data corruption, training issues, security issues, and user-created problems.

Managing users covers the following tasks:

- Creating user accounts
- Modifying user accounts
- Removing user accounts
- Granting access to files and directories
- Restricting access to files and directories
- Enforcing security policies
- Setting permissions on files and directories

Some user management tasks can be learned from this book, while others are purely experiential and on-the-job training for you. No two user environments are exactly alike, and no two user experiences are exactly alike. In this chapter, you learn some preemptive user management methods, but problems still occur. The techniques you learn in this chapter will get you started on being able to handle an array of user-related problems.

User and Group ID Numbering Conventions

There are some guidelines associated with creating and maintaining user accounts on Linux systems, as shown in Table 4-1. These aren't hard and fast rules, but they're generally followed on most corporate systems.

Table 4-1. Numbering conventions for user and group accounts

UID	GID	Description
0	0	Root
1–999	1–999	System/service accounts
1000+	1000+	User accounts

User account UID and GID numbers typically begin at 1000 and increment by one for each new account. The UID and GID for the root user are always 0; no other user on the system has these user and group IDs.

System and service accounts aren't human user accounts and typically don't have an interactive shell associated with them. These accounts are given UIDs and GIDs ranging from 1–999. These separations make system housekeeping much easier than randomly assigning UIDs and GIDs to user accounts.

Creating User Accounts

Like most tasks in Linux, there's more than one way to create user accounts. For this book, I stick with the two mainstream methods of creating accounts: `useradd` and `adduser`.

Adding Users with useradd

The `useradd` command is the standard command-line Linux method of adding new users to a system. The `useradd` command is simple; all you really need to supply is a username as an argument:

```
# useradd jsmith
```

This creates the home directory, */home/jsmith*, fills it with the default complement of hidden environment files, and places an entry into */etc/passwd*. When I create a user account with `useradd`, I supply a single argument and bit of information (the user's full name) that otherwise requires me to edit the */etc/passwd* file:

```
# useradd -c "Jane Smith" jsmith
```

The `-c` option writes the information you supply to it to the fifth field of the /etc/passwd file. If you wish to supply more information, such as phone number, email address, or whatever you wish to include, use commas (,) to separate the information:

```
# useradd -c "Jane Smith,Room 26,212-555-1000,jsmith@example.com" jsmith
```

The new user's *etc/passwd* entry:

```
jsmith:x:1007:1007:Jane Smith,Room 26,212-555-1000,jsmith@example.com:/home/
jsmith:/bin/bash
```

The individual fields in a user's *etc/passwd* entry are as follows (from left to right):

- Username
- *etc/shadow* password field
- User ID
- Primary group ID
- The comment field
- Home directory
- Default shell

Passwords are not stored in the *etc/passwd* file. The *etc/shadow* field refers to the *etc/shadow* file that contains each user's encrypted password and is readable only by the root user. Note the *etc/shadow* file's permissions are 000 on Red Hat Enterprise Linux–based systems. The file permissions vary among distributions but are never readable by regular users:

```
----------. 1 root root 1547 Jul 17 10:55 /etc/shadow
```

Although Jane Smith's user account is created, her home directory exists, and there's an entry in the *etc/passwd* file for the account, Jane can't log into the system. Do you know why? It's because the account has no password. As the sysadmin, you have to supply an initial password to Jane so that the user can log in. Since you haven't supplied a password for the account, the *etc/shadow* entry shows that there is no password:

```
jsmith:!!:18825:0:99999:7:::
```

Use the passwd command to supply a password to the account:

```
# passwd jsmith
Changing password for user jsmith.
New password:
Retype new password:
passwd: all authentication tokens updated successfully.
```

Now, you have to give the password to Jane before she can successfully log into the system.

Adding Users with adduser

On some Linux distributions, `adduser` is a symbolic link to `useradd`:

```
lrwxrwxrwx. 1 root root 17 Oct 26 2020 /usr/sbin/adduser -> /usr/sbin/useradd
```

On other distributions, `adduser` is an interactive Perl script that steps you through adding a new user, and `useradd` is a separate utility with its standard switches and arguments.

Modifying User Accounts

There's rarely such a thing as a static user account. Therefore, the `usermod` command exists to assist you in making those required changes without editing */etc/passwd*, a home directory, or configuration files. The `usermod` command is the catchall for changing all things user account related. The following is an abbreviated list of modifications that you can make with the `usermod` command:

- Add the user to a supplementary group
- Change the user's comment field in */etc/passwd*
- Change the user's home directory
- Set an account expiry date
- Remove an expiry date
- Change a user's login name (username)
- Lock/unlock a user's account
- Move the contents of a user's home directory
- Change a user's login shell
- Change a user's ID

Some of these options are more frequently used than others. For example, it's completely reasonable to change a user's login shell, lock and unlock an account, set or remove an expiry date, or add a user to a supplementary group. Changing a user's ID once it's set during account creation is rare, as is relocating a user's home directory.

In the following sections, I give examples of the most commonly requested user account changes. Check the man page for details if you need to alter other aspects of a user's account.

Adding a Supplementary Group

When you create a new user account, the system assigns the user a user ID (UID) and a primary group ID (GID). (They can be the same sequential number, but that isn't always the case.) For example, for the account created earlier for Jane Smith, the UID is 1007, and the GID is 1007:

```
jsmith:x:1007:1007:
```

Jane's primary GID is 1007, but she might also work in an area of the company, such as IT, engineering, or application development, that requires her to have access to a group-owned directory. For this exercise, Jane works in the engineering department as an associate engineer. The engineering department's shared directory GID is 8020. Using usermod, here's how to grant Jane access to that group's shared directory:

```
# usermod -a -G 8020 jsmith
```

This adds Jane's user account to the engineering group in the */etc/group* file:

```
engineering:x:8020:bjones,kdoe,vkundra,adundee,jsmith
```

Now Jane can access the engineering group's shared directory. To correctly add Jane's account to a new group, use the -a (append) and the -G (supplementary group) together. For example, if you want Jane to access the finance department's shared directory, you must append her to that group. When adding a user, you can use the GID number or the group's name:

```
# usermod -a -G finance jsmith
```

 You must use the -a (append) and the -G (supplementary group) together. If you don't use the -a option, your user will be removed from all other supplementary groups and added only to the one you specify.

A user can be a member of several other groups. For example, a user might be in the finance department (GID 8342) but also require access to human resources (GID 8901) information. You can also add a user to more than one group at once:

```
# usermod -a -G 8342,8901 jsmith
```

This command adds Jane Smith to the finance and the human resources group with a single command.

Changing the User Comments Field

Changing the user comments (GECOS) field is a common task. You can edit the */etc/passwd* file directly, although it comes with significant risk. The rule of thumb is that if there's a tool to perform some action or task, you should use it rather than directly editing configuration files. You can easily change the GECOS field using the usermod command and the -c option.

Let's say the company has recently hired a second person named Jane Smith, so you need to distinguish between them by adding a middle initial to the first Jane Smith's GECOS field:

```
# usermod -c "Jane R Smith" jsmith
```

This command replaces Jane Smith with Jane R Smith.

The -c option tells the usermod command that you're editing the "comments" field. You can also change this information using the chfn command:

```
# chfn -f "Janie Smith" jsmith
```

The chfn command changes your finger information. Finger is an old daemon that ran on early Unix systems and some Linux systems and supplied information about users. Almost no one uses it these days because of security issues, but the information is still referred to as finger information. The -f option changes the user's full name field for the specified account. There are other options for office (-o), office phone (-p), and home phone (-h). Generally, only the user's full name or the service's name and purpose are used for the GECOS field.

Setting an Expiration (Expiry) Date on an Account

If a user gives notice at a company, moves to a different business unit, or goes on parental leave, sysadmins might decide to disable that user's account for security reasons until the person returns or before removing the account from a system:

```
# usermod -e 2021-07-23 rsmith
```

Rob Smith's account will be disabled (expired) on the specified date in the format YYYY-MM-DD. The -e option sets the account for expiration.

Changing a User's Login Shell

The default Linux shell is bash, but some users prefer to use a different shell, so they request that their default shell be changed to one of the many other available shell options. There are three methods of changing a user's default shell: usermod, chsh, and directly editing */etc/passwd*. Direct editing of the */etc/passwd* file is not recommended.

The usermod command method uses the -s option, the new shell, and the username to make the change:

```
# usermod -s /bin/sh jsmith
```

The updated */etc/passwd* file is shown here:

```
jsmith:x:1007:1007:Janie Smith:/home/jsmith:/bin/sh
```

Only a user with root privileges may edit the */etc/passwd* file or use the usermod command. However, any user may change their shell with the chsh command:

```
$ chsh -s /bin/zsh
Changing shell for jsmith.
Password:
Shell changed.
```

The resulting */etc/passwd* entry is as follows:

```
jsmith:x:1007:1007:Janie Smith:/home/jsmith:/bin/zsh
```

For other changes, consult the man page for usermod.

> At the end of any man page, you'll find a list of related alternative commands, links to external documentation, and configuration files referenced in the "See Also" section. These are handy to explore and might prove more efficient for making changes. The following is the "See Also" section excerpted from the usermod man page (*https://oreil.ly/nqaH_*):
>
> See Also
>
> chfn(1), chsh(1), passwd(1), crypt(3), gpasswd(8), group-add(8), groupdel(8), groupmod(8), login.defs(5), user-add(8), userdel(8).

Now that you've learned to create and modify user accounts, let's discuss how to remove user accounts.

Removing User Accounts

Fortunately, system administrators and developers who give names to commands do so in a way that makes them easy to remember. Command names often describe their functions. The useradd command is one such example. To remove a user account from a system, you use the userdel command, which is just as easy to use as useradd is.

To remove a user account from your system, issue the userdel command and supply the username for the account:

```
# userdel jsmith
```

This command removes the user's entry from */etc/passwd* and from */etc/shadow* but leaves the user's home directory (*/home/jsmith*) intact. Why do you think that's a good option? Sysadmins often leave a user's home directory intact after a user has separated from a company or has changed jobs within the company but no longer requires access to a system. Retaining the user's home directory ensures that only the root user can access any documents left by the user that might be important to the company.

If you make nightly backups of users' home directories, you don't necessarily need to retain the user's home directory. The following userdel command removes the user's home directory and all files inside it:

```
# userdel -r jsmith
```

 Destructive Linux commands, such as userdel and rm, are irreversible and can't be undone once executed. Always be sure that you have the correct user account before pressing the Enter key—and have good backups.

When it's time to change passwords, you need to know how to force users to do it. Our next section shows you how.

Forcing Password Changes

It's a matter of trust that the user will change their password when you provide them with an initial password. Sysadmins who regularly audit their users' passwords realize that this "honor system" level of trust doesn't work 100% of the time. You can easily audit a user's account settings using the chage command. The -l option lists the current settings for the specified user account:

```
# chage -l rsmith
Last password change                                    : Jul 17, 2021
Password expires                                : never
Password inactive                                : never
Account expires                                : never
Minimum number of days between password change     : 0
Maximum number of days between password change     : 99999
Number of days of warning before password expires     : 7
```

As you can see, this account's password never expires, which is a security violation that needs to be fixed. In addition to a regular forced change, you should also set a minimum change period. For example, as shown in the following code listing, I set the rsmith account to force a password change every 90 days (-M 90) with a minimum number of days between password changes to 1 (-m 1). Setting a minimum number of days ensures that users don't change their passwords 10 times (or whatever the number of the system's remembered passwords is set to) to reset it to their original password, which amounts to no net password change.

```
# chage -m 1 -M 90 rsmith

# chage -l rsmith
Last password change                        : Jul 17, 2021
Password expires                            : Oct 15, 2021
Password inactive                           : never
Account expires                             : never
Minimum number of days between password change    : 1
Maximum number of days between password change    : 90
Number of days of warning before password expires    : 7
```

The expiration date set by the system is 90 days after the last password change. If the last password change is in the past, the user must change their password on the next login.

 From the chage man page (*https://oreil.ly/-NeGX*): "The chage command changes the number of days between password changes and the last password change date. The system uses this information to determine when users must change their passwords."

Passwords are a weak form of authentication because they can be guessed, cracked, or read in plain text if users write them down. Thus, you must ensure that passwords are changed often and not reused.

Handling Service Accounts

Nothing stirs controversy among sysadmins and security administrators like the mere mention of service accounts. I'm not sure what all the controversy is about because every Linux system has more than 30 service accounts.

An example of a service account is the *nobody* account, which is the Kernel Overflow User account:

```
nobody:x:65534:65534:Kernel Overflow User:/:/sbin/nologin
```

Generally, you can spot a service account because in the */etc/passwd* file, you see that the user account has no assigned shell. Service accounts have */sbin/nologin,* where the user's shell should be. This means that the service accounts have no interactive shell or passwords. That doesn't mean their passwords are blank or null, they simply don't exist. In other words, if a user account has */sbin/nologin* as their shell, they can't log into the system with any password. And no user, not even the root user, can su or sudo to those accounts:

```
# su - nobody
This account is currently not available.
```

Because service accounts have no interactive shell and no method of switching to one via su or sudo, there's no security violation associated with having service accounts on a system. The controversy comes from the fact that some system administrators don't know that service accounts don't usually have interactive shells or passwords. Services may require an interactive shell account for their service to function. For those services, extreme scrutiny and other security measures should be in place to thwart potential clandestine logins on those accounts.

Managing Groups Rather Than Users

When managing permissions for a set of users, it's more convenient to define and manage a group than to manage each user separately. Group management allows you to do the following:

- Manage permissions on assets such as folders and files
- Manage permissions according to job function
- Change permissions for a large number of users rather than for each user individually
- Easily add users to and remove users from a group's shared folders and files
- Restrict permissions to sensitive folders and files

It's very difficult to manage permissions for individual users because if those permissions need to change, you have to trace permissions for that user on every system on which they have an account. Managing permissions for groups allows sysadmins to manage fine-grained user access on a more global level.

For example, if you have a user who works in the human resources (HR) department and then moves to the finance department, it's easy to remove that user from the HR group and add them to the finance group. The user immediately has access to all shared files and folders that other finance group members do. And the user no longer has access to HR files and folders.

You learned earlier in this chapter how to add users to supplementary groups. You should practice adding directories to the system, adding a group account, setting that particular group ownership to the directory, and then adding users to the group. You can then su - *username*, becoming that user to test your permissions settings.

The following is one possible scenario for you to work through to learn group management. This example assumes you already have a finance group and users assigned to it. Notice that during this example, the root user exits and returns to a regular account that is part of the finance group. And users can change group ownership and permissions of files they own:

```
$ su - root
Password:

# mkdir /opt/finance

# chgrp finance /opt/finance

# ls -la /opt
total 0
drwxr-xr-x.  3 root root     21 Aug 11 21:56 .
dr-xr-xr-x. 18 root root    239 Aug 11 21:08 ..
drwxr-xr-x.  2 root finance    6 Aug 11 21:56 finance

# chmod 770 /opt/finance

# ls -la /opt
total 0
drwxr-xr-x.  3 root root     21 Aug 11 21:56 .
dr-xr-xr-x. 18 root root    239 Aug 11 21:08 ..
drwxrwx---.  2 root finance    6 Aug 11 21:56 finance

# exit
logout

$ cd /opt/finance

$ touch budget.txt

$ ls -la
total 0
drwxrwx---. 2 root   finance 24 Aug 11 21:58 .
drwxr-xr-x. 3 root   root    21 Aug 11 21:56 ..
-rw-rw-r--. 1 khess  khess    0 Aug 11 21:58 budget.txt

$ chgrp finance budget.txt

$ ls -la
total 0
drwxrwx---. 2 root   finance 24 Aug 11 21:58 .
drwxr-xr-x. 3 root   root    21 Aug 11 21:56 ..
```

```
-rw-rw-r--. 1 khess finance  0 Aug 11 21:58 budget.txt

$ chmod 660 budget.txt

$ ls -la
total 0
drwxrwx---. 2 root  finance 24 Aug 11 21:58 .
drwxr-xr-x. 3 root  root    21 Aug 11 21:56 ..
-rw-rw----. 1 khess finance  0 Aug 11 21:58 budget.txt
```

If you understand everything that's going on in this example, then you're ready to move on to the next chapter. If you haven't yet mastered these concepts, work through the chapter examples again and return to this exercise. Remember that creating users, groups, and directories and changing permissions are daily tasks for sysadmins, and practicing these skills is the only way to acquire them and become comfortable using them.

Summary

This chapter taught you how to create, remove, and change user accounts. You also learned how to set up service accounts and had a brief overview of managing groups. In the next chapter, you will learn about Linux networking, from the basics of why networks are important to more-complex concepts such as network troubleshooting.

## CHAPTER 5

Connecting to a Network

A standalone Linux system is powerful, but the scope of what the system is ultimately capable of is limited. Only a single operator or administrator can use a standalone system simultaneously. While the system can still run multiple workloads, its services are restricted to local access.

Linux is a multitasking, multiuser operating system. One of its most outstanding values is being networked with other computers to allow multiple users to run various workloads simultaneously. Connecting a Linux system to a network enables it to become part of a local network, a grid, a cloud, or the global internet.

In this chapter, you will learn how to select an IP addressing scheme for your network and some advantages and disadvantages of the static and dynamic options. You also learn the security implications of connecting systems to a network. You will learn how to, as much as possible, prevent security breaches by implementing good security practices, such as using secure protocols, turning off unnecessary services and daemons, and keeping systems patched and updated.

Plugging into a Network

There's no great skill required to plug a server system into an existing network. These days, as soon as a new system comes online, a Dynamic Host Configuration Protocol (DHCP) server provides it with an IP address, subnet mask, gateway, Domain Name System (DNS) servers, and some basic routing information. There are two schools of thought concerning DHCP and servers. The first claims that all server systems should have static IP addresses, and the second asserts that all systems should use DHCP for IP address distribution and management. I've always configured servers, printers, and networking equipment with static IP addresses near the lower end of the IP address pool. For me, it makes good organizational sense to do so rather than relying on DHCP and DNS services to maintain order for services that users rely on so heavily.

In the following sections, I describe the two IP addressing schemes—static and dynamic—and the advantages and disadvantages of each. The example network for each has the following IP addressing information:

- Network: 192.168.1.0/24
- Gateway: 192.168.1.254 (static IP address)
- DNS: 192.168.1.1, 192.168.1.2 (static IP addresses)

This example network is for learning purposes and is only practical for the smallest of companies or groups of users. This scheme will only work for small companies because there are only 251 usable IP addresses on this network after subtracting the gateway address and two DNS server addresses (254 – 3 = 251). A user might have as many as five devices that consume IP addresses, and it's easy to see that it doesn't take long to exhaust such a small pool.

Assigning a static IP address varies among Linux distributions. For these examples, I use Debian and CentOS distributions.

Static IP Addressing

A static IP address is a "hard-coded" IP address embedded into a configuration file. The IP address does not change unless it's changed manually. Static IP addresses do not depend on or use DHCP services. When assigning static IP addresses to systems, you should decide on a reserved block of IP addresses that you use for servers, network equipment (switches, routers, WiFi access points), printers, and any IP-capable system that is not mobile. Workstations, laptops, tablets, phones, and other mobile devices should use DHCP.

For example, using the network parameters mentioned in the preceding section, I reserve 192.168.1.1 through 192.168.1.25 for servers, network equipment, printers, and other stationary systems. As you note, the addresses 192.168.1.1 and .2 are already used on this reserved list. You can exclude a range of IP addresses in your DHCP configuration so that these addresses are not part of the available IP address pool.

One of the advantages of using a static pool of IP addresses is that network services are stable. If you set up some inventory service and monitoring on your network, which I highly recommend, having those statically addressed systems will save some headaches for you. You'll be able to compare inventories over time, see what's changed, measure growth, and plan for changes. Another advantage is that you can find critical systems even if DNS and DHCP are down. A static IP address gives you the stability you need, irrespective of any other services' status.

Some network services require static IP addresses for the server systems on which they reside. Services such as FTP, web, VPN, database, Active Directory, and DNS require static IP addresses or are recommended to have them. The primary disadvantage and argument against static IP addressing is management. The argument is that managing static IP addresses is labor-intensive and might cause conflicts elsewhere on the network. I don't see this as a problem for most sysadmins because the equipment you assign static IP addresses to lasts for years, and their locations are stable. You don't typically move a server to different locations within a company; you never move them offsite to use and then return them as you do laptops, tablets, and mobile phones. A reserved pool that's excluded from your DHCP pool prevents potential conflicts with other systems.

Dynamic IP Addressing

Using a DHCP service eliminates many of the IP address management problems that plagued system administrators in the days before DHCP. Assigning static IP addresses and keeping up with them for more than a few systems becomes a management nightmare. Static IP addresses made a little more sense when users only had desktop systems. But these days, with laptops, tablets, and mobile phones, a static IP address would likely mean that the user would have network access only on their corporate network, that they would experience IP conflicts if they ever connected to another network, or that they would have to know how to change their systems from static to dynamically assigned IP addresses each time they connected to a different network.

For example, if your laptop has a static IP address for your corporate network of 192.168.1.50, and you take that laptop to a remote location, such as your home, to do some work, then your home would have to use the same IP addressing scheme as your office. If it does, your laptop might conflict with a dynamically assigned IP address for your television, someone's mobile phone, or some other IP-capable gadget. You might be able to work around the issue at home, but when you take that same laptop to a hotel and attempt to connect to your corporate VPN, chances are very good that you wouldn't be able to because of that statically assigned IP address. The hotel might use a 10.0.1.0 IP addressing scheme, so your laptop would never connect.

Device mobility is one great advantage of DHCP. The user never has to reconfigure anything no matter where the laptop connects to another network or the internet. The other advantage is that once you configure a DHCP pool of addresses, there's not much maintenance for you to do. You'll have to determine which lease duration best suits your users. I've seen lease durations range from 24 hours to 30 days. I don't have a particular preference, but if you use a long lease duration (more than a few days), you might have some occasional cleanup by removing duplicates, stale leases, and so on. DHCP is supposed to clean up after itself but doesn't always.

Whether to use static IP addressing, DHCP, or a mixture of the two is really up to your personal preference for IP address management. You can still use a pure DHCP scheme and reserve IP addresses by entering MAC addresses, making them statically assigned. The only time there's a problem is if you change network interface cards (NICs). You must remember to update the DHCP reservations list with the new NIC's MAC address.

 If you change network interface card (NIC or adapter) settings, such as changing from DHCP to a static IP address, you need to restart the adapter for those changes to take effect. Restart the adapter by issuing these commands:

```
$ sudo ifdown adapter_name
$ sudo ifup adapter_name
```

The adapter name varies by system, but some examples are eth0 and enp0s3.

The next section discusses the security-related repercussions of placing systems on the network and how you can apply best security practices to your systems.

Networking and Security

Two types of Linux systems can be considered secure: one powered off and one powered on but not connected to a network. The powered-off system is safe from over-the-network attacks, as are non-networked systems. The powered-off system's only security vulnerability is physical security. Someone with physical access to the system could steal, dismantle, or damage it. Non-networked systems are, as mentioned at the outset of the chapter, still somewhat useful but have limited use beyond a single operator.

Once you network a system, you've exposed it to over-the-network attacks. Malicious actors continuously scan IP address ranges, searching for vulnerable systems to exploit. While many servers are exposed to the internet via demilitarized zones (DMZs) (*https://oreil.ly/wxezB*) or are inside corporate or home firewall-protected networks, they are also susceptible to attack. Once inside your network, a malicious actor can perform automated scans of all connected systems, searching for vulnerabilities.

Additionally, creating user accounts on your system decreases security because of weak passwords, the potential for on-path attacks, and social engineering exploits that might compromise one's credentials to a malicious actor.

For these reasons, administrators must take the following measures:

- Only grant what's required for users to work (the principle of *least privilege*)
- Enforce strong security policies for passwords, keys, or multifactor authentication
- Regularly patch and update systems
- Perform periodic security audits on all systems, network equipment, and devices that access corporate resources

Preparing a System for Network Connectivity

When a system administrator provisions a new system and installs it into a rack, plugging in network cables or connecting a virtual machine to a virtual network is standard practice. We often rely on others to vet the systems' function, purpose, and security options. However, this is not always the case. New system installation is often automatically performed by provisioning a "standard build" from a prepared operating system image that could be months or years old. Using old images is a poor security practice. If the system is immediately connected to a network before it's fully updated and secured, it's vulnerable to attack and compromise before it begins its regular duties on the network.

A solution is to provision new systems on a private network where they can receive updates, patches, and secure configurations from an internal repository before being placed into a production network.

Pruning Your Systems

Pruning means removing any unnecessary services and daemons from your systems. There's no need to create problems for yourself by running a production system with multiple services that no one uses but that could leave your system vulnerable to attack. Only install what you need to provide services to your users or other systems.

At a minimum, you need to have an SSH daemon running on your systems so that you can log in and manage them remotely. If you find that some users require a special service that's only used occasionally or that leaves a system in a less than secure state, either turn on the service when needed and turn it off when it's no longer being used or place the service on a secure network that can only be accessed from a restricted number of systems.

Securing Network Daemons

Deciding which network daemons to install and support is generally easy because you know your system's intended purpose each time you build a system. If it's a web server, you know that you'll install a web service such as Apache or NGINX. You'll install MySQL, MariaDB, or some other database software if the system is a database server. The issue is that for a system to be useful, it must expose the corresponding TCP ports for its services. These network daemons are vulnerable to attack and, therefore, must be protected.

There are multiple methods of securing network daemons and services, but installing secure versions of the services you want to provide is the simplest method. For example, if your new system is a DNS server, use DNSSEC. If you configure a Lightweight Directory Access Protocol (LDAP) server, use LDAPS. And always use HTTPS for web servers secured with a certificate. Table 5-1 shows a partial list of secure services.

Table 5-1. Examples of secure services

Protocol	Port	Description
https	443/tcp	HTTP protocol over TLS/SSL
https	443/udp	HTTP protocol over TLS/SSL
ldaps	636/tcp	LDAP over SSL
ldaps	636/udp	LDAP over SSL
imaps	993/tcp	IMAP over SSL
imaps	993/udp	IMAP over SSL
pop3s	995/tcp	POP-3 over SSL
pop3s	995/udp	POP-3 over SSL

Using secure protocols and encryption doesn't guarantee security. Still, it's better than using nonsecure protocols with no encryption. Vulnerabilities frequently appear even for secure applications and protocols. Keeping your systems updated and patched helps prevent security breaches. Security patches are generally available before widespread damage can be done but not always, so you must remain vigilant in maintaining security.

The Secure Shell Daemon

The most common network daemon available on almost every Linux system is the Secure Shell (SSH) daemon. SSH provides a secure (encrypted) connection to a Linux system over the network. Although the SSH daemon (SSHD) has built-in security through its encrypted channel, its communications are still vulnerable to attack. There are multiple methods of securing the SSHD so that attacks are less fruitful for an attacker.

Limiting access to SSHD from specific hosts

There are two files that an administrator can use to limit access to any daemon: */etc/hosts.allow* and */etc/hosts.deny*. They require no service restart because they're not configuration files, and the system checks them each time a client accesses a service. The */etc/hosts.allow* file is the more important of the two because its settings override those in the */etc/hosts.deny* file.

An */etc/hosts.allow* file entry to enable SSH connectivity from a single IP address (192.168.1.50) is shown here:

```
sshd: 192.168.1.50
sshd: ALL: DENY
```

This entry will only accept SSH connections from 192.168.1.50 and will deny them from all other IP addresses. If you find that setting such an entry in */etc/hosts.allow* doesn't work for you, then you need to check for tcp_wrapper integration in sshd using the following command:

```
$ sudo ldd /path/to/binary | grep libwrap
```

If you receive no response, your sshd wasn't compiled with tcp_wrappers enabled and is likely deprecated for your distribution. This is, unfortunately, the case with many packaged sshd installations. The response you're looking for is similar to the following:

```
$ sudo ldd /usr/sbin/sshd | grep libwrap
        libwrap.so.0 => /lib/x86_64-linux-gnu/libwrap.so.0 (0x00007fc6c2ab2000)
```

You have three options if your sshd doesn't have tcp_wrappers support:

- Use other methods to secure sshd (firewall rules, iptables, nftables).
- Compile openssh_server with tcp_wrappers enabled.
- Find and replace your current sshd with an openssh_server package that has tcp_wrappers enabled.

To give you options for firewalld, iptables, and nftables, consider the following commands that perform similar functions to adding entries into */etc/hosts.allow* and */etc/hosts.deny*.

Implementing firewalld rules

If you use firewalld, first delete the ssh service from firewalld's rules:

```
$ sudo firewall-cmd --permanent --remove-service=ssh
```

Add a new zone rather than using the default zone:

```
$ sudo firewall-cmd --permanent --new-zone=SSH_zone
$ sudo firewall-cmd --permanent --zone=SSH_zone --add-source=192.168.1.50
$ sudo firewall-cmd --permanent --zone=SSH_zone --add-service=ssh
```

You must reload the firewall to make the new configuration active:

```
$ sudo firewall-cmd --reload
```

If you use iptables, you can restrict ssh access to a single IP address with a single command:

```
$ sudo iptables -A INPUT -p tcp -s 192.168.1.50 --dport 22 -j ACCEPT
```

For netfilter (nft), you add a new rule:

```
$ sudo nft insert rule ip filter input ip saddr 192.168.1.50 tcp dport 22 accept
```

However if you receive an error that reads as follows, either you must create a new table and chain for the rule, or use an existing chain:

```
Error: Could not process rule: No such file or directory.
```

Use the following commands to create a new table and chain named input:

```
$ sudo nft add table ip filter # create table

# next, create chain
$ sudo nft add chain ip filter input { type filter hook input priority 0\; }

$ sudo nft insert rule ip filter input ip saddr 192.168.1.50 tcp dport 22 accept
```

Note that chain names are case-sensitive. For example, if you had used the existing input chain, INPUT, you would not have received the error:

```
$ sudo nft insert rule ip filter INPUT ip saddr 192.168.1.50 tcp dport 22 accept
```

Restart nftables after you've made your changes:

```
$ sudo systemctl restart nftables
```

The nftables system replaces iptables and combines functionality from iptables, ip6tables, arptables, and ebtables into a single utility. You can read more about nftables on the netfilter homepage (*https://oreil.ly/1RXmC*).

You now have multiple methods of limiting access to the SSH daemon from random hosts. If you don't want to single out a specific IP address, you can isolate the target system by subnet using 192.168.1.0/24 instead of the individual IP address.

Be aware that opening access from an entire subnet might still place your system in significant danger if an intruder infiltrates your network. Ideally, you should limit access to one or two hosts so that logs and monitoring systems are likelier to detect a breach.

You can also configure the SSH daemon to limit access to certain users using the */etc/ssh/sshd_config* file. You must prevent the root user from using SSH. You learn how to prevent root SSH access in the next section.

Denying SSH access for the root user

You should, upon installation, deny SSH access to the root user. Some Linux systems deny root logins via SSH by default, while others allow it. The root user should never log into any system via SSH. A regular user should log in via SSH and then become root or use the sudo command to perform tasks as the root user.

You'll have to check your */etc/ssh/sshd_config* for the following line:

```
PermitRootLogin yes
```

Change the yes to no and restart the SSH service:

```
$ sudo systemctl restart sshd
```

The root user cannot login via SSH. The root user may directly log into the console.

Using keys rather than passwords for authentication

Password authentication is the least secure method for authenticating users. Using key files is much more secure and efficient. You must make the following changes to the */etc/ssh/sshd_config* file and restart sshd for the new configuration to take effect:

```
PasswordAuthentication yes
```

Change the yes to no and then look for the following two entries to ensure they're uncommented and set as shown:

```
PubkeyAuthentication yes
AuthorizedKeysFile .ssh/authorized_keys
```

Restart sshd to enable the new settings:

```
$ sudo systemctl restart sshd
```

On the client side (local system), users need to do the following to set up key pair authentication. Create the public/private key pair. This example is for the user **tux**, and the remote target system is 192.168.1.99:

```
$ ssh-keygen -t rsa

Generating public/private rsa key pair.
Enter file in which to save the key (/home/tux/.ssh/id_rsa):
Enter passphrase (empty for no passphrase):
Enter same passphrase again:
Your identification has been saved in /home/tux/.ssh/id_rsa.
Your public key has been saved in /home/tux/.ssh/id_rsa.pub.
The key fingerprint is:
SHA256:NVweugZXvDitzl0JGypcWTJOww/F54vmHUbX7r4U2LQ tux@server1
The key's randomart image is:
+---[RSA 2048]----+
|         . +=    |
|          .B=+.. |
|         .o*@.+ ..|
|         +*o* * +|
|        .S.o+ B E |
|        o.o + * o|
|         + + + + |
|          o o o .|
|              oo|
+----[SHA256]-----+
```

Copy the generated keys to a remote host:

```
$ ssh-copy-id tux@192.168.1.99
/usr/bin/ssh-copy-id: INFO: Source of key(s) to be installed: "/home/tux/...
/usr/bin/ssh-copy-id: INFO: attempting to log in with the new key(s), to f...
/usr/bin/ssh-copy-id: INFO: 1 key(s) remain to be installed -- if you are ...
tux@192.168.1.99's password:

Number of key(s) added:        1
```

Now try logging into the target system with ssh tux@192.168.1.99 and check to ensure that only the key(s) you want exist on the target system:

```
$ ssh tux@192.168.1.99

Last login: Sun Sep 26 13:48:19 2021 from 192.168.0.10
[tux@server1 ~]$
```

User tux has successfully logged into the remote host, server1 (192.168.1.99), using a secure key pair rather than a password.

Remote connectivity: client to server

When connecting to a secure protocol service, your client software communicates on a secure channel with the service daemon. You don't have to have users do anything special to negotiate a secure communications link between the client and the service daemon.

It's just as important to keep client software up to date as it is for you, as an administrator, to update the software on servers. I suggest you set up `cron` jobs on each user system to automatically download and install updates and configure each new system to receive regular updates with no user interaction required. Be sure to schedule any required reboots for nighttime or when the user's system is idle.

Summary

In this chapter, you learned about selecting an IP addressing scheme for your network and some advantages and disadvantages of the static and dynamic options. You also now know the security implications of connecting systems to your network. You should understand the dangers and how to, as much as possible, prevent security breaches by implementing some good security practices, such as using secure protocols, turning off unnecessary services and daemons, and keeping systems patched and updated.

In the next chapter, you will learn how to install software via a package manager, update your system, and install software from source code.

## CHAPTER 6

Installing and Uninstalling Software

Installing and uninstalling software are basic system administrator tasks. You might not perform them daily, but these are regular tasks for you and your team to complete. Most often, you'll install updates, which can be automated. Any new software you install should be accompanied by a business justification, a change control record, and a written understanding of security implications, if any, from the requesting party. Installing software with known vulnerabilities is an easy pathway for malicious actors to compromise your systems.

Uninstalling software also requires a change control record because of the potential danger of removing a package, directory, or library required by some other critical system or service function.

There are three software installation methods: installing from repositories using a package manager, installing individual packages downloaded to the local filesystem, and compiling source code. This chapter covers all three methods. There are two standard methods of uninstalling software: using the package management tool and, in the case of compiled software, using an uninstall process. A third, nonstandard uninstall method is manually uninstalling software by removing directories, libraries, and binaries.

Manual software removal is a tedious task that only senior-level sysadmins should perform. The sections in this chapter teach you how to install software by a particular method and then uninstall software by that same method.

Before I discuss installing and uninstalling software, I'll show you how to update your system. Because updating is so important, it's worth discussing first, and you should update before performing other tasks because of the high value of updating your system. You should always update your system when troubleshooting to check whether a simple update resolves your issues. A quick system update might alleviate the need to remove or install new software to solve a problem.

 All demonstrations and examples in this chapter use CentOS 8.3 (server1) and Ubuntu Server 20.04 LTS (server2). I perform all tasks on server1 first and then on server2, noting any differences between the two systems. The software package used in the examples is Lynx, a lightweight text-based browser.

Updating Your System

I've mentioned keeping your system updated multiple times in this book. It's an important task to remember. It should be one of your top priorities. Updates are a part of standard maintenance. Many system administrators apply updates weekly, which is good practice. But don't hesitate to apply patches, updates, and upgrades as needed to mitigate vulnerabilities. Security is your top priority. The following two sections illustrate how to apply updates to your systems.

Applying Red Hat Enterprise Linux–Based System Updates

Red Hat Enterprise Linux–based systems use the YUM/DNF utility to maintain updates and software installation from repositories. From the official Red Hat documentation (*https://oreil.ly/R2Mca*):

> YUM/DNF (yum/dnf) is the primary tool for getting, installing, deleting, querying, and managing Red Hat Enterprise Linux RPM software packages from official Red Hat software repositories, as well as other third-party repositories. YUM/DNF is used in Red Hat Enterprise Linux versions five and newer.

DNF is the latest incarnation of the utility, so I've combined the two. According to the documentation, DNF is YUM version 4 and is the tool to use from Red Hat Enterprise Linux version 8 onward. To begin an update, issue the yum or dnf command:

```
$ sudo yum update
Last metadata expiration check: 1:52:37 ago on Sun 07 Nov 2021 07:14:51 PM CST.
Dependencies resolved.
================================================================================
 Package                      Architecture   Version      Repository     Size
================================================================================
Installing:
 kernel                       x86_64         4.18.0...    baseos         5.9 M
 kernel-core                  x86_64         4.18.0...    baseos          36 M
 kernel-modules               x86_64         4.18.0...    baseos          28 M
Upgrading:
 NetworkManager               x86_64         1:1.30...    baseos         2.6 M
 NetworkManager-config-server noarch         1:1.30...    baseos         129 k
```

```
NetworkManager-libnm        x86_64          1:1.30...       baseos          1.8 M
NetworkManager-team         x86_64          1:1.30...       baseos          146


Removing:
 kernel                     x86_64          4.18.0...       @BaseOS         0
 kernel-core                x86_64          4.18.0...       @BaseOS         60 M
 kernel-modules             x86_64          4.18.0...       @BaseOS         20 M

Transaction Summary
================================================================================
Install     21 Packages
Upgrade    256 Packages
Remove       3 Packages

Total download size: 404 M
Is this ok [y/N]:
```

Agree to the installation here to have your target packages upgraded to the latest stable versions. To automate subsequent updates, use the -y option to answer "yes" to any prompts. The following demonstrates using the -y option with the dnf command:

```
$ sudo dnf -y update
```

This automatically accepts the installation and does not prompt you interactively. This is a great option for use in scripts. The next section provides you with the equivalent update action on Debian-based systems.

Applying Debian-Based System Updates

You apply updates to Debian-based systems with a command analogous to the DNF one you used for Red Hat Enterprise Linux–based systems, using the Debian apt utility, as shown here. You'll also receive a similar response if your system requires updates.

```
$ sudo apt update
```

If your system doesn't require updates, apt's response will look similar to the following:

```
Hit:1 http://us.archive.ubuntu.com/ubuntu focal InRelease
Get:2 http://us.archive.ubuntu.com/ubuntu focal-updates InRelease [114 kB]
Get:3 http://us.archive.ubuntu.com/ubuntu focal-backports InRelease [101 kB]
Get:4 http://us.archive.ubuntu.com/ubuntu focal-security InRelease [114 kB]
Fetched 328 kB in 52s (6,311 B/s)
Reading package lists... Done
Building dependency tree
Reading state information... Done
All packages are up to date.
```

There are no special update commands for patches, security updates, or application version upgrades; this single command takes care of all updates regardless of type or priority on both systems. Your system checks for updates from all configured repositories and applies them when available. It's a good practice to check weekly or more frequently for updates and apply them during a scheduled maintenance window or as necessary for critical security updates.

The rest of this chapter focuses on installing software as on-demand service requests from your users, your management, or other sources.

Installing Software from Repositories

Installing software from a repository is the easiest method of installing software on a Linux system. The reason that it's the easiest method is because the repository automatically meets your dependencies without you having to do anything except request an installation. For example, if you want to install the Apache HTTP Server on a system, there are several dependencies that you must satisfy before it installs. The repository contains all of your dependent packages, gathers, and installs them as they're called for in support of your primary package. I use the text-based Lynx browser for the following installation demonstrations.

Installing an Application

On a CentOS system, enter the following command:

```
$ sudo yum install lynx
Last metadata expiration check: 1:00:58 ago on Fri 05 Nov 2021 10:50:41 AM CDT.
No match for argument: lynx
Error: Unable to find a match: lynx
```

If you receive this error, it means that the package, lynx, in this case, doesn't exist by that name. You'll have to search for the package name or repository that contains the package you want. For example, I had to perform the following steps to install lynx:

```
$ sudo dnf install dnf-plugins-core
```

This installs three packages: dnf-plugins-core, python3-dnf-plugins-core, and yum-utils. Then, use the following command to enable the PowerTools repository where lynx resides:

```
$ sudo dnf config-manager --set-enabled powertools
```

Now, proceed with the installation of lynx and its dependencies:

```
$ sudo dnf install lynx
CentOS Linux 8 - PowerTools                              2.4 kB/s | 2.4 MB     16:50
Last metadata expiration check: 0:14:39 ago on Fri 05 Nov 2021 12:09:08 PM CDT.
Dependencies resolved.
================================================================================
```

```
      Package                Architecture   Version         Repository       Size
================================================================================
Installing:
 lynx                        x86_64         2.8.9-2.el8     powertools       1.6 M
Installing dependencies:
 centos-indexhtml            noarch         8.0-0.el8       baseos           246 k

Transaction Summary
================================================================================
Install  2 Packages

Total download size: 1.8 M
Installed size: 6.5 M
Is this ok [y/N]:
```

Agree to the installation to continue:

```
Is this ok [y/N]: y
Downloading Packages:
(1/2): lynx-2.8.9-2.el8.x86_64.rpm                  208 kB/s | 1.6 MB     00:07
(2/2): centos-indexhtml-8.0-0.el8.noarch.rpm         30 kB/s | 246 kB     00:08
--------------------------------------------------------------------------------
Total                                               207 kB/s | 1.8 MB     00:09
Running transaction check
Transaction check succeeded.
Running transaction test
Transaction test succeeded.
Running transaction
  Preparing        :                                                       1/1
  Installing       : centos-indexhtml-8.0-0.el8.noarch                     1/2
  Installing       : lynx-2.8.9-2.el8.x86_64                               2/2
  Running scriptlet: lynx-2.8.9-2.el8.x86_64                               2/2
  Verifying        : centos-indexhtml-8.0-0.el8.noarch                     1/2
  Verifying        : lynx-2.8.9-2.el8.x86_64                               2/2

Installed:
  centos-indexhtml-8.0-0.el8.noarch               lynx-2.8.9-2.el8.x86_64

Complete!
```

This process installed the Lynx application and its dependency, `centos-indexhtml`.

On an Ubuntu system, enter the following command:

```
$ sudo apt install lynx
Reading package lists... Done
Building dependency tree
Reading state information... Done
The following additional packages will be installed:
  libidn11 lynx-common
The following NEW packages will be installed:
  libidn11 lynx lynx-common
0 upgraded, 3 newly installed, 0 to remove and 0 not upgraded.
Need to get 1,586 kB of archives.
```

```
After this operation, 5,731 kB of additional disk space will be used.
Do you want to continue? [Y/n]
```

Note the two dependencies: *libidn11* and *lynx-common*. The system installs the dependencies before the target package. Continue by responding yes (y) to the prompt:

```
Do you want to continue? [Y/n] y
Get:1 http://us.archive.ubuntu.com/ubuntu focal/main amd64 libidn11 amd64 1.33...
Get:2 http://us.archive.ubuntu.com/ubuntu focal/universe amd64 lynx-common all...
Get:3 http://us.archive.ubuntu.com/ubuntu focal/universe amd64 lynx amd64 2.9....
Fetched 1,586 kB in 4min 29s (5,890 B/s)
Selecting previously unselected package libidn11:amd64.
(Reading database ... 107982 files and directories currently installed.)
Preparing to unpack .../libidn11_1.33-2.2ubuntu2_amd64.deb ...
Unpacking libidn11:amd64 (1.33-2.2ubuntu2) ...
Selecting previously unselected package lynx-common.
Preparing to unpack .../lynx-common_2.9.0dev.5-1_all.deb ...
Unpacking lynx-common (2.9.0dev.5-1) ...
Selecting previously unselected package lynx.
Preparing to unpack .../lynx_2.9.0dev.5-1_amd64.deb ...
Unpacking lynx (2.9.0dev.5-1) ...
Setting up libidn11:amd64 (1.33-2.2ubuntu2) ...
Setting up lynx-common (2.9.0dev.5-1) ...
Setting up lynx (2.9.0dev.5-1) ...
update-alternatives: using /usr/bin/lynx to provide /usr/bin/www-browser ...
Processing triggers for libc-bin (2.31-0ubuntu9.2) ...
Processing triggers for man-db (2.9.1-1) ...
Processing triggers for mime-support (3.64ubuntu1) ...
```

The `apt` package manager installed the `lynx` package and its dependencies. That's all there is to install from a repository. Use the package installer and name the application packages you want to install, and the package manager takes care of everything for you. In the next section, you learn how to uninstall a software package.

Uninstalling an Application

The following simple process uninstalls a target package using a package manager on Red Hat Enterprise Linux–based systems. The Red Hat Package Manager, `rpm`, installs, uninstalls, and queries individual packages and their dependencies. The `-e` option erases (removes) target packages from the system. As you'll see next, when there are no errors from removing a package, the system gives no response. The `autoremove` step automatically removes unused dependencies. Your system might have more than one unused dependency. It's generally safe to remove them:

```
$ sudo rpm -e lynx
$ sudo dnf autoremove
Last metadata expiration check: 0:31:32 ago on Fri 05 Nov 2021 01:52:28 PM CDT.
Dependencies resolved.
================================================================================
```

```
Package                  Architecture      Version       Repository      Size
================================================================================
Removing:
 centos-indexhtml        noarch            8.0-0.el8     @baseos         505 k

Transaction Summary
================================================================================
Remove  1 Package

Freed space: 505 k
Is this ok [y/N]: y
Running transaction check
Transaction check succeeded.
Running transaction test
Transaction test succeeded.
Running transaction
  Preparing        :                                                     1/1
  Erasing          : centos-indexhtml-8.0-0.el8.noarch                   1/1
  Verifying        : centos-indexhtml-8.0-0.el8.noarch                   1/1

Removed:
  centos-indexhtml-8.0-0.el8.noarch

Complete!
```

This process removed the lynx package and its dependency, centos-indexhtml.

The following process uses Ubuntu's apt with the purge option:

```
$ sudo apt purge lynx
Reading package lists... Done
Building dependency tree
Reading state information... Done
The following packages were automatically installed and are no longer required:
  libidn11 lynx-common
Use 'sudo apt autoremove' to remove them.
The following packages will be REMOVED:
  lynx*
0 upgraded, 0 newly installed, 1 to remove and 0 not upgraded.
After this operation, 1,992 kB disk space will be freed.
Do you want to continue? [Y/n] y
(Reading database ... 108095 files and directories currently installed.)
Removing lynx (2.9.0dev.5-1) ...
(Reading database ... 108082 files and directories currently installed.)
Purging configuration files for lynx (2.9.0dev.5-1) ...
```

The purge option removes the lynx package but not the dependencies. As shown in the preceding output, you must run sudo apt autoremove to erase those files from the system. If you use the remove option, then apt only removes the binaries from the system, which leaves configurations and other files intact. In the next section, you learn how to install and remove individual packages using a system's package manager.

Installing and Uninstalling Individual Software Packages

You need software packages from other sources, such as vendor websites, GitHub, and SourceForge that aren't part of any repository. You must install these individual packages manually at the command line. Rather than using repository commands to install these packages, you use the local package manager utilities such as `rpm` and `dpkg`.

 Be sure to read any documentation that accompanies your target package before attempting to install it. Check for dependencies, configurations, and any security warnings. You'll need to satisfy dependencies before installing the target package.

Installing an Individual Software Package Manually

The examples in this section use the `downloadonly` option to download without installing packages from repositories to simplify locating a package for this demonstration. It doesn't matter what the source is for packages, only that you have them downloaded to your system and install them manually at the command line.

On a CentOS system, enter the following command:

```
$ sudo dnf --downloadonly install lynx
Last metadata expiration check: 0:20:15 ago on Sat 06 Nov 2021 08:11:31 AM CDT.
Dependencies resolved.
================================================================================
 Package              Architecture      Version        Repository      Size
================================================================================
Installing:
 lynx                 x86_64            2.8.9-2.el8     powertools      1.6 M
Installing dependencies:
 centos-indexhtml     noarch            8.0-0.el8       baseos          246 k

Transaction Summary
================================================================================
Install  2 Packages

Total download size: 1.8 M
Installed size: 6.5 M
DNF will only download packages for the transaction.
Is this ok [y/N]:y
Downloading Packages:
(1/2): lynx-2.8.9-2.el8.x86_64.rpm                287 kB/s | 1.6 MB     00:05
(2/2): centos-indexhtml-8.0-0.el8.noarch.rpm       37 kB/s | 246 kB     00:06
--------------------------------------------------------------------------------
Total                                             252 kB/s | 1.8 MB     00:07
Complete!
```

```
The downloaded packages were saved in cache until the next successful transact...
You can remove cached packages by executing 'dnf clean packages'.
```

When you download packages using this method, they're stored in a subdirectory of the */var/cache/dnf* directory. The subdirectory to which packages download depends on the repository that the packages originate from. For example, packages can download to any of the following on my CentOS system:

```
/var/cache/dnf/appstream-a520ed22b0a8a736
/var/cache/dnf/AppStream-a520ed22b0a8a736
/var/cache/dnf/baseos-929b586ef1f72f69
/var/cache/dnf/BaseOS-929b586ef1f72f69
/var/cache/dnf/epel-6519ee669354a484
/var/cache/dnf/epel-modular-95d9a0c53e492cbd
/var/cache/dnf/extras-2770d521ba03e231
/var/cache/dnf/powertools-25a6a2b331e53e98
```

In this example, the lynx package downloaded to */var/cache/dnf/powertools-25a6a2b3 31e53e98/packages* and centos-indexhtml downloaded to */var/cache/dnf/baseos-929b586ef1f72f69/packages*.

I will attempt to install the lynx package first, which will fail because of its dependency on the centos-indexhtml package:

```
$ sudo rpm -i lynx-2.8.9-2.el8.x86_64.rpm
error: Failed dependencies:
        redhat-indexhtml is needed by lynx-2.8.9-2.el8.x86_64
```

 Since CentOS is a Red Hat Enterprise Linux binary-compatible distribution, our centos-indexhtml package is equivalent to the redhat-indexhtml package. It will work because the package names are analogous.

Heeding the preceding error, install the centos-indexhtml package first and then proceed to install the lynx package:

```
$ sudo rpm -i centos-indexhtml-8.0-0.el8.noarch.rpm
```

The package installs without error:

```
$ sudo rpm -i lynx-2.8.9-2.el8.x86_64.rpm
```

The lynx package was installed successfully. The rpm switch (-i) means *install*.

For Ubuntu systems, the manual download and install process proceeds as follows:

```
$ sudo apt install --download-only lynx
Reading package lists... Done
Building dependency tree
Reading state information... Done
```

```
The following additional packages will be installed:
  libidn11 lynx-common
The following NEW packages will be installed:
  libidn11 lynx lynx-common
0 upgraded, 3 newly installed, 0 to remove and 0 not upgraded.
Need to get 960 kB/1,586 kB of archives.
After this operation, 5,731 kB of additional disk space will be used.
Do you want to continue? [Y/n]y
Get:1 http://us.archive.ubuntu.com/ubuntu focal/main amd64 libidn11 amd64 1.33...
Get:2 http://us.archive.ubuntu.com/ubuntu focal/universe amd64 lynx-common all...
Get:2 http://us.archive.ubuntu.com/ubuntu focal/universe amd64 lynx-common all...
Fetched 214 kB in 2min 24s (1,491 B/s)
Download complete and in download only mode
```

On Debian-based systems such as Ubuntu, files downloaded this way reside in */var/cache/apt/archives* as *.deb* packages, and you can install them from that location. Note that the apt utility dialog stated that the packages "will be installed" but the final message, "Download complete and in download only mode" means that the packages downloaded but didn't install. In the following example, I attempt to install lynx and ignore the dependencies that downloaded with it:

```
$ sudo dpkg -i lynx_2.9.0dev.5-1_amd64.deb
Selecting previously unselected package lynx.
(Reading database ... 108026 files and directories currently installed.)
Preparing to unpack lynx_2.9.0dev.5-1_amd64.deb ...
Unpacking lynx (2.9.0dev.5-1) ...
dpkg: dependency problems prevent configuration of lynx:
 lynx depends on libidn11 (>= 1.13); however:
  Package libidn11 is not installed.
 lynx depends on lynx-common; however:
  Package lynx-common is not installed.

dpkg: error processing package lynx (--install):
 dependency problems - leaving unconfigured
Errors were encountered while processing:
 lynx
```

The system won't allow you to install without the dependencies that downloaded into the same directory with lynx:

```
$ ls -1 /var/cache/apt/archives
libidn11_1.33-2.2ubuntu2_amd64.deb
lynx_2.9.0dev.5-1_amd64.deb
lynx-common_2.9.0dev.5-1_all.deb
```

Install the dependencies first, and then install lynx:

```
$ sudo dpkg -i libidn11_1.33-2.2ubuntu2_amd64.deb
Selecting previously unselected package libidn11:amd64.
(Reading database ... 108039 files and directories currently installed.)
Preparing to unpack libidn11_1.33-2.2ubuntu2_amd64.deb ...
Unpacking libidn11:amd64 (1.33-2.2ubuntu2) ...
```

```
Setting up libidn11:amd64 (1.33-2.2ubuntu2) ...
Processing triggers for libc-bin (2.31-0ubuntu9.2) …

$ sudo dpkg -i lynx-common_2.9.0dev.5-1_all.deb
Selecting previously unselected package lynx-common.
(Reading database ... 108044 files and directories currently installed.)
Preparing to unpack lynx-common_2.9.0dev.5-1_all.deb ...
Unpacking lynx-common (2.9.0dev.5-1) ...
Setting up lynx-common (2.9.0dev.5-1) ...
Processing triggers for mime-support (3.64ubuntu1) ...
Processing triggers for man-db (2.9.1-1) ...

$ sudo dpkg -i lynx_2.9.0dev.5-1_amd64.deb
(Reading database ... 108136 files and directories currently installed.)
Preparing to unpack lynx_2.9.0dev.5-1_amd64.deb ...
Unpacking lynx (2.9.0dev.5-1) over (2.9.0dev.5-1) ...
Setting up lynx (2.9.0dev.5-1) ...
update-alternatives: using /usr/bin/lynx to provide /usr/bin/www-browser ...
```

The -i switch for the dpkg command means install, just as it does for the rpm utility.
Next, we will uninstall the same packages manually.

Uninstalling Individual Software Packages

To uninstall a manually installed package, you have to reverse the process. This means you uninstall in the opposite order, beginning with the last installed package. In other words, you must uninstall all dependencies before uninstalling the package itself. If there are dependencies, the system will instruct you which ones they are.

On a CentOS system, enter the following command:

```
$ sudo rpm -e centos-indexhtml
error: Failed dependencies:
    redhat-indexhtml is needed by (installed) lynx-2.8.9-2.el8.x86_64

$ sudo rpm -e lynx

$ sudo rpm -e centos-indexhtml
```

You have successfully uninstalled lynx and its dependency, centos-indexhtml.

On an Ubuntu system, you'll notice that when you attempt an uninstall of a package that you manually installed, there are no warnings about dependencies. To uninstall Lynx on Ubuntu, there are three packages, lynx, and its two dependencies: libidn11 and lynx-common.

Look at the differences when attempting to uninstall lynx and its dependencies individually from an Ubuntu system. These are three separate commands to demonstrate how packages and dependencies are or are not removed, depending on which command you use. I've answered no (n) to each for this demonstration:

```
$ sudo apt purge lynx
Reading package lists... Done
Building dependency tree
Reading state information... Done
The following packages will be REMOVED:
  lynx*
0 upgraded, 0 newly installed, 1 to remove and 0 not upgraded.
After this operation, 1,992 kB disk space will be freed.
Do you want to continue? [Y/n]

$ sudo apt purge lynx-common
Reading package lists... Done
Building dependency tree
Reading state information... Done
The following packages will be REMOVED:
  lynx* lynx-common*
0 upgraded, 0 newly installed, 2 to remove and 0 not upgraded.
After this operation, 5,481 kB disk space will be freed.
Do you want to continue? [Y/n]

$ sudo apt purge libidn11
Reading package lists... Done
Building dependency tree
Reading state information... Done
The following packages will be REMOVED:
  libidn11* lynx*
0 upgraded, 0 newly installed, 2 to remove and 0 not upgraded.
After this operation, 2,242 kB disk space will be freed.
Do you want to continue? [Y/n]
```

And, if you remove only lynx from the system, lynx_common and libidn11 are left behind. Issuing the command sudo apt autoremove won't remove the unused dependencies as it did when you installed Lynx from a repository. The following section describes how to find dependencies for a specific software package.

Finding Package Dependencies

It helps to know a package's dependencies before you install it. This is how you find them on a Red Hat Enterprise Linux–based system:

```
$ dnf deplist lynx
CentOS Linux 8 - AppStream                              37 kB/s | 9.6 MB  04:28
CentOS Linux 8 - BaseOS                                 39 kB/s | 8.5 MB  03:44
CentOS Linux 8 - Extras                                7.8 kB/s |  10 kB  00:01
CentOS Linux 8 - PowerTools                            121 kB/s | 2.4 MB  00:20
Extra Packages for Enterprise Linux Modular 8 - x86_64  20 kB/s | 955 kB  00:48
Extra Packages for Enterprise Linux 8 - x86_64          29 kB/s |  11 MB  06:08
package: lynx-2.8.9-2.el8.x86_64
  dependency: libc.so.6(GLIBC_2.15)(64bit)
   provider: glibc-2.28-151.el8.x86_64
```

```
dependency: libcrypto.so.1.1()(64bit)
  provider: openssl-libs-1:1.1.1g-15.el8_3.x86_64
dependency: libcrypto.so.1.1(OPENSSL_1_1_0)(64bit)
  provider: openssl-libs-1:1.1.1g-15.el8_3.x86_64
dependency: libdl.so.2()(64bit)
  provider: glibc-2.28-151.el8.x86_64
dependency: libncursesw.so.6()(64bit)
  provider: ncurses-libs-6.1-7.20180224.el8.x86_64
dependency: libssl.so.1.1()(64bit)
  provider: openssl-libs-1:1.1.1g-15.el8_3.x86_64
dependency: libssl.so.1.1(OPENSSL_1_1_0)(64bit)
  provider: openssl-libs-1:1.1.1g-15.el8_3.x86_64
dependency: libtinfo.so.6()(64bit)
  provider: ncurses-libs-6.1-7.20180224.el8.x86_64
dependency: libz.so.1()(64bit)
  provider: zlib-1.2.11-17.el8.x86_64
dependency: redhat-indexhtml
  provider: centos-indexhtml-8.0-0.el8.noarch
dependency: rtld(GNU_HASH)
  provider: glibc-2.28-151.el8.i686
  provider: glibc-2.28-151.el8.x86_64
```

As mentioned earlier in this chapter, the system has already installed most of the
required dependencies. The required one, centos-indexhtml, doesn't stand out in
any particular way. The only way I know of to isolate any dependencies that your
system requires is to attempt an installation of the target package.

The following listing shows you the same dependency list query on an Ubuntu
system:

```
$ sudo apt show lynx
Package: lynx
Version: 2.9.0dev.5-1
Priority: extra
Section: universe/web
Origin: Ubuntu
Maintainer: Ubuntu Developers <ubuntu-devel-discuss@lists.ubuntu.com>
Original-Maintainer: Debian Lynx Packaging Team <pkg-lynx-maint@lists.aliot...
Bugs: https://bugs.launchpad.net/ubuntu/+filebug
Installed-Size: 1,992 kB
Provides: news-reader, www-browser
Depends: libbsd0 (>= 0.0), libbz2-1.0, libc6 (>= 2.15), libgnutls30 (>= 3.6.12...
Recommends: mime-support
Conflicts: lynx-ssl
Breaks: lynx-cur (<< 2.8.9dev8-2~), lynx-cur-wrapper (<< 2.8.8dev.8-2)
Replaces: lynx-cur (<< 2.8.9dev8-2~), lynx-cur-wrapper (<< 2.8.8dev.8-2)
Homepage: https://lynx.invisible-island.net/
Download-Size: 626 kB
APT-Manual-Installed: yes
APT-Sources: http://us.archive.ubuntu.com/ubuntu focal/universe amd64 Packages
```

```
Description: classic non-graphical (text-mode) web browser
  In continuous development since 1992, Lynx sets the standard for
  text-mode web clients. It is fast and simple to use, with support for
  browsing via FTP, Gopher, HTTP, HTTPS, NNTP, and the local file system.
```

If you're a Linux purist and like to compile your software so that you have maximum control, the next section demonstrates installing a software package from source code.

Installing Software from Source Code

Some system administrators prefer to install all software from source code (also referred to as "source") because it is the most flexible software installation method. Installing from source allows you to customize the installation for your specific needs. You can change installation paths, enable features, disable features, and make minute adjustments to every possible configuration option available for an application.

There are some downsides to installing from source code. The major downside is that you must satisfy dependencies for the software you install. This can be frustrating, time-consuming, and tedious. I have personally chased recursive dependencies to the point where I've forgotten the name of the original application I needed to install. Another downside is that you must install a full complement of development tools onto your systems, which consumes considerable disk space. Another downside is that upgrading to a newer version of the software installed from source code is just as difficult and time-consuming as installing the original version. And if a previous version isn't fully overwritten or removed, you can experience version conflicts that can be quite difficult to resolve.

Satisfying Prerequisites: Building a Development Environment

Before installing any application from source code, you'll need to set up a development environment by installing a code compiler and supporting software. The easiest method is to install a group of software packages from your Linux vendor's repositories.

For Red Hat Enterprise Linux–based systems, using the `groupinstall` option and identifying "`Development Tools`" as the installation target group is the best choice. Unfortunately, this group selection installs many unnecessary and potentially nonsecure packages for compiling source code at the command line, such as a list of graphical tools. For this reason, it's often desirable to set up a specific system dedicated to software development. To create a software development system, use the following command:

```
$ sudo dnf groupinstall "Development Tools"
Last metadata expiration check: 2:41:45 ago on Sun 07 Nov 2021 09:57:05 AM CST.
Dependencies resolved.
================================================================================
 Package                      Architecture  Version          Repository    Size
================================================================================
Upgrading:
 automake                     noarch        1.16.1-7.el8     appstream    713 k
 binutils                     x86_64        2.30-93.el8      baseos       5.8 M
 cpp                          x86_64        8.4.1-1.el8      appstream     10 M
 elfutils-libelf              x86_64        0.182-3.el8      baseos       216 k
 elfutils-libs                x86_64        0.182-3.el8      baseos       293 k
 gcc                          x86_64        8.4.1-1.el8      appstream     23 M

...

 xorg-x11-font-utils          x86_64        1:7.5-40.el8     appstream    103 k
 xorg-x11-fonts-ISO8859-1-100dpi noarch     7.5-19.el8       appstream    1.1 M
 xorg-x11-server-utils        x86_64        7.7-27.el8       appstream    198 k
 zlib-devel                   x86_64        1.2.11-17.el8    baseos        58 k
 zstd                         x86_64        1.4.4-1.el8      appstream    393 k
Installing weak dependencies:
 gcc-gdb-plugin               x86_64        8.4.1-1.el8      appstream    117 k
 kernel-devel                 x86_64        4.18.0-305...    baseos        18 M
Enabling module streams:
 javapackages-runtime                       201801
Installing Groups:
 Development Tools

Transaction Summary
================================================================================
Install  159 Packages
Upgrade   23 Packages

Total download size: 219 M
Is this ok [y/N]:
```

On Ubuntu systems, the equivalent installation uses the option build-essential to install all the necessary development tools on your system:

```
$ sudo apt install build-essential
Reading package lists... Done
Building dependency tree
Reading state information... Done
The following additional packages will be installed:
  binutils binutils-common binutils-x86-64-linux-gnu cpp cpp-9 dpkg-dev fakero...
g++ g++-9 gcc gcc-9 gcc-9-base libalgorithm-diff-perl libalgorithm-diff-xs-per...
libasan5 libatomic1 libbinutils libc-dev-bin libc6-dev libcc1-0 libcrypt-dev l...
libctf0 libdpkg-perl libfakeroot libfile-fcntllock-perl libgcc-9-dev libgomp1 ...
libitm1 liblsan0 libmpc3 libquadmath0 libstdc++-9-dev libtsan0 libubsan1 linux...
make manpages-dev
```

```
Suggested packages:
  binutils-doc cpp-doc gcc-9-locales debian-keyring g++-multilib g++-9-multili...
gcc-multilib autoconf automake libtool flex bison gdb gcc-doc gcc-9-multilib g...
bzr libstdc++-9-doc make-doc
The following NEW packages will be installed:
  binutils binutils-common binutils-x86-64-linux-gnu build-essential cpp cpp-9...
fakeroot g++ g++-9 gcc gcc-9 gcc-9-base libalgorithm-diff-perl libalgorithm-di...
libalgorithm-merge-perl libasan5 libatomic1 libbinutils libc-dev-bin libc6-dev...
libcrypt-dev libctf-nobfd0 libctf0 libdpkg-perl libfakeroot libfile-fcntllock-...
libgcc-9-dev libgomp1 libisl22 libitm1 liblsan0 libmpc3 libquadmath0 libstdc++...
libtsan0 libubsan1 linux-libc-dev make manpages-dev
0 upgraded, 41 newly installed, 0 to remove and 0 not upgraded.
Need to get 43.0 MB of archives.
After this operation, 189 MB of additional disk space will be used.
Do you want to continue? [Y/n]
```

Confirm the installation and continue. Installing groups of packages can take several minutes. Once your development environment is set up, you'll need to download the source code for Lynx. The instructions for installing from source are the same for any Linux distribution; however, I will perform this installation on both the CentOS and the Ubuntu systems and note any differences and errors in the text. Users may download, compile, and make the binaries, but only the root user can install binaries to the system directories.

Download, Extract, Compile, and Install Your Software

Download your compressed source code using a utility such as wget:

```
$ wget https://invisible-mirror.net/archives/lynx/tarballs/lynx2.8.9rel.1.tar.gz
```

Extract the source code from the compressed archive:

```
$ tar zxvf lynx2.8.9rel.1.tar.gz
```

Change the directory into the lynx source tree created by the extraction process:

```
$ cd lynx2.8.9rel.1
```

Before running configure, take a few minutes to look for and read the *README* file that often exists in source code trees. This file has valuable instructions and information about the source code and installation instructions. The *README* file usually refers to the *INSTALLATION* file describing installation options. I accept all the defaults for demonstration purposes and simply run the configure script. If all dependencies are met, the configuration checks will go without error, create the makefile, and then drop you back at your shell prompt. This process can take a few minutes to complete:

```
$ ./configure
```

Both configure scripts failed with the following error:

```
checking for screen type... curses
checking for specific curses-directory... no
checking for extra include directories... no
checking if we have identified curses headers... none
configure: error: No curses header-files found
```

When you encounter errors, the configure script (configure) stops but keeps its place so that you may continue where you left off as you satisfy dependencies by running the script again. To satisfy the current dependency, I installed the ncurses-devel package (sudo dnf -y install ncurses-devel) on the CentOS system. The configure script completed successfully. For the Ubuntu system, I installed the lib32ncurses-dev package (sudo apt install lib32ncurses-dev), and the configure script completed successfully.

According to the *INSTALLATION* file, you now must run the make command to compile the sources. This process will take a few minutes to complete:

```
$ make
```

After satisfying the failed dependencies in the configure script, both compilations successfully completed. To install Lynx to its proper location and set the correct permissions, run sudo make install:

```
$ sudo make install
/bin/sh -c "P=`echo lynx|sed 's,x,x,'`; \
if test -f /usr/local/bin/$P ; then \
    mv -f /usr/local/bin/$P /usr/local/bin/$P.old; fi"
/usr/bin/install -c lynx /usr/local/bin/`echo lynx|sed 's,x,x,'`
/usr/bin/install -c -m 644 ./lynx.man /usr/.../man1/`echo lynx|sed 's,x,x,'`.1
** installing ./lynx.cfg as /usr/local/etc/lynx.cfg
** installing ./samples/lynx.lss as /usr/local/etc/lynx.lss

Use make install-help to install the help-files
Use make install-doc to install extra documentation files
```

At this point, most instructions advise you to run make clean to remove all of the object code and other temporary files from your system:

```
$ make clean
rm -f WWW/Library/*/*.[aoib]
rm -f WWW/Library/*/.created
cd ./WWW/Library/Implementation && make  DESTDIR="" CC="gcc" clean
make[1]: Entering directory '/home/khess/lynx2.8.9rel.1/.../Implementation'
rm -f core *.core *.leaks *.[oi] *.bak tags TAGS
rm -f dtd_util
rm -f ./*.o
make[1]: Leaving directory '/home/khess/lynx2.8.9rel.1/.../Implementation'
cd ./src && make  DESTDIR="" CC="gcc" clean
make[1]: Entering directory '/home/khess/lynx2.8.9rel.1/src'
rm -f lynx core *.core *.leaks *.i *.o *.bak tags TAGS test_*
```

```
cd chrtrans && make  DESTDIR="" CC="gcc" clean
make[2]: Entering directory '/home/khess/lynx2.8.9rel.1/src/chrtrans'
rm -f makeuctb *.o *uni.h *uni2.h *.i
make[2]: Leaving directory '/home/khess/lynx2.8.9rel.1/src/chrtrans'
make[1]: Leaving directory '/home/khess/lynx2.8.9rel.1/src'
rm -f *.b ./src/lynx *.leaks cfg_defs.h LYHelp.h lint.*
rm -f help_files.sed
rm -f core *.core
```

It's a matter of preference to run this command. If you need to remove compiled soft-ware from your system, the next section steps you through the process of doing so.

Uninstalling a Source-Installed Software Package

If your source trees exist with your original makefile intact, you can uninstall a package quite easily, but you must have the makefile to do so. If you don't want to keep all your source trees on your system for every compiled program, make a backup of the makefile, such as copying it to a backup directory with the name *makefile.lynx289r1* or similar. The makefile must be in your current directory when uninstalling:

```
$ sudo make uninstall
rm -f /usr/local/bin/`echo lynx|sed 's,x,x,'`
rm -f /usr/local/share/man/man1/`echo lynx|sed 's,x,x,'`.1
rm -f /usr/local/etc/lynx.cfg
rm -f /usr/local/etc/lynx.lss
/bin/sh -c 'if test -d "/usr/local/share/lynx_help" ; then \
    WD=`cd "/usr/local/share/lynx_help" && pwd` ; \
    TAIL=`basename "/usr/local/share/lynx_help"` ; \
    HEAD=`echo "$WD"|sed -e "s,/${TAIL}$,,"` ; \
    test "x$WD" != "x$HEAD" && rm -rf "/usr/local/share/lynx_help"; \
    fi'
/bin/sh -c 'if test -d "/usr/local/share/lynx_doc" ; then \
    WD=`cd "/usr/local/share/lynx_doc" && pwd` ; \
    TAIL=`basename "/usr/local/share/lynx_doc"` ; \
    HEAD=`echo "$WD"|sed -e "s,/${TAIL}$,,"` ; \
    test "x$WD" != "x$HEAD" && rm -rf "/usr/local/share/lynx_doc"; \
    fi'
/bin/sh -c 'if test -d "/usr/local/share/lynx_help" ; then \
    WD=`cd "/usr/local/share/lynx_help" && pwd` ; \
    TAIL=`basename "/usr/local/share/lynx_help"` ; \
    HEAD=`echo "$WD"|sed -e "s,/'${TAIL}'$,,"` ; \
    test "x$WD" != "x$HEAD" ; \
    cd "/usr/local/share/lynx_help" && rm -f COPYING COPYHEADER ; \
    fi'
```

If you don't have your makefile or it isn't in your current directory, you receive the following error:

```
$ sudo make uninstall
make: *** No rule to make target 'uninstall'.  Stop.
```

You can re-create the makefile if you extract the same version of the source tree that you previously used and can remember your configure options. Otherwise, you can use the preceding uninstall results to guide you in uninstalling manually.

Summary

This chapter walked you through installing software from different sources: repositories, local package files, and source code. You'll find that installing software is easy enough with a little practice. Please remember that the responsibility of keeping your systems running smoothly and securely rests with you. Just because installing software is quick and easy doesn't mean that you should ignore its impact on system performance, security, and disk usage.

The next chapter teaches you how to add disk space to your systems.

## CHAPTER 7

Managing Storage

In this chapter, you learn how to add storage to your systems. You'll see how to add a new disk drive to the system and make it available. You will also explore the logical volume manager and how to manipulate logical volumes, as well as learn about disk formatting, partitioning, and mounting.

In the first section, I cover some general concepts related to disks, filesystems, volumes, partitions, directories, and filesystem mounting.

Administering Linux Storage

The price of disk space has decreased so much in recent years that space is no longer a high-value commodity. You can buy multiterabyte disks for a few dollars per gigabyte. So system administrators rarely have to threaten to implement quotas or other arbitrary limits on disk space. Workstations and laptops often have as much space as servers, so space is no longer at a premium, and managing it is far less of a problem than it was just a few years ago. For example, many sysadmins now bypass old backup methods such as tape for faster and cheaper disk-to-disk backups.

But even though disk space is cheap and available, sysadmins still need to monitor users' disk usage. You don't want individuals filling up shared disk spaces or home directories with their music, videos, or other large files, because they waste corporate-owned space and prolong backup times. This section discusses disk-related terminology and how Linux system administrators interpret those terms. The specifics of how to work with each of these items are covered later in the chapter.

Disks

Disks (disk drives) are the devices that we refer to as hard drives or hard disk drives (HDDs), but *disks* can also refer to solid-state drives (SSDs) and USB thumb drives. System administrators make entire disks available to Linux systems using internal connections, USB connectivity, or an over-the-network technology such as Ethernet or fiber optic cabling. Before accessing a disk on Linux systems, a system administrator must mount the disk on a directory. For example, to mount a new disk identified by the system as */dev/sdd*, the sysadmin creates a new directory, such as */software*, and mounts the entire disk on that directory or *mount point*:

```
$ sudo mount /dev/sdd1 /software
```

The disk device */dev/sdd1* is now mounted on the directory */software* and is accessible.

 The entire disk device is */dev/sdd* but initializing the disk requires at least one partition, so if disk */dev/sdd* has only a single partition, its name will be */dev/sdd1*. Details of this process appear later in this chapter.

Once the administrator prepares the disk by partitioning and establishing a filesystem on it, users may access space made available to them.

Filesystems

A *filesystem* is an organizational construct that allows for file storage and retrieval for an operating system. A filesystem is a data structure the operating system uses to keep track of files on a disk or partition. It is how the files are organized on the disk. A filesystem is a partition or entire disk that stores files.

Contemporary Linux systems give administrators a broad choice of filesystems, although many sysadmins stick with ZFS, XFS, or ext4 when creating new partitions. There are many other filesystems available for specific needs and applications.

Mounting and Mount Points

Only the root user, or a user with sudo privileges, may mount a filesystem. Mounting a filesystem on a directory is roughly analogous to assigning a drive letter to a disk in Windows. Linux uses directories rather than drive letters, and those directories are referred to as mount points. In the example in "Disks", a new disk, */dev/sdd,* was mounted on the directory */software. /software* is the mount point.

Linux systems provide a generic mount point, */mnt*, onto which you may temporarily mount disks. You shouldn't use the */mnt* directory for a permanent mount point because another system administrator might mount another filesystem over it, hiding the original contents.

Mount points need not be directories off of the root directory. They can be subdirectories. For example, you could mount the */dev/sdd* disk onto */opt/software*:

```
$ sudo mount /dev/sdd1 /opt/software
```

A mount point (directory) must exist before mounting a disk or filesystem onto it.

There's nothing special about a mount point directory. It's the same as any other directory on the filesystem. Create a new directory, set its permissions, and mount the filesystem or disk onto it.

Don't mount filesystems or disks onto existing system directories such as */tmp*, */var*, */usr*, */etc*, etc. Doing so will cause erratic system behavior and possibly catastrophic failure.

To cause disks to mount automatically at boot time, you must create an entry in the */etc/fstab* file that includes the new disk or filesystem and the mount point. For example, to automatically mount the */dev/sdd1* partition onto the */opt/software* directory, the */etc/fstab* entry looks like the following:

```
UUID=324ddbc2-353b-4221-a80e-49ec356678dc /opt/software    xfs    defaults    0 0
```

If you don't create this entry, the */dev/sdd1* won't mount automatically upon reboot. This isn't a problem if that's your intent or if you only have a few systems, but if you manage dozens or hundreds of systems, you need to set up */etc/fstab* for each filesystem or disk you wish to mount automatically.

Physical and Logical Volumes

When sysadmins speak of physical and logical volumes, they refer to logical volume management (LVM). Figure 7-1 shows a visual reference of the Logical Volume Manager. A physical volume is a partition or disk managed by a logical volume. The physical volume looks exactly like a disk partition. For example, the partition */dev/sdd1* is also the physical volume */dev/sdd1*.

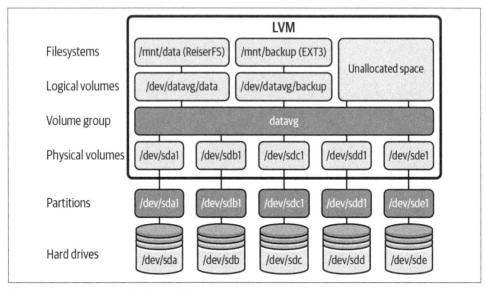

Figure 7-1. The Logical Volume Manager

A volume group contains physical volumes. A logical volume is equivalent to a partition on a disk, but you create logical volume partitions from volume groups. Logical volumes contain filesystems that are named, and those names can be descriptive.

Another way of thinking about logical volumes is that volume groups are analogous to disks, and logical volumes are analogous to disk partitions.

The advantages of abstracting physical volumes into logical ones are that you have the flexibility of spanning multiple disks to create large volume groups and can dynamically resize (shrink and grow) logical volumes without taking the system offline to do so.

Checking Space

Sysadmins should keep a close eye on disk space usage. Log files can grow to fill filesystems if something goes wrong on a system, such as a buffer overflow. Users often fill filesystems and shared spaces with nonwork files. Developers also often download gigabytes of code and other files without discussing their needs with the sysadmins or anyone else. You can quickly check disk space using the *disk free* (df) command:

```
$ df -h
Filesystem           Size  Used Avail Use% Mounted on
/dev/mapper/cl-root   6.2G  3.3G  3.0G  53% /
/dev/sdb1             1.5G   43M  1.4G   3% /opt/software
/dev/sda1             976M  250M  660M  28% /boot
```

The df command lets you know at a glance how much available space there is on your mounted filesystems. The -h switch means human-readable, which means M for megabytes, G for gigabytes, etc. Monitoring systems or your own scripts can alert you to filesystems that fill beyond a given threshold. For example, setting a 90% threshold would trigger an alert that a particular filesystem is at or over 90% capacity.

The disk usage (du) command is very handy for checking individual directories and provides a breakdown of what's consuming space. For example, the following command checks the space consumed by the /var/log directory:

```
$ sudo du -h /var/log
0      /var/log/private
0      /var/log/samba/old
0      /var/log/samba
36K     /var/log/sssd
28K     /var/log/tuned
2.3M     /var/log/audit
0     /var/log/chrony
3.3M     /var/log/anaconda
10M     /var/log
```

You can see at a glance which directories consume the most disk space. This is important if you're auditing your system's disk space before removing unneeded files.

Swap Space

Swap space is a special type of Linux disk partition that extends a system's memory beyond the limits of physical random access memory (RAM). Your system's kernel uses swap space to write inactive programs from memory to disk, freeing up memory for active programs. If a user or process activates those swapped programs, the system writes them from disk back into memory.

Expanding swap space is not a remedy for solving memory problems. If your system has memory constraints, one accepted solution is to add more physical RAM rather than increasing swap space or adding another swap partition. A system's overuse of swap space creates a condition known as *thrashing*. Thrashing occurs when too many programs are running, the swap partition is too small, or the system has insufficient physical RAM to support its processes.

I discuss how to create and manage swap space later in this chapter.

RAM-Based Temporary Space (ramfs and tmpfs)

Ramfs and *tmpfs* are filesystems whose files exist in memory and are not written to disk. The *tmpfs* system is the newer and preferred RAM-based temporary filesystem, and *tmpfs* is the default for all contemporary Linux distributions. One reason for the transition away from *ramfs* to *tmpfs* is that *ramfs* allowed itself to fill to capacity.

Tmpfs has limit checking to prevent reaching its maximum capacity. *Tmpfs* adds the feature of writing files to available swap space to save resources.

The following listings show the *tmpfs* mount information for both CentOS and Ubuntu systems, respectively:

```
$ mount | grep tmpfs
devtmpfs on /dev type devtmpfs (rw,nosuid,seclabel,size=397220k,nr_inodes=9930...
tmpfs on /dev/shm type tmpfs (rw,nosuid,nodev,seclabel)
tmpfs on /run type tmpfs (rw,nosuid,nodev,seclabel,mode=755)
tmpfs on /sys/fs/cgroup type tmpfs (ro,nosuid,nodev,noexec,seclabel,mode=755)
tmpfs on /run/user/1000 type tmpfs (rw,nosuid,nodev,relatime,seclabel,size=828...

$ mount | grep tmpfs
udev on /dev type devtmpfs (rw,nosuid,noexec,relatime,size=456144k,nr_inodes=1...
tmpfs on /run type tmpfs (rw,nosuid,nodev,noexec,relatime,size=100480k,mode=755)
tmpfs on /dev/shm type tmpfs (rw,nosuid,nodev)
tmpfs on /run/lock type tmpfs (rw,nosuid,nodev,noexec,relatime,size=5120k)
tmpfs on /sys/fs/cgroup type tmpfs (ro,nosuid,nodev,noexec,mode=755)
tmpfs on /run/snapd/ns type tmpfs (rw,nosuid,nodev,noexec,relatime,size=100480...
tmpfs on /run/user/1000 type tmpfs (rw,nosuid,nodev,relatime,size=100480k,mode...
```

The purpose of *tmpfs* is to write temporary files and caches to memory rather than to disk because of the speed differences between RAM and disk. RAM is many times faster than the fastest SSD. The downside of *tmpfs* is that if you reboot or unmount *tmpfs*, the data you have stored there is lost. Programs, processes, and users may all write to this temporary space. Similar to disk-based filesystems, a warning of "no space left on device" occurs when files, from whatever sources, have filled the allotted space.

Adding a New Disk to a System

In this section, I show you the steps required to add a new disk to a system and prepare the disk for use. First, I describe how to add a disk to a physical system. Then I demonstrate the same procedure but using a virtual disk. You'll also learn how to create a filesystem on the disk and mount it as a single usable directory. I also demonstrate how to set up a logical volume on a disk.

 You must have root privileges to perform these system-level functions.

Installing the Disk

You can simply attach a hard drive without powering it down for physical systems with hot-swappable disk interfaces. If your system doesn't have hot-swappable interfaces, shut it down before adding a new disk. Once you've physically added the disk, power on the system (if required) and log in to set it up.

For those who use virtual machines (VMs), shut down your VM, add a new disk, and restart it. From then on, the process is the same for physical and virtual systems.

 I can't demonstrate adding a new virtual disk because there are too many virtual platforms available from which to choose. It generally involves selecting storage, attaching a virtual disk to a virtual controller, adjusting the size of the disk, and saving the configuration.

Prepping the Disk for Use

You must first determine the new disk's device name. The system assigns the device name automatically. Use the `fdisk` command to display all attached disks and partitions:

```
$ sudo fdisk -l

Disk /dev/sda: 8 GiB, 8589934592 bytes, 16777216 sectors
Units: sectors of 1 * 512 = 512 bytes
Sector size (logical/physical): 512 bytes / 512 bytes
I/O size (minimum/optimal): 512 bytes / 512 bytes
Disklabel type: dos
Disk identifier: 0x38e117ab

Device     Boot    Start      End   Sectors Size Id Type
/dev/sda1  *        2048  2099199   2097152   1G 83 Linux
/dev/sda2        2099200 16777215  14678016   7G 8e Linux LVM


Disk /dev/sdb: 1.5 GiB, 1550843904 bytes, 3028992 sectors
Units: sectors of 1 * 512 = 512 bytes
Sector size (logical/physical): 512 bytes / 512 bytes
I/O size (minimum/optimal): 512 bytes / 512 bytes
Disklabel type: dos
Disk identifier: 0xd268486b
```

In the preceding listing, the system identified the new disk device as */dev/sdb*. Now that you've identified the disk's device name, you can begin initializing it using the `fdisk` command:

```
$ sudo fdisk /dev/sdb

Welcome to fdisk (util-linux 2.32.1).
Changes will remain in memory only, until you decide to write them.
Be careful before using the write command.


Command (m for help): n

Partition type
   p   primary (0 primary, 0 extended, 4 free)
   e   extended (container for logical partitions)
Select (default p): <ENTER>
Partition number (1-4, default 1): <ENTER>
First sector (2048-3028991, default 2048): <ENTER>
Last sector, +sectors or +size{K,M,G,T,P} (2048-3028991, default 3028991): <EN...

Created a new partition 1 of type 'Linux' and of size 1.5 GiB.

Command (m for help): w

The partition table has been altered.
Failed to add partition 1 to system: Device or resource busy

The kernel still uses the old partitions. The new table will be used at the ne...
Syncing disks.

$ sudo fdisk -l
Disk /dev/sda: 8 GiB, 8589934592 bytes, 16777216 sectors
Units: sectors of 1 * 512 = 512 bytes
Sector size (logical/physical): 512 bytes / 512 bytes
I/O size (minimum/optimal): 512 bytes / 512 bytes
Disklabel type: dos
Disk identifier: 0x38e117ab

Device     Boot    Start       End  Sectors Size Id Type
/dev/sda1  *        2048  2099199  2097152   1G 83 Linux
/dev/sda2        2099200 16777215 14678016   7G 8e Linux LVM


Disk /dev/sdb: 1.5 GiB, 1550843904 bytes, 3028992 sectors
Units: sectors of 1 * 512 = 512 bytes
Sector size (logical/physical): 512 bytes / 512 bytes
I/O size (minimum/optimal): 512 bytes / 512 bytes
Disklabel type: dos
Disk identifier: 0xd268486b

Device     Boot Start     End Sectors  Size Id Type
/dev/sdb1       2048 3028991 3026944  1.5G 83 Linux
```

You can ignore the message Failed to add partition 1 to system: Device or resource busy. You can see that the partition */dev/sdb1* does exist on the system. You have initialized the disk and created partition */dev/sdb1*. Now you must create the filesystem. The following command formats the */dev/sdb1* partition using XFS:

```
$ sudo mkfs.xfs /dev/sdb1
meta-data=/dev/sdb1              isize=512    agcount=4, agsize=94592 blks
         =                       sectsz=512   attr=2, projid32bit=1
         =                       crc=1        finobt=1, sparse=1, rmapbt=0
         =                       reflink=1
data     =                       bsize=4096   blocks=378368, imaxpct=25
         =                       sunit=0      swidth=0 blks
naming   =version 2              bsize=4096   ascii-ci=0, ftype=1
log      =internal log           bsize=4096   blocks=2560, version=2
         =                       sectsz=512   sunit=0 blks, lazy-count=1
realtime =none                   extsz=4096   blocks=0, rtextents=0
```

The following command lists all block devices and filesystems:

```
$ sudo lsblk -f
NAME          FSTYPE        LABEL UUID        MOUNTPOINT
loop0         squashfs                        /var/lib/snapd/snap/asciinema/16
loop1         squashfs                        /var/lib/snapd/snap/core/10577
loop2         squashfs                        /var/lib/snapd/snap/core/10583
sda
├─sda1        ext4          1825fee2...       /boot
└─sda2        LVM2_member   PqHcgi-X...
  ├─cl-root xfs             41b93d34...       /
  └─cl-swap swap            6b31789a...       [SWAP]
sdb
└─sdb1        xfs           ca2701e0...
sr0
```

The lsblk command also displays the devices' universally unique identifiers (UUIDs), which you need for the last step of the disk preparation process: mounting the filesystem.

You can also display the UUID by issuing the blkid command with the device name as the argument:

```
$ sudo blkid /dev/sdb1
```

Next, create a directory on which you want to mount the new partition. I use */opt/software* as the mount point in this example:

```
$ sudo mkdir /opt/software
```

Mount the */dev/sdb1* partition onto the */opt/software* directory:

```
$ sudo mount /dev/sdb1 /opt/software
```

Check to see if the preceding mount command worked correctly by using the mount command without any switches:

```
$ mount | grep sdb1
/dev/sdb1 on /opt/software type xfs (rw,relatime,seclabel,attr2,inode64,logbuf...
```

The partition */dev/sdb1* successfully mounted on */opt/software*. Now you need to make this mount "permanent," which means it will survive a system reboot. Edit the */etc/fstab* file and enter the following information:

```
UUID=ca2701e0-3e75-4930-b14e-d83e19a5cffb /opt/software    xfs    defaults   0 0
```

Save the file. The */dev/sdb1* partition will mount automatically once you reboot the system. Debian-derived systems handle this */etc/fstab* syntax a bit differently. On the Ubuntu system, this */etc/fstab* entry looks like the following:

```
/dev/disk/by-uuid/ca2701e0-3e75-4930-b14e-d83e1... /opt/software xfs defaults 0 0
```

To allow users to access the drive, alter the permissions of */opt/software* or create subdirectories with appropriate permissions.

Implementing Logical Volumes

Logical volumes give you much flexibility in allocating disk space. The capability of resizing live partitions is a huge feature because adding or removing disk space from a partition doesn't require any system downtime. You should still schedule a maintenance window when resizing a logical volume because there is still potential for something to go wrong during the process. If you make a mistake, you could lose data or possibly have to rebuild the entire logical volume. Disasters are somewhat unlikely, but they can happen.

Resizing isn't the only notable feature of logical volumes. A logical volume can span disks, meaning you can create a very large logical volume from multiple disks. A few years ago, administrators were reluctant to create volumes that span multiple disks because spinning, mechanical hard drives are prone to failure. But using SSDs deprecates the "don't span" rule. SSDs fail too, but their lifespans and reliability make it much more reasonable to span when necessary.

This section demonstrates how to set up a logical volume from a raw disk. (You can convert a currently used disk to a logical volume, but you will lose all the data in the process.)

Identifying available disks

To check your system for available (unused) disks or disks that you want to convert to logical volumes, use the `lsblk` command:

```
$ lsblk
NAME        MAJ:MIN RM   SIZE RO TYPE MOUNTPOINT
loop0         7:0    0   8.5M  1 loop /var/lib/snapd/snap/asciinema/16
loop1         7:1    0  97.9M  1 loop /var/lib/snapd/snap/core/10577
loop2         7:2    0  97.9M  1 loop /var/lib/snapd/snap/core/10583
sda           8:0    0     8G  0 disk
├─sda1        8:1    0     1G  0 part /boot
└─sda2        8:2    0     7G  0 part
  ├─cl-root 253:0    0   6.2G  0 lvm  /
  └─cl-swap 253:1    0   820M  0 lvm  [SWAP]
sdb          8:16    0   1.5G  0 disk
sr0          11:0    1  1024M  0 rom
```

From the listing, in the line containing the disk, `sdb` shows that it is online and available for use:

```
sdb          8:16    0   1.5G  0 disk
```

First, you must create the physical volume (PV), which is the basic block device onto which you'll build logical volumes. Use the `pvcreate` command and the device name to initialize the disk as a physical volume:

```
$ sudo pvcreate /dev/sdb
WARNING: dos signature detected on /dev/sdb at offset 510. Wipe it? [y/n]: y
  Wiping dos signature on /dev/sdb.
  Physical volume "/dev/sdb" successfully created.
```

List all physical volumes and confirm that *dev/sdb* is among them using the pvs (PV Show) command:

```
$ sudo pvs
  PV         VG Fmt  Attr PSize  PFree
  /dev/sda2  cl lvm2 a--  <7.00g     0
  /dev/sdb      lvm2 ---   1.44g 1.44g
```

Use the `pvdisplay` command to see details about your physical volume:

```
$ sudo pvdisplay /dev/sdb
  "/dev/sdb" is a new physical volume of "1.44 GiB"
  --- NEW Physical volume ---
  PV Name               /dev/sdb
  VG Name
  PV Size               1.44 GiB
  Allocatable           NO
  PE Size               0
  Total PE              0
  Free PE               0
  Allocated PE          0
  PV UUID               yl6k0u-cymt-p4jd-VXro-Lit1-EkLe-Jqjc94
```

If your disk or filesystem is already mounted when you attempt to use pvcreate, you'll receive the following error:

```
$ sudo pvcreate /dev/sdb
  Can't open /dev/sdb exclusively.  Mounted filesystem?
```

You'll need to unmount *dev/sdb* (umount /dev/sdb) before proceeding.

The second step is to create a volume group (VG) from the physical volume */dev/sdb* using the vgcreate command. Give the VG a name, as I've done here with *vgsw*:

```
$ sudo vgcreate vgsw /dev/sdb
  Volume group "vgsw" successfully created

$ sudo vgs
  VG    #PV #LV #SN Attr   VSize  VFree
  cl      1   2   0 wz--n- <7.00g    0
  vgsw    1   0   0 wz--n-  1.44g 1.44g

$ sudo vgdisplay vgsw
  --- Volume group ---
  VG Name               vgsw
  System ID
  Format                lvm2
  Metadata Areas        1
  Metadata Sequence No  1
  VG Access             read/write
  VG Status             resizable
  MAX LV                0
  Cur LV                0
  Open LV               0
  Max PV                0
  Cur PV                1
  Act PV                1
  VG Size               1.44 GiB
  PE Size               4.00 MiB
  Total PE              369
  Alloc PE / Size       0 / 0
  Free  PE / Size       369 / 1.44 GiB
  VG UUID               AsQkWT-UpSu-3dYk-5EWT-DbQR-SovE-2oAmlR
```

As depicted in Figure 7-1, you create volume groups from physical volumes. In this demonstration, I only used one physical volume. Now that you have a volume group, you must create logical volumes. Creating the logical volume is the third step in this process.

For this demonstration, I begin by deciding how much space to allocate to the logical volume. I decide to use 1 GB of the 1.5 GB disk. It's now time to create the logical volume using the lvcreate command.

The general syntax of the `lvcreate` command is as follows:

```
$ sudo lvcreate -L size -n lvname vg
```

You must provide the size parameter in gigabytes or megabytes, by adding a trailing G or M, respectively. The `lvname` is the name you want to use for this logical volume (`software-lv`) and you must supply the volume group name (`vgsw`) from which you want to create the logical volume (`software-lv`):

```
$ sudo lvcreate -L 1G -n software-lv vgsw
WARNING: xfs signature detected on /dev/vgsw/software-lv at offset 0.
Wipe it? [y/n]: y
  Wiping xfs signature on /dev/vgsw/software-lv.
  Logical volume "software-lv" created.
```

From the preceding message, you see that the disk or partition had previously held an `xfs signature`, which means it's not a new disk or partition but a recycled one.

 There's no problem with using a previously used disk but realize that all the information on it will be overwritten and unrecoverable in this process.

Use the `lvs` and `lvdisplay` commands to list details about your logical volumes:

```
$ sudo lvs
  LV          VG   Attr       LSize    Pool Origin Data%  Meta%  Move Log ...
  root        cl   -wi-ao---- <6.20g
  swap        cl   -wi-ao---- 820.00m
  software-lv vgsw -wi-a----- 1.00g

$ sudo lvdisplay /dev/vgsw/software-lv
  --- Logical volume ---
  LV Path                /dev/vgsw/software-lv
  LV Name                software-lv
  VG Name                vgsw
  LV UUID                ebB3ST-3E7k-BShG-8oPi-sj0c-yXXr-C7EgAw
  LV Write Access        read/write
  LV Creation host, time server1, 2021-12-10 07:34:56 -0600
  LV Status              available
  # open                 0
  LV Size                1.00 GiB
  Current LE             256
  Segments               1
  Allocation             inherit
  Read ahead sectors     auto
  - currently set to     8192
  Block device           253:2
```

You must use the full path to the logical volume device (/dev/vgsw/software-lv) when you filter by the logical volume name:

```
$ sudo lvs /dev/vgsw/software-lv
    LV      VG    Attr          LSize Pool Origin ...
    software-lv vgsw -wi-a----- 1.00g
```

The fourth step in this process is to create a filesystem on your logical volume. You perform this task by using the same command that you would use for any partition:

```
$ sudo mkfs.xfs /dev/vgsw/software-lv
meta-data=/dev/vgsw/software-lv  isize=512    agcount=4, agsize=65536 blks
         =                       sectsz=512   attr=2, projid32bit=1
         =                       crc=1        finobt=1, sparse=1, rmapbt=0
         =                       reflink=1
data     =                       bsize=4096   blocks=262144, imaxpct=25
         =                       sunit=0      swidth=0 blks
naming   =version 2             bsize=4096   ascii-ci=0, ftype=1
log      =internal log          bsize=4096   blocks=2560, version=2
         =                       sectsz=512   sunit=0 blks, lazy-count=1
realtime =none                  extsz=4096   blocks=0, rtextents=0
```

Create a mount point for your filesystem:

```
$ sudo mkdir /sw
```

Mount the filesystem onto the mount point:

```
$ sudo mount /dev/vgsw/software-lv /sw

$ mount | grep software
/dev/mapper/vgsw-software--lv on /sw type xfs \
(rw,relatime,seclabel,attr2,inode64,logbufs=8,logbsize=32k,noquota)
```

Check available space on the device:

```
$ df -h /sw
Filesystem                   Size  Used Avail Use% Mounted on
/dev/mapper/vgsw-software--lv 1014M   40M  975M   4% /sw
```

The final step is to add the filesystem and its mount point to /etc/fstab to mount the logical volume automatically at boot time. My entry looks like the following:

```
/dev/vgsw/software-lv /sw      xfs     defaults        0 0
```

Don't use the UUID for defining logical volumes in /etc/fstab. Instead, use the device name (/dev/vgsw/software-lv).

The logical volume will mount automatically on reboot. The next section describes how to increase the size of, or extend, a logical volume.

Extending a logical volume

For the logical volume that I configured in this scenario, I used 1 GB of the 1.5 GB total disk size for */dev/vgsw/software-lv*. To extend this volume, you can use one of the following general commands:

```
$ sudo lvextend -L +size(M or G) lvname
$ sudo lvextend -l +100%FREE lvname
```

In this example, I'll use the -l (extents) option rather than a specific size to consume the rest of the free space on the device:

```
$ df -h /sw
Filesystem                      Size  Used Avail Use% Mounted on
/dev/mapper/vgsw-software--lv 1014M    40M  975M   4% /sw

$ sudo lvextend -l +100%FREE /dev/vgsw/software-lv

$ sudo lvextend -l +100%FREE /dev/vgsw/software-lv
Size of logical volume vgsw/software-lv changed from 1.00 GiB (256 extents)
to 1.44 GiB (369 extents).
Logical volume vgsw/software-lv successfully resized.
```

The lvextend command extends the logical volume to its maximum capacity but a df shows the same amount of available space:

```
$ df -h /sw
Filesystem                      Size  Used Avail Use% Mounted on
/dev/mapper/vgsw-software--lv 1014M    40M  975M   4% /sw
```

You have extended the logical volume but not the filesystem. Now resize the filesystem using the xfs_growfs command with no size parameter. By not specifying a size parameter with -D size, xfs_growfs will extend the filesystem to its maximum value:

```
$ sudo xfs_growfs /dev/vgsw/software-lv
meta-data=/dev/mapper/vgsw-software--lv isize=512    agcount=4, agsize=65536 blks
         =                              sectsz=512   attr=2, projid32bit=1
         =                              crc=1        finobt=1, sparse=1, rmapbt=0
         =                              reflink=1
data     =                              bsize=4096   blocks=262144, imaxpct=25
         =                              sunit=0      swidth=0 blks
naming   =version 2                     bsize=4096   ascii-ci=0, ftype=1
log      =internal log                  bsize=4096   blocks=2560, version=2
         =                              sectsz=512   sunit=0 blks, lazy-count=1
realtime =none                          extsz=4096   blocks=0, rtextents=0
data blocks changed from 262144 to 377856

$ df -h /sw
Filesystem                      Size  Used Avail Use% Mounted on
/dev/mapper/vgsw-software--lv  1.5G    43M  1.4G   3% /sw
```

You cannot shrink an XFS volume.

You have successfully extended the filesystem, and your logical volume is ready to use. The actual available size is 1.44 GB (shown as 1.4G in the preceding example) because of filesystem overhead.

Decommissioning and Disk Disposal

Decommissioning includes the wiping or destruction of disks before disposal. The decommissioning process differs from company to company but generally follows these steps:

- Notification
- "Scream" test
- Power down
- Disk wiping
- Unracking
- Palletizing
- Disposal

The timeline for each of these steps varies. The following sections provide details for each step.

Notification

Stakeholders, system administrators, network administrators, storage administrators, and management all receive multiple decommissioning notifications for a list of systems. Large companies generally send the list out weekly for a period of three to four weeks (the actual time varies from company to company and is a matter of policy). These notifications give stakeholders and others a chance to take possession of a system or to prevent its decommissioning via email and then a discussion during a governance meeting. If no one speaks up on behalf of any listed system, the process proceeds to the "scream" test phase.

Scream Test

The so-called "scream" test is a period of two or more weeks where a system administrator or data center staff member unplugs a given system from the network but doesn't power down listed systems. The plan is that during this time if someone screams about a system being down, it would be plugged back into the network, and its operations would continue as before. The next governance meeting would remove the system from the decommissioning list.

Power Down

The next milestone in the decommissioning process is the power-down phase, which lasts two or more weeks. System administrators power down all listed systems. This period is a second chance for interested parties to claim a system or to notify the governance committee that the system needs to remain in operation.

Disk Wiping

After several weeks of notifications and waiting, the governance committee finalizes the list and submits it to system administrators for disk wiping. The system administrator powers on each system and uses a disk-wiping utility to overwrite every local disk. Leveraged or shared storage such as storage area network (SAN), network-attached storage (NAS), or nonlocal disk storage is not included in this process. This process ensures no data is left on a system's local storage.

 I have relied on Darik's Boot and Nuke (DBAN) utility (*https://oreil.ly/PnMgA*) for years to wipe disks for decommissioning and disposal. It is a free, open source utility for hard disk drives (HDDs). This product is *not* for solid-state drives (SSDs).

Unracking and Palletizing

Once a system's disks have been wiped, the list goes to data center personnel for unracking. Technicians remove the systems from data center racks and place them onto shipping pallets. Once a pallet is full, the technician labels it, and it goes into a disposal queue.

Disposal

The disposal process may consist of bidding, where companies bulk purchase palletized systems for sale or redeployment. Sometimes the systems go to a recycling facility where technicians remove disks, CPUs, memory, and other salvageable components for individual or bulk resale. System disposal can also mean that those whole systems are disposed of by crushing or shredding and sold as recyclable material.

Summary

This chapter covered multiple aspects of disk management, including general disk-related information, adding a new disk to a system, logical volume management, and decommissioning and disposal.

In the next chapter, I cover two important tasks for system administrators: health and housekeeping.

## CHAPTER 8

Maintaining System Health

Maintaining system health is a broad topic that includes preventative maintenance, housekeeping, patching, security tasks, user maintenance, and monitoring and mitigating various types of sprawl. Maintaining the health of your systems is an active task, not a passive one.

Monitoring can help. Automating periodic cleanup of certain areas can help. Automating updates can help, but you must actively watch logs, check space and sprawl, and take care of user maintenance tasks. Many of these tasks require eyes on screens and hands on keyboards. Far fewer system administrators would be required if you could automate every aspect of system health maintenance.

This chapter covers both automated and manual system health maintenance tasks.

Keeping Your System Clutter-Free

Housekeeping is something that no one loves to do. It's tedious, time-consuming, and can anger users to the point of reporting your behavior to management, which is never a good thing. As long as you comply with corporate policy and don't apply any of your own, you'll have material to refer your angry users to. The rules for decluttering a system are the same for any maintenance you do: have a good backup available if you remove a critical file or directory by accident. The following sections detail how to keep your systems clutter-free.

Cleaning the /tmp Directory

The *tmp* directory is a shared directory. It's shared with all users, applications, and system processes. Anyone may write to this directory, which is bad for administrators because having unlimited access to a system directory can have fatal consequences. If the original administrator didn't create the *tmp* directory as a separate filesystem with access to limited space, users or applications can potentially fill up all of the space. The */tmp* directory should never be a part of the same partition as / for this reason.

The */tmp* directory is tricky from a housekeeping perspective for sysadmins because there are no restrictions on users, applications, or the system. Because any user may write to it, they might expect that it's extra, available free space where they can store downloads and other files. To make this directory a less desirable location to store files, you should create a `cron` job to run every night, after backups, to remove any nonsystem files.

 In many enterprises, automated scripts remove user-created files from the */tmp* directory every night, and most exclude */tmp* directories from backups.

The solution to the */tmp* dilemma if you don't want to create a separate filesystem and mount it on */tmp* is to enable *tmp.mount*. This service creates a temporary filesystem (tmpfs) and mounts it as */tmp*. One of the features is that it's volatile storage (RAM) and filling it up won't cause stability issues on your system.

To enable *tmp.mount* on your system, complete the following steps.

First, check your */tmp* directory mount point to see if you need to configure *tmp.mount*:

```
$ df -h /tmp
Filesystem          Size  Used Avail Use% Mounted on
/dev/mapper/cl-root 6.2G  3.3G  3.0G  53% /
```

As you can see, my */tmp* has the flaw of being a subdirectory of the / filesystem. Enable *tmp.mount* and then start it:

```
$ sudo systemctl enable tmp.mount
Created symlink /etc/systemd/system/local-fs.target.wants/tmp.mount
→ \ /usr/lib/systemd/system/tmp.mount.

$ sudo systemctl start tmp.mount

$ df -h /tmp
Filesystem      Size  Used Avail Use% Mounted on
tmpfs           405M     0  405M   0% /tmp
```

Now, the */tmp* directory is no longer a subdirectory of /. Enabling *tmp.mount* makes this configuration persistent, which means it is a permanent change and will be automatically created each time the system is booted.

The next section deals with keeping the */home* directory usable for everyone.

Making /home a Livable Space for Everyone

The *home* directory is a shared directory because it contains all users' home directories, except for the root user. For example, suppose you have users tux, penguin, and gentoo on your system. Their home directories will look like the following:

```
/home/tux
/home/penguin
/home/gentoo
```

On systems where the */home* directory is on the same filesystem as the / directory, there is a potential that users can fill up / and cause system problems, much the same as filling up */tmp*, as discussed in the previous section. Because of the nature of files contained in */home*, you can't create and mount a volatile filesystem for it. The */home* directory must be a permanently mounted filesystem, preferably not part of /. If it is part of /, there are two approaches to correct it. The first entails the following:

- Shrinking an existing LVM filesystem
- Creating a partition and filesystem
- Mounting that filesystem as */home*

The second approach involves the following:

- Installing a new disk
- Creating a new partition
- Mounting that new partition as */home*

For the demonstration in this chapter, I'll use the second approach of installing a new disk for */home*.

The steps to complete this are as follows:

1. Create or install a new disk.
2. Create a new partition on the disk.
3. Make the filesystem on the new partition.
4. Mount the new partition on */mnt*.
5. Copy or move all files from */home* to */mnt*.
6. Remove all files from */home*.
7. Unmount the new partition from */mnt*.
8. Mount the new partition on */home*.
9. Add an entry for */home* in */etc/fstab*.

I added a 1 GB disk to my VM to demonstrate these steps. The following sections explain how to complete each step in this process.

Create a new partition on the disk

Identify the new disk by listing all disk block devices on the system:

```
$ lsblk | grep disk
sda                  8:0    0    8G  0 disk
sdb                  8:16   0  1.5G  0 disk
sdc                  8:32   0    1G  0 disk
```

The sdc (*/dev/sdc*) device is the new disk. It is the 1 GB disk I added to the virtual machine. To create a new partition on the disk, use the fdisk utility:

```
$ sudo fdisk /dev/sdc

Welcome to fdisk (util-linux 2.32.1).
Changes will remain in memory only, until you decide to write them.
Be careful before using the write command.

Device does not contain a recognized partition table.
Created a new DOS disklabel with disk identifier 0x3c239df6.

Command (m for help): n
Partition type
   p   primary (0 primary, 0 extended, 4 free)
   e   extended (container for logical partitions)
Select (default p): p
Partition number (1-4, default 1):
First sector (2048-2097151, default 2048):
Last sector, +sectors or +size{K,M,G,T,P} (2048-2097151, default 2097151):

Created a new partition 1 of type 'Linux' and of size 1023 MiB.

Command (m for help): w
The partition table has been altered.
Calling ioctl() to re-read partition table.
Syncing disks.
```

List the sdc block device to verify that the partition */dev/sdc1* exists:

```
$ lsblk | grep sdc
sdc                  8:32   0    1G  0 disk
└─sdc1               8:33   0 1023M  0 part
```

The */dev/sdc1* partition exists and is ready to have a filesystem created on it.

Create the filesystem

For the */home* directory, format it as the `ext4` filesystem type:

```
$ sudo mkfs.ext4 /dev/sdc1

mke2fs 1.45.6 (20-Mar-2020)
Creating filesystem with 261888 4k blocks and 65536 inodes
Filesystem UUID: bcd18fcc-3774-4b94-be0a-e2abf8aa4d31
Superblock backups stored on blocks:
    32768, 98304, 163840, 229376

Allocating group tables: done
Writing inode tables: done
Creating journal (4096 blocks): done
Writing superblocks and filesystem accounting information: done
```

Verify that you correctly created the `ext4` filesystem on */dev/sdc1*:

```
$ lsblk -o NAME,FSTYPE,SIZE | grep sdc
sdc                              1G
└─sdc1            ext4         1023M
```

Mount the new partition

To use the new partition, you must mount it. I use */mnt* as the temporary mount point to copy files from */home* to the new partition I will eventually mount as */home*. If I mount */dev/sdc1* onto */home* now, I can't copy the files because mounting on */home* hides its files from view. Mounting a device onto a nonempty directory hides its contents and makes its files inaccessible:

```
$ sudo mount /dev/sdc1 /mnt

$ mount | grep sdc
/dev/sdc1 on /mnt type ext4 (rw,relatime,seclabel)
```

Copy files from /home to /mnt

Copy all files from the */home* directory to preserve all (`-a`) permissions, links, and timestamps:

```
$ sudo cp -a /home/* /mnt

$ ls -la /home
total 0
drwxr-xr-x.  4 root   root    32 Nov  3  2020 .
dr-xr-xr-x. 19 root   root   258 Dec 10 08:37 ..
drwx------.  2 1001   1001    62 Nov 13  2020 diane
drwx------.  7 khess  khess  273 Dec 14 21:03 khess
```

```
$ ls -la /mnt
total 28
drwxr-xr-x.  5 root   root    4096 Dec 15 08:33 .
dr-xr-xr-x. 19 root   root     258 Dec 10 08:37 ..
drwx------.  2 1001   1001    4096 Nov 13  2020 diane
drwx------.  7 khess  khess   4096 Dec 14 21:03 khess
drwx------.  2 root   root   16384 Dec 15 08:17 lost+found
```

Remove all files from /home

The reason that I remove all files from the original *home* directory is that it releases disk space back to the */* filesystem, which is one of the reasons why we're going through this exercise. The following command removes all directories under */home* without removing the */home* directory. There's no need to remove */home*:

```
$ sudo rm -rf /home/*
```

Unmount /dev/sdc1 from /mnt

Unmount */dev/sdc1* from */mnt*:

```
$ sudo umount /mnt
```

Mount the new partition on /home

Mount the new partition onto the */home* directory:

```
$ sudo mount /dev/sdc1 /home
```

The true test of this exercise is to log in as a user and check if everything works as expected.

Create the /etc/fstab entry

The */home* directory won't mount automatically after a system reboot because */home* is on a different partition that is not listed in */etc/fstab*. You must create an */etc/fstab* entry for it.

My */etc/fstab* entry for */dev/sdc1* is as follows:

```
/dev/sdc1    /home                ext4    defaults    0 0
```

This */etc/fstab* entry makes the mount persistent.

The next section deals with archiving and removing "stale" and duplicated files from shared directories.

Decluttering Shared Directories

Keeping shared directories free of clutter is difficult. It might be impossible, but there are some things you can do to confront the issue using system tools and some planning. This section explores some utilities that can simplify decluttering and housekeeping.

Deduplicating Files with fdupes

fdupes is a popular deduplication utility. fdupes finds duplicate files in a given set of directories. The fdupes man page (*https://oreil.ly/XERaf*) describes the command's function as follows:

> Searches the given path for duplicate files. Such files are found by comparing file sizes and MD5 signatures, followed by a byte-by-byte comparison.

You can install fdupes from your distribution's repositories, but it's better to grab the patched version from a GitHub repository using the following steps:

```
$ git clone https://github.com/tobiasschulz/fdupes
$ cd fdupes
$ make fdupes
$ sudo make install
```

This patched version has more options such as the one you're most likely to use as a system administrator in a production environment. When you use fdupes on a directory, you can just look at the duplicates, delete the duplicates (not recommended), or remove the duplicates but provide soft links to one of the files (recommended). This solution presents a problem only if the original file no longer exists. But providing a soft link to one of the files is far less invasive than removing the duplicates, which may result in tickets, phone calls, and reprimands. Examples 8-1 through 8-3 illustrate how to use fdupes to find duplicates, generate a report, and then only provide links to one of the files.

Example 8-1. List duplicate files and their sizes

```
$ fdupes -rS /opt/shared
29 bytes each:
/opt/shared/docs/building/test.rtf
/opt/shared/docs/building/test.txt
/opt/shared/a/b/list.txt
/opt/shared/a/b/c/stuff.doc
/opt/shared/a/todo.list
/opt/shared/one/foo.lst
/opt/shared/x/y/listed.here
```

```
20 bytes each:
/opt/shared/docs/hr/list.txt
/opt/shared/x/got.txt
/opt/shared/a/b/none.doc
```

The -r option is recursive, which means check the specified directory and all its subdirectories. The -S option means to report the file sizes.

In Example 8-2, the -m option tells fdupes to print a report of any duplicates found.

Example 8-2. Generate a duplicate file report using the -m option

```
$ fdupes -mr /opt/shared
8 duplicate files (in 2 sets), occupying 214 bytes.
```

In Example 8-3, fdupes replaces duplicate files with hard links using the -L option. Only the first found file in each group of duplicates remains intact.

Example 8-3. Provide links to one of the files

```
$ fdupes -rL /opt/shared
[+] /opt/shared/docs/building/test.rtf
[h] /opt/shared/docs/building/test.txt
[h] /opt/shared/a/b/list.txt
[h] /opt/shared/a/b/c/stuff.doc
[h] /opt/shared/a/todo.list
[h] /opt/shared/one/foo.lst
[h] /opt/shared/x/y/listed.here

[+] /opt/shared/docs/hr/list.txt
[h] /opt/shared/x/got.txt
[h] /opt/shared/a/b/none.doc
```

Using the selective delete option, -d, you're prompted for which file(s) you want to keep. Again, deleting files is highly discouraged. Proceed at your own risk:

```
$ fdupes -rd /opt/shared
[1] /opt/shared/a/b/goo.txt
[2] /opt/shared/a/false.doc
[3] /opt/shared/one/two/three/three
[4] /opt/shared/docs/building/test.rtf
[5] /opt/shared/x/y/new.txt
[6] /opt/shared/docs/building/test.txt
[7] /opt/shared/a/b/list.txt
[8] /opt/shared/a/b/c/stuff.doc
[9] /opt/shared/a/todo.list
[10] /opt/shared/one/foo.lst
[11] /opt/shared/x/y/listed.here

Set 1 of 2, preserve files [1 - 11, all]:
```

This option removes files except for the one(s) you preserve and does not create links. Check the online help and man pages for `fdupes` for other options.

Tackling /home File Sprawl with Quotas

Some system administrators and users find that using quotas is a harsh solution to dealing with file sprawl. I find it a good solution that works well in various situations to help deal with users who chronically use up more than their fair share of disk space. You can implement quotas on any directory, but you certainly want to consider it for shared directories and *home*.

The first task is to install `quota`, if your system doesn't have it:

```
$ sudo yum install quota
$ sudo apt install quota
```

To use the `quota` system, you'll need to have an `xfs` filesystem handy and mounted. Mine, for example, is *home*. Create an entry in *etc/fstab* for the `xfs` filesystem. Here is the *etc/fstab* entry for *home* where I want to enforce quotas:

```
/dev/sdc1     /home                   xfs     defaults,usrquota,grpquota     0 0
```

Next, create two new empty files on *home*: *quota.group* and *quota.user*. These two files must exist in any directory that's configured for quotas, which are used by the `quota` system:

```
$ sudo touch /home/quota.group /home/quota.user
```

Then, enable quotas with the `quotaon` command:

```
$ sudo quotaon /home
quotaon /home
quotaon: Enforcing group quota already on /dev/sdc1
quotaon: Enforcing user quota already on /dev/sdc1
quotaon: Enable XFS project quota accounting during mount
```

The system is now ready to apply quotas to users' accounts. The following command sets a very low `quota` value for demonstration purposes. The soft limit is 50 MB, and the hard limit is 80 MB. You receive a warning when you exceed the soft limit, but the `quota` system prevents you from exceeding the hard limit. You can also limit the number of inodes (file metadata structures) that a user may consume. The inode limit is a bit harsher because a user might generate thousands of tiny text files that only amount to a few megabytes, but it limits the number of files users can create. There are hard and soft limits for inodes as well.

```
[root@server1 home1]# sudo xfs_quota -x -c \
'limit -u bsoft=50m bhard=80m isoft=60 \ ihard=80 djones' /home
```

The following is an example of what the user sees when they exceed a quota. The head command creates a 51 MB file to illustrate how quotas truncate files that exceed a set quota limit:

```
$ su - djones
Password:
Last login: Mon Jan 10 20:16:49 CST 2022 on pts/0
[djones@server1 ~]$ head -c 51MB /dev/urandom > fillit.txt
[djones@server1 ~]$ head -c 51MB /dev/urandom > fillit1.txt
head: error writing 'standard output': Disk quota exceeded
$ ls -l
total 81892
-rw-rw-r--. 1 djones djones 32854016 Jan 10 20:21 fillit1.txt
-rw-rw-r--. 1 djones djones 51000000 Jan 10 20:21 fillit.txt
```

You can see that when the user reached their hard limit, the system truncated the files they attempted to create (*fillit1.txt*). If no quota had been placed on the user, they would have had two 51 MB files.

Quotas prevent users from consuming more than a given amount of space on a filesystem or directory. Still, they should only be enforced on users who violate company policy or egregiously store personal files on company systems. You can easily remove a quota limit from a user's account by setting all limits to 0:

```
$ sudo xfs_quota -x -c 'limit -u bsoft=0 bhard=0 isoft=0 ihard=0 djones' /home
[sudo] password for khess:
[khess@server1 home]$ su - djones
Password:
Last login: Mon Jan 10 20:20:41 CST 2022 on pts/0
[djones@server1 ~]$ head -c 51MB /dev/urandom > fillit2.txt
[djones@server1 ~]$ ls -l
total 131700
-rw-rw-r--. 1 djones djones        0 Jan 10 20:21 blah.txt
-rw-rw-r--. 1 djones djones 32854016 Jan 10 20:21 fillit1.txt
-rw-rw-r--. 1 djones djones 51000000 Jan 10 22:37 fillit2.txt
-rw-rw-r--. 1 djones djones 51000000 Jan 10 20:21 fillit.txt
```

Now there are no warnings (or truncations) about exceeding limits. The djones account no longer has quota limits imposed on it.

That's a good introduction to quotas, what they can do for you as an administrator, and how they can keep your users in check with their space usage. The next topic to explore is patching, an essential task for any administrator wanting to keep their system running smoothly.

Patching Your Way to a Healthy System

Patching, to the new system administrator, might sound like you're putting duct tape on a system to hold it together temporarily while you locate the real fix for a problem. Patching is an essential task and perhaps is a misnomer for what it is: updating system utilities, daemons, and applications with fixes supplied by developers. A software patch fixes a specific problem. A good example is applying a patch to the SSH daemon to resolve new vulnerabilities that can render a system susceptible to attack and compromise.

Patching isn't always security-focused. Often, patches fix a stability problem, plug a memory leak, or repair a broken feature. Remember that patching a Linux system rarely means that you'll have to initiate a reboot, but if you update a service, you'll want to restart that service unless the patching process takes care of that for you. If the patching process restarts a service, a message will appear on the screen informing you of the restart. To be safe, I often reboot after a major patch event to ensure that the system and its services receive a restart. A *major* patch event includes multiple fixes and often a kernel update. If you are inside your maintenance window and have updated several services, the kernel, or other critical system software, I suggest you reboot the system.

Some system administrators automate their patching by setting up a `cron` job to periodically check for and install patches. That scenario works, but you should have a test system or two that you manually update to see what's to be updated, how the system reacts to those updates, and how the system responds after a reboot. You don't want or need any surprises from a bad patch session.

Now, let's look at how to patch two types of Linux systems—a Red Hat–based system and a Debian-based system.

Patching a Red Hat Enterprise Linux–Based System

To initiate patches on a Red Hat Enterprise Linux–based system, use `yum` or `dnf`. For this demonstration, I use `yum`, but `dnf` is the preferred command for versions 8 and above of Red Hat Enterprise Linux:

```
$ sudo yum update
Last metadata expiration check: 0:23:24 ago on Sun 30 Jan 2022 08:27:15 AM CST.
Dependencies resolved.
================================================================
 Package          Arch       Version        Repo        Size
================================================================
Installing:
 kernel           x86_64     4.18.0-348...  baseos      7.0 M
 kernel-core      x86_64     4.18.0-348...  baseos      38 M
 kernel-modules   x86_64     4.18.0-348...  baseos      30 M
```

```
Upgrading:
 NetworkManager         x86_64      1:1.32.10-...       baseos          2.6 M

...

 openssh                x86_64      8.0p1-10.el8        baseos          522 k
 openssh-clients        x86_64      8.0p1-10.el8        baseos          668 k
 openssh-server         x86_64      8.0p1-10.el8        baseos          485 k
 openssl                x86_64      1:1.1.1k-5...       baseos          709 k
 openssl-libs           x86_64      1:1.1.1k-5...       baseos          1.5 M

...

 yum                    noarch      4.7.0-4.el8         baseos          205 k
 yum-utils              noarch      4.0.21-3.el8        baseos          73 k
Installing dependencies:
 libbpf                 x86_64      0.4.0-1.el8         baseos          110 k
Removing:
 kernel                 x86_64      4.18.0-240...       @BaseOS         0
 kernel-core            x86_64      4.18.0-240...       @BaseOS         62 M
 kernel-modules         x86_64      4.18.0-240...       @BaseOS         21 M

Transaction Summary
================================================================================
Install    4 Packages
Upgrade  287 Packages
Remove     3 Packages

Total download size: 558 M
Is this ok [y/N]:
```

As you can see from the truncated listing above, it's been a while since I last updated this system (287 packages require upgrading). I included the parts I want you to see, such as a new kernel update and the new OpenSSH server (SSHD), to demonstrate that I will reboot this system after the updates. I prefer to install manually by not providing the -y option so that I can view everything that needs an upgrade before I proceed.

The default behavior for YUM/DNF updates is not installing them. You receive the following prompt:

```
Is this ok [y/N]:
```

The updates will not install if you press the Enter key because the N is the default response. You must explicitly approve the installation by answering with a y here.

It's generally OK to proceed with updates on production systems if you've installed and verified them on test systems first. Installing patches not verified on test systems might cause stability problems or application/library conflicts, especially if you run older versions of some programs.

Patching a Debian-Based Linux System

Patching a Debian-based system is similar to patching a Red Hat Enterprise Linux–based system with a couple of subtle differences. The first difference is that you use the apt command to install updates to the system:

```
$ sudo apt update
Hit:1 http://us.archive.ubuntu.com/ubuntu focal InRelease
Get:2 http://us.archive.ubuntu.com/ubuntu focal-updates InRelease [114 kB]
Get:3 http://us.archive.ubuntu.com/ubuntu focal-backports InRelease [108 kB]
Get:4 http://us.archive.ubuntu.com/ubuntu focal-security InRelease [114 kB]
Fetched 336 kB in 1s (407 kB/s)
Reading package lists... Done
Building dependency tree
Reading state information... Done
20 packages can be upgraded. Run 'apt list --upgradable' to see them.
khess@server2:~$ sudo apt upgrade
Reading package lists... Done
Building dependency tree
Reading state information... Done
Calculating upgrade... Done
The following packages will be upgraded:
  cloud-init command-not-found libasound2 libasound2-data libnetplan0 libssl1.1
linux-firmware netplan.io openssh-client openssh-server openssh-sftp-server ...
python3-commandnotfound python3-software-properties rsync software-propertie...
ubuntu-advantage-tools ufw update-notifier-common wget
20 upgraded, 0 newly installed, 0 to remove and 0 not upgraded.
Need to get 120 MB of archives.
After this operation, 20.3 MB of additional disk space will be used.
Do you want to continue? [Y/n]
```

The other difference is in the approval procedure. Notice the Do you want to continue? [Y/n] prompt. The Y is capitalized, which means that if you press the Enter key, the updates will install in your system. Remember that when updating a Red Hat Enterprise Linux–based system, if you press the Enter key, the updates don't install. But also note that apt doesn't have an automatic approval option (-y) like yum or dnf.

 unattended-upgrades is a package you can install that will allow you to update your Debian-based system automatically.

As stated earlier, you should always install updates and upgrades on test systems first. If you set up automated updates, this is more difficult to do unless you create a clever schedule for updating your systems similar to the following:

Test systems
    Manual updates every Tuesday

Development systems
    Manual updates every other Thursday

Production systems
    Monthly updates last Sunday of the month

This schedule, or similar, allows you to check automated updates before installing them to your production systems. If you have an automation or enterprise management tool that allows you to suspend `cron` jobs in case of a problem, you can better control your automated patching. If you don't have such a tool and have more than a handful of systems to manage, I suggest you explore an automation tool such as Ansible to deliver new configuration files, scripts, and so on to your systems.

An automation system also helps when applying zero-day or other emergency patches to your systems. Patching, like backups, needs your close attention. Keeping your systems running smoothly and securely by regularly applying the latest patches is vital to your system administrator duties.

Securing Your Systems

While regular patching should be part of an overall security plan, there are some basic security settings unrelated to the topic of patching that I will cover in this section. Again, an automated system such as Ansible can help greatly in saving time and effort in maintaining the security of dozens, hundreds, or thousands of systems.

Not all systems can be treated equally when applying security measures. For example, your DMZ (internet-facing) systems, database systems, web servers, application servers, and file storage systems each (as a group) need different security settings. You can rarely apply a single security policy covering every type of system. A few general security measures apply to every system regardless of function, but to state that you're going to set up a single, generic security plan is unrealistic. You must apply security configurations to each system type to focus on specific vulnerabilities.

For example, can you think of particular security settings that apply to web servers but not file servers? In the case of a web server, you'll need to implement certificates to secure your web communications. You should concentrate on securing shared directories and user accounts on a file server. Are you going to allow Samba shares on your file servers? Are you going to allow uploads onto your web servers? How you and your users interact with a system dictates its security concerns, not the fact that it's a generic Linux system.

Table 8-1 shows some example security guidelines for your Linux systems with specific purposes and workloads.

Table 8-1. Linux service security guidelines

Purpose/workload	Examples	Security measure
All servers	Miscellaneous services	SSH, */etc/hosts.allow* and */etc/hosts.deny* restrictions, firewall, SELinux
Web server	Apache, NGINX, IHS, others	TLS, certificates, HTTPS
Database server	MySQL, PostgreSQL, others	Tunnel over SSH, restrict connections to localhost
File server	Samba shares, NFS shares, SSH	Active Directory integration for Samba, two-factor authentication
Application server	Tomcat, WebSphere, others	HTTPS, TLS, certificates
Mail server	SMTP, IMAP, POP-3 protocols	Use secured protocols and mail services

As you can see in Table 8-1, there are certain security features that you should implement on every system regardless of purpose unless there's some vendor-related reason that you shouldn't. You should lock down every system and be as restrictive as possible while maintaining functionality and accessibility for your users.

Maintaining User and Group Accounts

User account maintenance goes beyond adding and removing accounts. It also includes developing an account naming convention, creating policies that set standards for how long to disable accounts before they're removed, how long to retain a user's home directory after they've left the group or the company, retiring of group accounts, and the retiring or reusing of user and group IDs. All of these activities prevent user account sprawl. Here are some examples of account sprawl:

- Disabled accounts left on systems past policy limits
- Home directories left on systems past policy limits
- Active, terminated user accounts left on systems
- Group accounts with no members
- Disabled or removed accounts that remain in */etc/sudoers*
- Active temporary accounts left on systems
- Active service accounts with shells or passwords

Setting Up a Naming Convention

One of the easiest methods of circumventing account sprawl is to create a user account naming convention. A naming convention prevents sprawl by setting a standard by which you and your team create user accounts. For example, you now have a working system if you set your naming convention as the first initial and the first seven characters of the last name. The exception is when two or more people have the same first and last names. In these cases, you'd opt for using the first initial of the first name, a middle initial, and the first six characters of the last name.

Table 8-2 shows examples of the standard naming convention.

Table 8-2. Standard account naming convention

First name	Last name	Username
José	Alvarez	jalvarez
Paula	Anderson	panderso
Vivek	Kundra	vkundra
Sylvia	Goldstein	sgoldste

Table 8-3 shows examples of repeated name exceptions.

Table 8-3. Repeated name exceptions

First name	Last name	Username
José	Alvarez	jalvarez
José	Alvarez	jqalvare
Paula	Anderson	panderso
Paula	Anderson	pmanders

If your users have no middle names, then you can work backward from the end of the alphabet, as shown in Table 8-4.

Table 8-4. Account name workarounds for users without middle names

First name	Last name	Username
Paula	Anderson	panderso
Paula	Anderson	pzanders
Paula	Anderson	pyanders
Paula	Anderson	pxanders

You can certainly develop your own naming convention, but I've seen this one work at other enterprises, so it's worth a mention here. I've also seen other companies use a number system to avoid duplicate usernames. For example, if you have two users named Vivek Kundra, the first one created on a system is created as `vkundra` and the second Vivek Kundra is `vkundra2`.

The whole point of a naming convention is to develop a system and then stick to it. Having a naming convention prevents administrators from creating random user accounts that could duplicate other accounts.

For example, suppose you create a user account for Sylvia Goldstein as `sgoldste` and another system administrator creates an account as `sylviag`. You now have a security problem because you have a single user with two accounts on the same system, plus the problem of user account sprawl.

User account sprawl is not a minor issue. Suppose Sylvia logs in and uses both accounts to create files, install software, and possibly create dependencies for groups she's a member of. Now the problem is far more complex than simply moving files from one account to another, changing user and group ownership, and removing the lesser-used account from the system.

If the system administrators had a naming convention, the second administrator might not have created the second account. Next, I discuss creating an account retention policy, another method to prevent account sprawl.

Creating Account Retention Policies

An account retention policy is a good security practice and housekeeping practice. Nothing flags security scans like active accounts that no one has accessed in more than 90 days. Some highly secure environments will force a password change every 45 days, disable accounts after 90 days of inactivity, and remove accounts that remain inactive for six months. This type of aggressive account retention policy won't fit every environment, but it certainly protects and challenges users of sensitive systems to maintain their accounts or let them go.

I'm not suggesting that you adopt a policy as strict as this one. Still, you should have some type of retention policy in place that you provide to your users as part of an overall security and employment education program.

Your account retention policy should be a written policy as well as a system-level policy. A system-level policy means that you must configure system-wide settings for inactive account lockout and removal.

Changing inactive account status

To work toward a system solution, audit the default value for the number of days after a password expires that the system disables the account, also known as the INACTIVE variable:

```
$ sudo useradd -D | grep INACTIVE
INACTIVE=-1
```

The -1 means there's no default inactive value set.

Set the inactive value according to your company's security policy. If you have no security policy addressing this value, set it to 15 days. Some sysadmins set this value to 30. The purpose of this setting is to disable inactive accounts and protect system security:

```
$ sudo useradd -D -f 15
```

This sets the system-wide default inactive value to 15 days. If users receive the message that they need to update their password, they have 15 days before the system disables the account:

```
$ sudo useradd -D | grep INACTIVE
INACTIVE=15
```

If a user attempts to log into a system and fails, you can check their account status:

```
$ sudo passwd -S username
$ sudo passwd -S ndavis
ndavis PS 2022-02-13 0 99999 7 15 (Password set, SHA512 crypt.)
```

This user is in good standing. Perhaps they attempted to log into a host other than the one they intended or typed in an incorrect password. However, another user, asmith, contacted you complaining that they couldn't log into the same system:

```
$ sudo passwd -S asmith
asmith LK 2022-02-12 0 99999 7 15 (Password locked.)
```

User asmith is locked out of the system. You will have to unlock their account before they can log in again:

```
$ sudo passwd -u asmith
passwd: Success
```

The user may log in again. Next, I will demonstrate how to take account protection further with the chage command.

Protecting user accounts

The chage command has several options for further protecting your user accounts by forcing regular password changes, setting a minimum password change duration, and so on. This section shows how to alter those settings to protect your users and systems.

There are three parameters that I change for all users on the systems that I manage: `Inactive days`, `Minimum number of days between password changes`, and `Maximum number of days between password changes`. I change them according to company policy, if one exists. Otherwise, I change them to my "defaults":

```
Inactive days:                                     15
Minimum number of days between password changes:   1
Maximum number of days between password changes:   90

$ sudo chage -m 1 -M 90 --inactive 15 asmith

$ sudo chage --list asmith
Last password change                         : Feb 13, 2022
Password expires                             : May 14, 2022
Password inactive                            : May 29, 2022
Account expires                              : never
Minimum number of days between password change  : 1
Maximum number of days between password change  : 90
Number of days of warning before password expires  : 7
```

This sets the user's password to expire every 90 days. If they don't change it, their account will be disabled 15 days after the change password date. If they change their password when prompted, they won't be able to change it again until one day later.

You can only change one user at a time using the `chage` command. This can become cumbersome if you have more than a few users on a few servers. A scripted version that covers all users is far more efficient. I've provided my script as follows:

```
#!/bin/bash
egrep ^[^:]+:[^\!*] /etc/shadow | cut -d: -f1 | grep -v root > user-list.txt
for user in `more user-list.txt`
do
chage -m 1 -M 90 -I 15 $user
done
```

Retiring Group Accounts

Group accounts that remain on the system once they're empty and inactive are a common source of account sprawl but easily remedied. The `groupmems` command can save you a lot of time and frustration by answering who, if anyone, is a member of a specific group:

```
$ sudo groupmems -g operations -l
ajones bhaas

$ sudo groupmems -g hr -l
asmith
```

The `groupmems` command options used in the example are `-g` for the group name and `-l` for list.

If there are no group members, the command displays no output:

```
$ sudo groupmems -g engineering -l
$
```

On this system, the engineering group should be retired (removed from the system because it's empty). But before removing the group, you must find out if the engineering group left any files they own:

```
$ sudo find / -group engineering
find: '/proc/3368/task/3368/fd/7': No such file or directory
find: '/proc/3368/task/3368/fdinfo/7': No such file or directory
find: '/proc/3368/fd/6': No such file or directory
find: '/proc/3368/fdinfo/6': No such file or directory
/shared/engineering
/shared/engineering/one
/shared/engineering/two
/shared/engineering/three
/shared/engineering/four
/shared/engineering/five
/shared/engineering/six
/shared/engineering/seven
/shared/engineering/eight
/shared/engineering/nine
/shared/engineering/ten
```

You should transfer the files to another user or change ownership to root to secure them and then remove the empty group account:

```
$ sudo groupdel engineering
```

You have successfully removed the engineering account. You can re-create it in the future if you need to.

Now that I've covered sprawl, I will discuss monitoring your system's health.

Monitoring System Health

System monitoring doesn't explicitly fall under the sprawl umbrella but is part of maintaining system health. There are dozens of commercial monitoring tools that you can purchase, but `sysstat` is a free one native to Linux. It's easy to install, and on Red Hat–based systems, it self-configures and begins collecting data immediately. On Debian-based systems, you must enable `sysstat` to collect data manually.

To enable `sysstat`'s System Activity Report (`sar`) utility to begin collecting data, edit the */etc/default/sysstat* file and change the line that reads `ENABLED="false"` to `ENABLED="true"`.

Then restart the `sysstat` service:

```
$ sudo service sysstat restart
```

Give the system some time to begin generating activity reports. You'll learn how to generate activity reports later in this chapter.

The `sysstat` package contains new binaries for checking performance and formatting system statistics information. Table 8-5 lists the binaries and their functions. I copied the descriptions of each binary from their respective man pages.

Table 8-5. Binaries in the `sysstat` package

Binary	Name	Description
cifsiostat	CIFS statistics	The `cifsiostat` command displays statistics about read and write operations on CIFS filesystems.
iostat	CPU and device I/O statistics	The `iostat` command is used for monitoring system input/output device loading by observing the time the devices are active in relation to their average transfer rates.
mpstat	Processor-related statistics	The `mpstat` command writes to standard output activities for each available processor, processor 0 being the first one.
pidstat	Task statistics	The `pidstat` command monitors individual tasks currently managed by the Linux kernel.
sadf	sar data formatting	The `sadf` command is used for displaying the contents of data files created by the `sar` command. But unlike `sar`, `sadf` can write its data in many different formats (CSV, XML, etc.).
sar	System activity reporter	The `sar` command writes to standard output the contents of selected cumulative activity counters in the operating system.
tapestat	Tape statistics	The `tapestat` command is used for monitoring the activity of tape drives connected to a system.

If you're familiar with the `vmstat` command, which isn't part of `sysstat`, you know how the other "stat" commands work. For example, `vmstat`, on every Linux system, requires that you provide a time delay interval between snapshots in seconds and a specific number (count) of snapshots, with 5 being the typical value used:

```
vmstat [options] [delay [count]]
```

The first run of the `vmstat` command gives averages since the last reboot:

```
$ vmstat 5 5
procs -----------memory---------- ---swap-- -----io---- -system-- ------cpu-----
 r  b   swpd   free   buff  cache   si   so    bi    bo   in   cs us sy id wa st
 3  0  44616 343888    244 334676    0    0     1     1    1   24  0  0 100  0  0
 0  0  44616 343768    244 334676    0    0     0     0   48   91  0  0 100  0  0
 0  0  44616 343768    244 334676    0    0     0     2   53  104  0  0 100  0  0
 1  0  44616 343768    244 334676    0    0     0     4   78  141  0  0 100  0  0
 0  0  44616 343768    244 334676    0    0     0     0   75  141  0  0 100  0  0
```

This vmstat command ran every five seconds with five snapshots. The other "stat" commands work the same way. You provide a delay and a count. The following is an iostat command example with two snapshots and a five-second delay:

```
$ iostat 5 2
Linux 4.18.0-348.7.1.el8_5.x86_64 (server1)   02/13/2022   _x86_64_  (1 CPU)

avg-cpu:  %user   %nice %system %iowait  %steal   %idle
           0.01    0.00    0.24    0.01    0.00   99.74

Device             tps    kB_read/s    kB_wrtn/s    kB_read    kB_wrtn
sda               0.16         0.98         1.34    1592993    2187576
scd0              0.00         0.00         0.00          1          0
sdc               0.00         0.01         0.00       8975       2786
sdb               0.00         0.00         0.00       2921       2048
dm-0              0.17         0.94         1.33    1529818    2170543
dm-1              0.02         0.02         0.06      38232      94228
loop0             0.00         0.00         0.00       1192          0
loop1             0.00         0.00         0.00        253          0
loop2             0.00         0.00         0.00       1202          0
dm-2              0.00         0.00         0.00       1223       2048

avg-cpu:  %user   %nice %system %iowait  %steal   %idle
           0.00    0.00    0.50    0.00    0.00   99.50

Device             tps    kB_read/s    kB_wrtn/s    kB_read    kB_wrtn
sda               0.00         0.00         0.00          0          0
scd0              0.00         0.00         0.00          0          0
sdc               0.00         0.00         0.00          0          0
sdb               0.00         0.00         0.00          0          0
dm-0              0.00         0.00         0.00          0          0
dm-1              0.00         0.00         0.00          0          0
loop0             0.00         0.00         0.00          0          0
loop1             0.00         0.00         0.00          0          0
loop2             0.00         0.00         0.00          0          0
dm-2              0.00         0.00         0.00          0          0
```

Gathering System Activity Reports

The sar command is comprehensive and versatile in its collection, reporting, and saving of system activity information. You can use it like the "stat" commands by supplying an interval and a count, issuing an option such as -b to display I/O statistics, or combining the two to display your selected performance counter at a specific interval.

I'll begin with an example of using sar with a switch. Staying with the -b example, here is a partial report of I/O statistics:

```
$ sar -b
Linux 4.18.0-348.7.1.el8_5.x86_64 (server1)   02/13/2022   _x86_64_   (1 CPU)

12:00:15 AM       tps      rtps      wtps    bread/s    bwrtn/s
12:10:15 AM      0.22      0.03      0.19       2.32       4.30
12:20:15 AM      0.10      0.00      0.10       0.00       0.79
12:30:15 AM      0.16      0.00      0.16       0.00       1.76
12:40:15 AM      0.08      0.00      0.08       0.00       0.5
...
12:20:15 PM      0.08      0.00      0.08       0.00       0.73
12:30:15 PM      0.10      0.00      0.10       0.00       0.87
12:40:15 PM      0.08      0.00      0.08       0.00       0.78
12:50:15 PM      0.11      0.00      0.11       0.00       0.90
Average:         0.25      0.11      0.14       6.29       2.35
```

As you can see from the report, data display begins at midnight, which is why I had to truncate it. The following is an example of I/O statistical data using -b with a count of five and a time delay of five seconds:

```
$ sar -b 5 5
Linux 4.18.0-348.7.1.el8_5.x86_64 (server1)   02/13/2022   _x86_64_   (1 CPU)

12:57:13 PM       tps      rtps      wtps    bread/s    bwrtn/s
12:57:18 PM      0.00      0.00      0.00       0.00       0.00
12:57:23 PM      0.00      0.00      0.00       0.00       0.00
12:57:28 PM      0.00      0.00      0.00       0.00       0.00
12:57:33 PM      0.00      0.00      0.00       0.00       0.00
12:57:38 PM      0.00      0.00      0.00       0.00       0.00
Average:         0.00      0.00      0.00       0.00       0.00
```

Finally, you can issue sar with a count and an interval:

```
$ sar 5 5
Linux 4.18.0-348.7.1.el8_5.x86_64 (server1)   02/13/2022   _x86_64_   (1 CPU)

01:02:11 PM     CPU     %user     %nice   %system   %iowait    %steal     %idle
01:02:16 PM     all      0.00      0.00      0.20      0.00      0.00     99.80
01:02:21 PM     all      0.00      0.00      0.40      0.00      0.00     99.60
01:02:26 PM     all      0.00      0.00      0.20      0.00      0.00     99.80
01:02:31 PM     all      0.00      0.00      0.20      0.00      0.00     99.80
01:02:36 PM     all      0.00      0.00      0.20      0.00      0.00     99.80
Average:        all      0.00      0.00      0.24      0.00      0.00     99.76
```

The default output from the sar command is CPU statistics. To display other statistics, you must use a switch, such as -b for I/O data.

The next section demonstrates how to run system activity reports and save sar data into files.

Formatting System Activity Reports

Displaying sar data enables you to see snapshots and performance from the last 24 hours, but what if you want to capture that data to a file (the system activity report) in a specific format such as CSV or XML? The sadf command is available to you for this purpose.

To help distinguish between the sadf and sar options, remember that sadf options are first in the command, and then sar options follow the double hyphen. Refer to the man pages for all available options for both commands.

My favorite sadf command uses the -d switch to create a comma-separated file that's perfect for ingesting into a database:

```
$ sadf -d
# hostname;interval;timestamp;CPU;%user;%nice;%system;%iowait;%steal;%idle
server1;600;2022-02-13 06:10:15 UTC;-1;0.01;0.00;0.24;0.01;0.00;99.74
server1;600;2022-02-13 06:20:15 UTC;-1;0.00;0.00;0.21;0.01;0.00;99.78
server1;600;2022-02-13 06:30:15 UTC;-1;0.01;0.02;0.23;0.01;0.00;99.74
server1;600;2022-02-13 06:40:15 UTC;-1;0.00;0.00;0.22;0.01;0.00;99.77
```

The system activity logs reside in */var/log/sa* and have filenames of "sa" immediately followed by a number representing the day of the month. For a system activity log for the tenth of the month, the datafile is *sa10*. You can specify an activity log datafile from another date:

```
$ sadf -d /var/log/sa/sa10 -- -d
# hostname;interval;timestamp;DEV;tps;rkB/s;wkB/s;areq-sz;aqu-sz;await;...
server1;600;2022-02-10 06:10:15 UTC;dev8-0;0.35;8.46;2.17;30.81;0.00;0.62;...
server1;600;2022-02-10 06:10:15 UTC;dev11-0;0.00;0.00;0.00;0.00;0.00;0.00;...
server1;600;2022-02-10 06:10:15 UTC;dev8-32;0.00;0.00;0.00;0.00;0.00;0.00;...
server1;600;2022-02-10 06:10:15 UTC;dev8-16;0.00;0.00;0.00;0.00;0.00;0.00;...
server1;600;2022-02-10 06:10:15 UTC;dev253-0;0.30;8.35;2.27;35.42;0.00;0.90;...
server1;600;2022-02-10 06:10:15 UTC;dev253-1;0.03;0.11;0.00;4.00;0.00;1.00;...
server1;600;2022-02-10 06:10:15 UTC;dev7-0;0.00;0.00;0.00;0.00;0.00;0.00;...
server1;600;2022-02-10 06:10:15 UTC;dev7-1;0.00;0.00;0.00;0.00;0.00;0.00;...
server1;600;2022-02-10 06:10:15 UTC;dev7-2;0.00;0.00;0.00;0.00;0.00;0.00;...
server1;600;2022-02-10 06:10:15 UTC;dev253-2;0.00;0.00;0.00;0.00;0.00;0.00;...
```

sysstat logs reside in */var/log/sa* on some Linux distributions, but on others those logs reside in */var/log/sysstat*.

The -- option tells the `sadf` command that the options that follow it are `sar` command options and not `sadf` options. In the command `sadf -d /var/log/sa/sa10 -- -d`, the `-d` option following the -- will display `sar` device information. Perhaps a less confusing example is to display network information from the `sar` command:

```
$ sadf -d /var/log/sa03 -- -n DEV
# hostname;interval;timestamp;IFACE;rxpck/s;txpck/s;rxkB/s;txkB/s;rxcmp/s;...
server1;600;2022-02-10 06:10:15 UTC;lo;0.00;0.00;0.00;0.00;0.00;...
server1;600;2022-02-10 06:10:15 UTC;enp0s3;0.50;0.01;0.12;0.00;0.00;...
server1;600;2022-02-10 06:20:15 UTC;lo;0.00;0.00;0.00;0.00;0.00;...
server1;600;2022-02-10 06:20:15 UTC;enp0s3;0.42;0.00;0.10;0.00;0.00;...
server1;600;2022-02-10 06:30:15 UTC;lo;0.00;0.00;0.00;0.00;0.00;...
server1;600;2022-02-10 06:30:15 UTC;enp0s3;0.47;0.00;0.10;0.00;0.00;...
```

The `-n` is the `sar` option for network activity. DEV means the network device, such as `lo` (loopback), `eth0`, `enp0s3`, and so on.

Summary

I've only scratched the surface of system health, and this chapter could be an entire book. Health monitoring is extremely vital in maintaining SLAs for your customers. Keeping track of system health is an essential system administrator task that affects capacity and performance, security, and standard system housekeeping. It's so important that some large enterprises dedicate entire teams to it.

In Chapter 9, I cover nonhealth system monitoring and network inventory systems.

Monitoring Your System

Monitoring is not optional. It's essential. Every system administrator must monitor their system's performance, health, and security with a vigilant eye. It's impossible to manually monitor your systems and also perform your other administrative tasks, so you must rely on automated software, specific system configurations, and a reporting system to update you on each system's status.

This chapter explores native monitoring tools and guides you in gathering performance and health statistics for your systems.

Maintaining Vigilance on CPU, Memory, and Disk Performance and Capacity

The three primary monitoring focal points in Linux systems are CPU, memory, and disk performance.

Network capacity on local area networks (LANs) isn't usually much of an issue, especially with gigabit network speeds. Many data centers/server rooms use 10-gigabit connections so that system-to-system communications are practically instantaneous and backups, even huge ones, are of no consequence. That said, checking network performance will only require a few minutes of your day, so why not include it? The data exists and is freely available to you, so display it, study it, and act on it if you see a negative trend.

This chapter focuses on CPU, memory, and disk performance and capacity.

Tracking CPU Usage

The CPU is often at the top of the list of system components to monitor. It's at the top of the list because it's the system's powerhouse. Suppose your system's CPU continuously operates above 80% utilization. In that case, it's possible that your system doesn't have enough CPU to power the operating system and all of a host's running applications. It's also conceivable that an application coding problem or security breach issue sends your CPU's utilization into the "red" zone.

There are numerous tools available to help you monitor and assess CPU utilization. The simplest and most readily available are top and ps. These commands are part of the standard build on every Linux distribution.

The top commands

As a system administrator, you've possibly encountered top or one of its related commands, such as atop or htop. The top utility is standard on most Linux distributions, but you'll have to install atop and htop packages from your distribution's repositories. The top commands give you a real-time view of your system's "top" processes. By default, top lists those that consume the most CPU at the top of the view.

top. All users may issue the top command and change sorting options from CPU (default) to memory, time, and PID, as shown in Figure 9-1.

```
top - 22:31:33 up 3 min,  1 user,  load average: 0.14, 0.22, 0.10
Tasks: 124 total,   2 running, 122 sleeping,   0 stopped,   0 zombie
%Cpu(s):  0.0 us,  0.3 sy,  0.0 ni, 99.3 id,  0.0 wa,  0.3 hi,  0.0 si,  0.0 st
MiB Mem :    809.2 total,    417.9 free,    170.0 used,    221.3 buff/cache
MiB Swap:    820.0 total,    820.0 free,      0.0 used.    518.6 avail Mem

    PID USER      PR  NI    VIRT    RES    SHR S  %CPU  %MEM     TIME+ COMMAND
    307 root      20   0       0      0      0 I   0.3   0.0   0:00.31 kworker/0:3-events
   1584 khess     20   0  275204   4440   3796 R   0.3   0.5   0:00.12 top
      1 root      20   0  174996  13384   8888 S   0.0   1.6   0:02.52 systemd
      2 root      20   0       0      0      0 S   0.0   0.0   0:00.01 kthreadd
      3 root       0 -20       0      0      0 I   0.0   0.0   0:00.00 rcu_gp
      4 root       0 -20       0      0      0 I   0.0   0.0   0:00.00 rcu_par_gp
      5 root      20   0       0      0      0 I   0.0   0.0   0:00.00 kworker/0:0-events
      6 root       0 -20       0      0      0 I   0.0   0.0   0:00.00 kworker/0:0H-events_highpri
      7 root      20   0       0      0      0 I   0.0   0.0   0:00.20 kworker/0:1-ata_sff
      8 root      20   0       0      0      0 I   0.0   0.0   0:00.00 kworker/u2:0-events_unbound
      9 root       0 -20       0      0      0 I   0.0   0.0   0:00.00 mm_percpu_wq
     10 root      20   0       0      0      0 S   0.0   0.0   0:00.15 ksoftirqd/0
     11 root      20   0       0      0      0 R   0.0   0.0   0:00.17 rcu_sched
     12 root      rt   0       0      0      0 S   0.0   0.0   0:00.00 migration/0
     13 root      rt   0       0      0      0 S   0.0   0.0   0:00.00 watchdog/0
     14 root      20   0       0      0      0 S   0.0   0.0   0:00.00 cpuhp/0
     16 root      20   0       0      0      0 S   0.0   0.0   0:00.00 kdevtmpfs
     17 root       0 -20       0      0      0 I   0.0   0.0   0:00.00 netns
     18 root      20   0       0      0      0 S   0.0   0.0   0:00.00 rcu_tasks_trace
     19 root      20   0       0      0      0 S   0.0   0.0   0:00.00 rcu_tasks_rude_
     20 root      20   0       0      0      0 S   0.0   0.0   0:00.00 kauditd
```

Figure 9-1. The top command sorted by % CPU

Use Shift + M to switch to memory usage mode, as shown in Figure 9-2.

```
top - 22:32:50 up 5 min,  1 user,  load average: 0.04, 0.16, 0.09
Tasks: 124 total,   1 running, 123 sleeping,   0 stopped,   0 zombie
%Cpu(s):  0.3 us,  0.0 sy,  0.0 ni, 99.0 id,  0.3 wa,  0.3 hi,  0.0 si,  0.0 st
MiB Mem :    809.2 total,    417.5 free,    170.3 used,    221.4 buff/cache
MiB Swap:    820.0 total,    820.0 free,      0.0 used.    510.2 avail Mem

    PID USER      PR  NI    VIRT    RES    SHR S  %CPU  %MEM     TIME+ COMMAND
    942 root      20   0  507752  42236  18704 S   0.0   5.1   0:01.19 firewalld
    939 root      20   0  438888  40832  39048 S   0.0   4.9   0:00.11 sssd_nss
    965 root      20   0  705400  31568  15556 S   0.0   3.8   0:00.62 tuned
    926 polkitd   20   0 1631840  27620  17248 S   0.0   3.3   0:00.15 polkitd
    958 root      20   0  601572  18348  15980 S   0.0   2.2   0:00.12 NetworkManager
    935 root      20   0  437552  15448  12604 S   0.0   1.9   0:00.25 sssd_be
    915 root      20   0  428896  14152  12056 S   0.0   1.7   0:00.06 sssd
      1 root      20   0  174996  13384   8888 S   0.0   1.6   0:02.52 systemd
    734 root      20   0  116808  11392   8428 S   0.0   1.4   0:00.27 systemd-udevd
   1539 root      20   0  153444  10452   9180 S   0.0   1.3   0:00.05 sshd
   1543 khess     20   0   89444   9736   8320 S   0.0   1.2   0:00.12 systemd
    944 root      20   0   92184   9556   7460 S   0.0   1.2   0:00.04 systemd-logind
    704 root      20   0   84508   8080   7136 S   0.0   1.0   0:00.16 systemd-journal
    968 root      20   0   92348   7048   6152 S   0.0   0.9   0:00.01 sshd
    930 rngd      20   0  154828   6276   5448 S   0.0   0.8   0:16.33 rngd
    924 root      20   0   50708   5976   4688 S   0.0   0.7   0:00.08 smartd
    913 dbus      20   0   64728   5500   4540 S   0.0   0.7   0:00.13 dbus-daemon
   1553 khess     20   0  153444   5436   4168 S   0.0   0.7   0:00.01 sshd
   1554 khess     20   0  235212   5308   3400 S   0.0   0.6   0:00.15 bash
   1547 khess     20   0  244512   4772      8 S   0.0   0.6   0:00.00 (sd-pam)
   1584 khess     20   0  275204   4440   3796 R   0.3   0.5   0:00.25 top
```

Figure 9-2. The top command is sorted by Memory consumption usage

To see how long your processes have run, use Shift + S to sort by time, as shown in Figure 9-3.

```
top - 08:01:45 up  9:34,  1 user,  load average: 0.00, 0.00, 0.00
Tasks: 120 total,   1 running, 119 sleeping,   0 stopped,   0 zombie
%Cpu(s):  0.0 us,  0.0 sy,  0.0 ni,100.0 id,  0.0 wa,  0.0 hi,  0.0 si,  0.0 st
MiB Mem :    809.2 total,    341.8 free,    174.4 used,    293.0 buff/cache
MiB Swap:    820.0 total,    819.7 free,      0.3 used.    507.2 avail Mem

    PID USER      PR  NI    VIRT    RES    SHR S  %CPU  %MEM     TIME+ COMMAND
   2008 khess     20   0  275200   5016   4224 R   0.3   0.6   0:00.18 top
      1 root      20   0  174996  13384   8888 S   0.0   1.6   0:02.94 systemd
      2 root      20   0       0      0      0 S   0.0   0.0   0:00.01 kthreadd
      3 root       0 -20       0      0      0 I   0.0   0.0   0:00.00 rcu_gp
      4 root       0 -20       0      0      0 I   0.0   0.0   0:00.00 rcu_par_gp
      6 root       0 -20       0      0      0 I   0.0   0.0   0:00.00 kworker/0:0H-events_highpri
      9 root       0 -20       0      0      0 I   0.0   0.0   0:00.00 mm_percpu_wq
     10 root      20   0       0      0      0 S   0.0   0.0   0:00.26 ksoftirqd/0
     11 root      20   0       0      0      0 I   0.0   0.0   0:00.26 rcu_sched
     12 root      rt   0       0      0      0 S   0.0   0.0   0:00.00 migration/0
     13 root      rt   0       0      0      0 S   0.0   0.0   0:00.01 watchdog/0
     14 root      20   0       0      0      0 S   0.0   0.0   0:00.00 cpuhp/0
     16 root      20   0       0      0      0 S   0.0   0.0   0:00.00 kdevtmpfs
     17 root       0 -20       0      0      0 I   0.0   0.0   0:00.00 netns
     18 root      20   0       0      0      0 S   0.0   0.0   0:00.00 rcu_tasks_trace
     19 root      20   0       0      0      0 S   0.0   0.0   0:00.00 rcu_tasks_rude_
     20 root      20   0       0      0      0 S   0.0   0.0   0:00.00 kauditd
     21 root      20   0       0      0      0 S   0.0   0.0   0:00.00 khungtaskd
     22 root      20   0       0      0      0 S   0.0   0.0   0:00.00 oom_reaper
     23 root       0 -20       0      0      0 I   0.0   0.0   0:00.00 writeback
     24 root      20   0       0      0      0 S   0.0   0.0   0:00.00 kcompactd0
```

Figure 9-3. Top processes sorted by time

Table 9-1 provides you with a few keyboard shortcuts to top's sorting options.

Table 9-1. Keyboard shortcuts for some sorting options

Key	Sorting
Shift + M	%MEM (memory usage)
Shift + P	%CPU (CPU usage—the default)
Shift + S	TIME (running time)

From a cursory glance at top's output, you might find it difficult to know which value is in focus. So it's often necessary to use one of the keyboard shortcuts to apply a known sorting scheme to reset your view. If I forget which sorting scheme I'm running, I cycle through CPU, memory, and time to check.

The standard top command is useful, but for many sysadmins, the displayed information isn't sufficient for informed decision-making. The atop and htop commands, not installed by default on most distributions, provide you with a broader view of what's happening.

atop. The atop utility is an advanced system and process monitor. atop displays standard top processes in the lower pane but provides insight into CPU, memory, disk, and network performance in the upper pane, as shown in Figure 9-4.

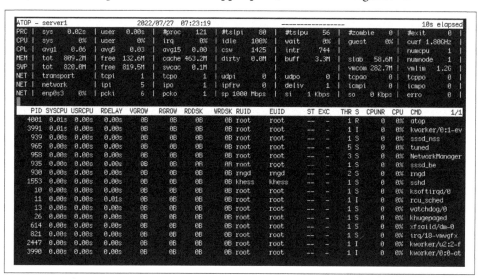

Figure 9-4. The atop command

The atop man page (*https://oreil.ly/Fu2Sw*) describes atop as follows:

> The program atop is an interactive monitor to view the load on a Linux system. It shows the occupation of the most critical hardware resources (from a performance point of view) on the system level, i.e., CPU, memory, disk, LVM, swap usage, and network. It also shows which processes are responsible for the indicated load concerning CPU and memory load on the process level.

You may run atop as a regular user or as the root user. Depending on which user (regular or root) executes the command, the command displays a message that informs you of which mode you're using.

When run as root:

```
*** System and Process Activity since Boot ***     Unrestricted view (privileged)
```

When run as a regular user:

```
*** System and Process Activity since Boot ***     Restricted view (unprivileged)
```

The views are the same for both modes. Still, in restricted view, there are actions that you can't take, such as using kill on processes that you don't own. As mentioned earlier, the atop utility appeals to sysadmins because it displays focused performance values for critical system parameters. These statistics are handy because you don't have to search for performance-specific data or use a potentially expensive third-party tool to extract the information. The atop utility is an essential part of a system administrator's toolbox.

htop. The htop utility is another system performance viewer that displays the same information as the standard top utility but is color-coded and has a convenient command menu. As you can see in Figure 9-5, the htop utility's current usage mode is highlighted (CPU%). The current mode is CPU usage. The menu helps execute specific commands without the administrator having to memorize keystrokes for each action.

```
CPU[|                          1.3%]    Tasks: 29, 16 thr; 1 running
Mem[||||||||||||||||||||||||||||||||||||||||159M/809M]    Load average: 0.00 0.00 0.00
Swp[                         12.3M/820M]    Uptime: 2 days, 09:58:50

  PID USER       PRI  NI  VIRT   RES   SHR S CPU%MEM%   TIME+  Command
 4133 root        20   0  235M  4496  3628 R  0.7  0.5  0:00.11 htop
    1 root        20   0  170M 12812  8316 S  0.0  1.5  0:05.03 /usr/lib/systemd/systemd --switched-root --system --dese
  704 root        20   0 86552  8656  7608 S  0.0  1.0  0:00.96 /usr/lib/systemd/systemd-journald
  734 root        20   0  114M 10108  7144 S  0.0  1.2  0:00.50 /usr/lib/systemd/systemd-udevd
  885 root        16  -4  147M  2160  1776 S  0.0  0.3  0:00.15 /sbin/auditd
  886 root        16  -4  147M  2160  1776 S  0.0  0.3  0:00.00 /sbin/auditd
  887 root        16  -4 48560  2208  1896 S  0.0  0.3  0:00.07 /usr/sbin/sedispatch
  888 root        16  -4  147M  2160  1776 S  0.0  0.3  0:00.00 /sbin/auditd
  912 libstorag   20   0 19740  1848  1692 S  0.0  0.2  0:00.48 /usr/bin/lsmd -d
  913 dbus        20   0 64728  5144  4184 S  0.0  0.6  0:00.71 /usr/bin/dbus-daemon --system --address=systemd: --nofor
  915 root        20   0  418M 12252 10156 S  0.0  1.5  0:00.30 /usr/sbin/sssd -i --logger=files
  918 root        20   0 18300  2144  1996 S  0.0  0.3  0:00.00 /usr/sbin/mcelog --ignorenodev --daemon --foreground
  924 root        20   0 50708  5800  4512 S  0.0  0.7  0:00.11 /usr/sbin/smartd -n -q never
  926 polkitd     20   0 1593M 23116 16888 S  0.0  2.8  0:00.19 /usr/lib/polkit-1/polkitd --no-debug
  927 dbus        20   0 64728  5144  4184 S  0.0  0.6  0:00.00 /usr/bin/dbus-daemon --system --address=systemd: --nofor
  930 rngd        20   0  151M  5556  4728 S  0.0  0.7  0:18.28 /usr/sbin/rngd -f --fill-watermark=0
  933 polkitd     20   0 1593M 23116 16888 S  0.0  2.8  0:00.00 /usr/lib/polkit-1/polkitd --no-debug
  934 polkitd     20   0 1593M 23116 16888 S  0.0  2.8  0:00.03 /usr/lib/polkit-1/polkitd --no-debug
  935 root        20   0  427M 13352 10508 S  0.0  1.6  0:01.82 /usr/libexec/sssd/sssd_be --domain implicit_files --uid
  936 polkitd     20   0 1593M 23116 16888 S  0.0  2.8  0:00.00 /usr/lib/polkit-1/polkitd --no-debug
  937 polkitd     20   0 1593M 23116 16888 S  0.0  2.8  0:00.00 /usr/lib/polkit-1/polkitd --no-debug
  938 rngd        20   0  151M  5556  4728 S  0.0  0.7  0:16.27 /usr/sbin/rngd -f --fill-watermark=0
  939 root        20   0  428M 25000 23196 S  0.0  3.0  0:01.93 /usr/libexec/sssd/sssd_nss --uid 0 --gid 0 --logger=file
  940 polkitd     20   0 1593M 23116 16888 S  0.0  2.8  0:00.00 /usr/lib/polkit-1/polkitd --no-debug
  942 root        20   0  495M 35664 13480 S  0.0  4.3  0:01.19 /usr/libexec/platform-python -s /usr/sbin/firewalld --no
  944 root        20   0 92184  8984  6888 S  0.0  1.1  0:00.48 /usr/lib/systemd/systemd-logind
  958 root        20   0  587M 16264 13896 S  0.0  2.0  0:07.91 /usr/sbin/NetworkManager --no-daemon
  963 root        20   0  587M 16264 13896 S  0.0  2.0  0:03.13 /usr/sbin/NetworkManager --no-daemon
  964 root        20   0  587M 16264 13896 S  0.0  2.0  0:00.01 /usr/sbin/NetworkManager --no-daemon
  965 root        20   0  688M 27436 11560 S  0.0  3.3  0:39.23 /usr/libexec/platform-python -Es /usr/sbin/tuned -l -P
  968 root        20   0 92348  5556  4660 S  0.0  0.7  0:00.01 /usr/sbin/sshd -D -oCiphers=aes256-gcm@openssh.com,chach
F1Help  F2Setup F3Search F4Filter F5Tree F6SortBy F7Nice -F8Nice +F9Kill  F10Quit
```

Figure 9-5. The htop *utility running in CPU usage mode*

ps

The ps command displays information about running processes. You can view your own processes, all processes, and the process table in different formats using command options or switches. The ps command is common to all Linux distributions.

To view all processes your user account owns, use the ps command with the -ux option:

```
$ ps -ux
USER    PID %CPU %MEM    VSZ   RSS TTY     STAT START   TIME COMMAND
khess  1550  0.0  1.1  89444  9600 ?       Ss   Jul31   0:00 /usr/lib/systemd/...
khess  1554  0.0  0.4 244512  3868 ?       S    Jul31   0:00 (sd-pam)
khess  1560  0.0  0.5 153444  4728 ?       S    Jul31   0:00 sshd: khess@pts/0
khess  1561  0.0  0.6 235212  5052 pts/0   Ss   Jul31   0:00 -bash
khess  4698  0.0  0.4 271452  4140 pts/0   R+   08:31   0:00 ps -ux
```

You may also view all processes by owner using the -aux switch combination:

```
$ ps -aux
USER    PID %CPU %MEM     VSZ   RSS TTY    STAT START   TIME COMMAND
root      1  0.0  1.6 174996 13372 ?      Ss   Jul31   0:04 /usr/lib/systemd/...
root      2  0.0  0.0      0     0 ?      S    Jul31   0:00 [kthreadd]
root      3  0.0  0.0      0     0 ?      I<   Jul31   0:00 [rcu_gp]
```

```
root      4  0.0  0.0       0      0 ?       I<   Jul31   0:00 [rcu_par_gp]
root      6  0.0  0.0       0      0 ?       I<   Jul31   0:00 [kworker/0:0H...
root      9  0.0  0.0       0      0 ?       I<   Jul31   0:00 [mm_percpu_wq]
```

The full process table is too long to show here, but you can see from the listing that the displayed results show processes in ascending order of process ID (PID). The top command in the previous section is a dynamic process table that you can order by CPU, memory, and other performance measurements.

The remaining utilities in this section are not as well-known as the top or ps commands but are important enough for you to learn about and explore the features and functions of each.

glances

glances, shown in Figure 9-6, is another top program. It is a cross-platform monitoring tool. The developer(s) rearranged and colorized the display, but the information is similar to what you see in the htop utility.

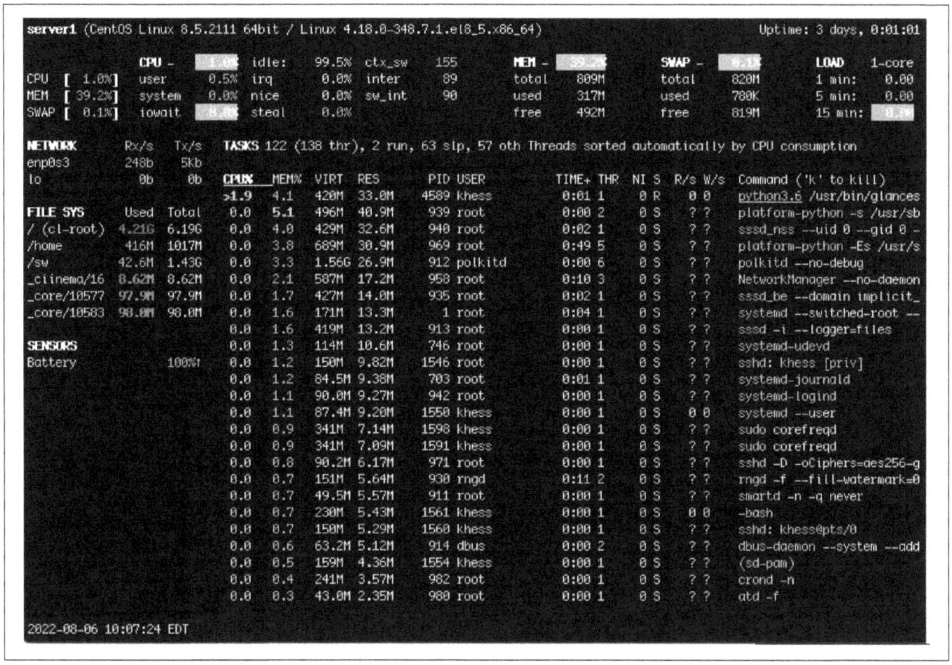

Figure 9-6. glances' dynamic display with CPU% focus

Press the M key (Shift is not required for shortcuts in glances) to change the focus from CPU% to MEM%, and press T to switch to TIME. Press C to return to CPU% on the display.

If your system is CPU-constrained or you suspect it to be CPU-constrained, don't use glances as your primary CPU performance check because it consumes about 15% of your CPU as opposed to top's 3%–5%.

You may also run glances in a client/server configuration, export data to multiple formats, and change its display settings. Consult the man page for a list of glances' features and options.

Exploring sysstat Monitoring

The sysstat (System Status) package is a native tool. In other words, it's a prepackaged, standard monitoring tool that's free and freely available on any Linux distribution. You can compile it from source code if you prefer, but it's generally available in package form for all major distributions.

The following is excerpted from the sysstat man page:

> The sysstat package contains the sar, sadf, mpstat, iostat, tapestat, pidstat, cifsiostat tools for Linux.

- sar is the system activity reporter utility.
- sadf is the system activity data formatter that displays data collected by sar in multiple formats (CSV, XML, etc.).
- iostat is the input/output statistics utility that displays CPU utilization and disk I/O statistics.
- tapestat displays tape and tape drive statistics.
- mpstat is the multi-processor statistics utility that displays global and per-processor statistics.
- pidstat reports statistics for Linux processes by process ID.
- cifsiostat is the CIFS (Samba/SMB) I/O statistics utility.

Reporting System Activity

The sar utility is the most used of the sysstat suite of commands. The system activity reporting tool displays performance statistics from midnight to the current time. By default, sar only displays the current day's metrics.

You can save the information collected by sar in a file in a binary format. The statistics reported by sar include I/O transfer rates, paging, process-related performance, interrupts, network activity, memory utilization, swap space utilization, CPU utilization, kernel activities, TTY statistics, and more. The sysstat package fully supports both single and multiprocessor systems.

Using the `sar` command with no options displays CPU statistics (default):

```
$ sar
Linux 4.18.0-348.7.1.el8_5.x86_64 (server1)    09/20/2022    _x86_64_    (1 CPU)

12:00:07 AM    CPU    %user    %nice    %system    %iowait    %steal    %idle
12:10:08 AM    all     0.01     0.20       0.53       0.05      0.00    99.22
12:20:00 AM    all     0.01     0.00       0.25       0.01      0.00    99.74
12:30:01 AM    all     0.00     0.00       0.24       0.01      0.00    99.75
12:40:02 AM    all     0.01     0.00       0.25       0.01      0.00    99.73

...

02:00:04 PM    all     0.01     0.00       0.26       0.01      0.00    99.73
02:10:05 PM    all     0.01     0.01       0.27       0.01      0.00    99.70
02:20:05 PM    all     0.01     0.00       0.26       0.01      0.00    99.72
02:30:06 PM    all     0.01     0.00       0.27       0.01      0.00    99.72
Average:       all     0.01     0.01       0.29       0.01      0.00    99.69
```

You can filter `sar` results using command options. For example, to display CPU statistics, use the `-u` option. The `-u` option displays the same results as the `sar` command with no options. Add the `ALL` keyword to include all CPU-related statistics:

```
$ sar -u ALL
Linux 4.18.0-348.7.1.el8_5.x86_64 (server1)    09/24/2022    _x86_64_    (1 CPU)

12:00:03 AM    CPU %usr %nice %sys %iowait %steal %irq %soft %guest %gnice %idle
12:10:01 AM    all 0.02 0.00  0.06 0.01     0.00   0.22 0.05  0.00   0.00   99.64
12:20:01 AM    all 0.01 0.00  0.03 0.01     0.00   0.21 0.05  0.00   0.00   99.69
12:30:02 AM    all 0.01 0.00  0.03 0.01     0.00   0.20 0.05  0.00   0.00   99.70
```

The `-B` option displays paging statistics:

```
$ sar -B
Linux 4.18.0-348.7.1.el8_5.x86_64 (server1)    09/24/2022    _x86_64_    (1 CPU)
```

The `-b` option reports I/O and transfer rate statistics:

```
$ sar -b
Linux 4.18.0-348.7.1.el8_5.x86_64 (server1)    09/24/2022    _x86_64_    (1 CPU)

12:00:03 AM      tps     rtps     wtps    bread/s    bwrtn/s
12:10:01 AM     0.53     0.13     0.40      11.42       6.52
12:20:01 AM     0.17     0.00     0.17       0.00       1.97
12:30:02 AM     0.16     0.00     0.16       0.00       1.97
12:40:03 AM     0.17     0.00     0.17       0.00       1.99
```

As demonstrated, the `sar` command is versatile and has many options for displaying system performance data. Refer to the `sar` man page for an extensive list of options. The next section covers displaying `sar` data in multiple formats using the `sadf` command.

Displaying System Activity Data in Multiple Formats

The `sadf` command sends `sar` data to different output types to make ingesting its data into a database or displaying it on a web page easier. For example, the following command displays `sar` data from the 21st of the month in a format that's easy to import into a database:

```
$ sadf -d /var/log/sa/sa21
# hostname;interval;timestamp;CPU;%user;%nice;%system;%iowait;%steal;%idle
server1;601;2022-09-21 04:10:04 UTC;-1;0.01;0.00;0.28;0.01;0.00;99.70
server1;601;2022-09-21 04:20:05 UTC;-1;0.01;0.00;0.26;0.01;0.00;99.72
server1;601;2022-09-21 04:30:06 UTC;-1;0.01;0.00;0.28;0.01;0.00;99.71
server1;601;2022-09-21 04:40:07 UTC;-1;0.01;0.00;0.27;0.01;0.00;99.71
...
```

In addition to using `sadf` with historical data, you can also use it with current data:

```
$ sadf -dh -- -p
# hostname;interval;timestamp;CPU;%user;%nice;%system;%iowait;%steal;%idle[...]
server1;598;2022-09-24 04:10:01 UTC;-1;0.02;0.00;0.33;0.01;0.00;99.64
server1;601;2022-09-24 04:20:01 UTC;-1;0.01;0.00;0.30;0.01;0.00;99.69
server1;601;2022-09-24 04:30:02 UTC;-1;0.01;0.00;0.29;0.01;0.00;99.70
server1;600;2022-09-24 04:40:03 UTC;-1;0.01;0.00;0.29;0.01;0.00;99.69
...
```

There are too many possible options for generating different data outputs using `sadf` to list here. Search online for more examples or experiment with options from the `sadf` man page. The next sections deal with specific statistics output from other `sysstat` utilities: `iostat`, `tapestat`, `mpstat`, `pidstat`, and `cifsiostat`. Their relevance depends on your hardware configuration. For example, very few, if any, businesses still use tape drives for backups.

Monitoring System I/O Device Loading with iostat

Like other "stat" commands, the first metric you see is a statistics summary or summary metric from the time since the system was last booted. Generally, you run the stat commands in multiples to see current statistics or use the `-y` option to ignore the summary metric. In this first example, the summary information is included; in the second, the summary is omitted.

Here it is with the summary information included:

```
$ iostat -d 2
Linux 4.18.0-348.7.1.el8_5.x86_64 (server1)     09/24/2022     _x86_64_    (1 CPU)

Device           tps    kB_read/s    kB_wrtn/s    kB_read    kB_wrtn
sda             0.26         1.59         2.05     312698     403049
sdc             0.01         0.04         0.01       8267       2797
sdb             0.00         0.02         0.01       3028       2048
scd0            0.00         0.00         0.00          1          0
```

```
dm-0                0.26           1.31           2.12         257071         416372
dm-1                0.00           0.01           0.01           2220           1172
dm-2                0.00           0.01           0.01           1330           2048

Device               tps       kB_read/s      kB_wrtn/s        kB_read        kB_wrtn
sda                 0.00           0.00           0.00              0              0
sdc                 0.00           0.00           0.00              0              0
sdb                 0.00           0.00           0.00              0              0
scd0                0.00           0.00           0.00              0              0
dm-0                0.00           0.00           0.00              0              0
dm-1                0.00           0.00           0.00              0              0
dm-2                0.00           0.00           0.00              0              0

Device               tps       kB_read/s      kB_wrtn/s        kB_read        kB_wrtn
sda                 0.00           0.00           0.00              0              0
sdc                 0.00           0.00           0.00              0              0
sdb                 0.00           0.00           0.00              0              0
scd0                0.00           0.00           0.00              0              0
dm-0                0.00           0.00           0.00              0              0
dm-1                0.00           0.00           0.00              0              0
dm-2                0.00           0.00           0.00              0              0
```

Here it is with the summary information omitted:

```
$ iostat -y -d 2
Linux 4.18.0-348.7.1.el8_5.x86_64 (server1)    09/24/2022    _x86_64_    (1 CPU)

Device               tps       kB_read/s      kB_wrtn/s        kB_read        kB_wrtn
sda                 0.00           0.00           0.00              0              0
sdc                 1.00           0.00           0.75              0              1
sdb                 0.00           0.00           0.00              0              0
scd0                0.00           0.00           0.00              0              0
dm-0                0.00           0.00           0.00              0              0
dm-1                0.00           0.00           0.00              0              0
dm-2                0.00           0.00           0.00              0              0

Device               tps       kB_read/s      kB_wrtn/s        kB_read        kB_wrtn
sda                 0.00           0.00           0.00              0              0
sdc                 0.00           0.00           0.00              0              0
sdb                 0.00           0.00           0.00              0              0
scd0                0.00           0.00           0.00              0              0
dm-0                0.00           0.00           0.00              0              0
dm-1                0.00           0.00           0.00              0              0
dm-2                0.00           0.00           0.00              0              0

Device               tps       kB_read/s      kB_wrtn/s        kB_read        kB_wrtn
sda                 0.00           0.00           0.00              0              0
sdc                 0.00           0.00           0.00              0              0
sdb                 0.00           0.00           0.00              0              0
scd0                0.00           0.00           0.00              0              0
dm-0                0.00           0.00           0.00              0              0
dm-1                0.00           0.00           0.00              0              0
dm-2                0.00           0.00           0.00              0              0
```

The statistics on a quiet virtual machine aren't very interesting, but at least you see which metrics the utility yields in its reports. Like the other `sysstat` utilities, `iostat` has several options you can glean from the man pages.

Kicking It Old-School with the tapestat Utility

I haven't used a tape drive in more than 15 years as of this writing. Virtual tape drives (hard disks masquerading as tape drives) have replaced the old streaming tape systems. I'm covering `tapestat` here for legacy purposes because there's always an old "unsupported" system lying about somewhere with a tape drive installed. The information on it is always more valuable than gold, and you might have to retrieve it. This section won't help you retrieve the information, but you can see some tape drive–related statistics from its operation.

This is the response I receive when I run `tapestat` on my Linux VM:

```
$ tapestat
Linux 4.18.0-348.7.1.el8_5.x86_64 (server1)     09/24/2022     _x86_64_    (1 CPU)

No tape drives with statistics found
```

That's the message you're likely to receive when you type the `tapestat` command. Tape drives are part of history and were not part of anyone's good old days. If you're still using one, your output will provide you with interesting and useful statistics.

Collecting Processor Statistics

Using the `mpstat` (multiprocessor statistics) utility, you can display multiprocessor and uniprocessor statistics for your systems. Issuing the `mpstat` command with no options displays a summary for all processors:

```
$ mpstat
Linux 5.4.0-125-generic (server2)     09/25/2022     _x86_64_    (2 CPU)

10:06:16 AM  CPU  %usr %nice %sys %iowait %irq  %soft %steal %guest %gnice  %idle
10:06:16 AM  all  0.92  0.01  0.91 0.20    0.00  0.25  0.00   0.00   0.00   97.72
```

You see that the system contains two processors, so you know that you can view individual processor performance. View individual processors by specifying option -P and the processor number. Remember that processor numbering begins with 0. For a two-processor system, you have processor 0 and processor 1. The following command displays statistics for processor 1:

```
$ mpstat -P 1
Linux 5.4.0-125-generic (server2)     09/25/2022     _x86_64_    (2 CPU)

10:12:43 AM  CPU  %usr %nice  %sys %iowait %irq  %soft %steal %guest %gnice  %idle
10:12:43 AM    1  0.71  0.01  0.64  0.14    0.00  0.08  0.00   0.00   0.00   98.43
```

You may also view all processors by specifying the ALL option:

```
$ mpstat -P ALL
Linux 5.4.0-125-generic (server2)     09/25/2022     _x86_64_    (2 CPU)

09:56:28 AM  CPU  %usr  %nice   %sys %iowait %irq %soft %steal %guest %gnice %idle
09:56:28 AM  all  2.05   0.02   2.01    0.44 0.00  0.44   0.00   0.00   0.00 95.05
09:56:28 AM    0  1.93   0.02   2.11    0.44 0.00  0.65   0.00   0.00   0.00 94.84
09:56:28 AM    1  2.16   0.02   1.91    0.43 0.00  0.22   0.00   0.00   0.00 95.25
```

Similar to other "stat" commands, you can request a display at an interval in seconds and a specified number of iterations. For example, the following executes mpstat every five seconds and three iterations:

```
$ mpstat 5 3
Linux 5.4.0-125-generic (server2)     09/25/2022     _x86_64_    (2 CPU)

10:26:53 AM  CPU  %usr %nice %sys  %iowait %irq %soft %steal %guest %gnice  %idle
10:26:58 AM  all  0.00  0.00 0.00     0.00 0.00  0.10   0.00   0.00   0.00  99.90
10:27:03 AM  all  0.00  0.00 0.00     0.00 0.00  0.10   0.00   0.00   0.00  99.90
10:27:08 AM  all  0.00  0.00 0.00     0.00 0.00  0.00   0.00   0.00   0.00 100.00
Average:     all  0.00  0.00 0.00     0.00 0.00  0.07   0.00   0.00   0.00  99.93
```

On a busier system, the numbers are far more informative. You can determine if a particular processor is at or above capacity and then selectively bind processes (changing the processor affinity of a process) to other processors to relieve the stress on CPU0. The next utility, pidstat, displays which processor a particular process is bound to.

Monitoring Linux Tasks with pidstat

The pidstat command is used to monitor individual tasks currently managed by the Linux kernel. The default command, with no options passed to it, displays only active tasks (tasks with nonzero statistics values) in the report:

```
$ pidstat
Linux 5.4.0-125-generic (server2)     09/25/2022     _x86_64_    (2 CPU)

11:19:08 AM   UID   PID   %usr %system  %guest    %wait   %CPU   CPU  Command
11:19:08 AM     0     1   0.02    0.04    0.00     0.01   0.06     0  systemd
11:19:08 AM     0     2   0.00    0.00    0.00     0.00   0.00     1  kthreadd
11:19:08 AM     0    10   0.00    0.01    0.00     0.00   0.01     0  ksoftirqd/0
11:19:08 AM     0    11   0.00    0.03    0.00     0.02   0.03     1  rcu_sched
11:19:08 AM     0    12   0.00    0.00    0.00     0.00   0.00     0  migration/0
11:19:08 AM     0    17   0.01    0.00    0.00     0.01   0.01     1  migration/1
11:19:08 AM     0    18   0.00    0.00    0.00     0.01   0.00     1  ksoftirqd/1
11:19:08 AM     0    30   0.00    0.00    0.00     0.00   0.00     1  khugepaged
...
```

A handy use of the `pidstat` utility is to check system usage by an individual user:

```
$ pidstat -d -U khess
Linux 5.4.0-125-generic (server2)      09/25/2022      _x86_64_     (2 CPU)

11:36:26 AM    USER     PID   kB_rd/s   kB_wr/s  kB_ccwr/s iodelay  Command
11:36:26 AM    khess    1131   0.03      0.00      0.00       1      systemd
11:36:26 AM    khess    1239   0.79      0.00      0.00       2      bash
```

The `pidstat` utility has significant value if you're tracking down a rogue user or process consuming too many system resources.

Watching Windows-Compatible Filesystem Statistics with cifsiostat

The `cifsiostat` command displays statistics about read and write operations on Common Internet File System (CIFS) or Samba filesystems. Many system administrators will maintain CIFS to be compatible with their Windows users. Windows users may map drive letters to CIFS shares, similar to mapping to a shared folder on a Windows system. Using CIFS makes it easier to maintain some compatibility between Windows desktop systems and Linux servers. CIFS may also make using Windows Server systems unnecessary because many Windows services may be duplicated using the protocol.

Use the `cifsiostat` command to display statistics:

```
$ cifsiostat

Filesystem:      rB/s   wB/s   rops/s   wops/s   fo/s   fc/s   fd/s
\\server2\common  0.00   0.00    0.00     0.00    1.00   1.00   0.00
```

If `cifsiostat` doesn't work on your systems, ensure that you have CIFS/Samba installed and operating correctly. Add Samba users to your system. Set up writeable/browseable shares. Start/restart and enable Samba using the following commands:

```
$ sudo systemctl enable smbd
$ sudo systemctl enable nmbd
$ sudo systemctl start smbd
$ sudo systemctl start nmbd
```

Also, be sure that the `cifs` kernel module is loaded:

```
$ modinfo cifs
```

Summary

In this chapter, you learned about monitoring your system's performance as well as the tools with which you can track those statistics. Unfortunately, there isn't a single tool that does everything. Many system administrators install commercial monitoring tools to remedy the lack of a global, free monitoring tool. There have been a few attempts in the past to create such free tools, but they were either abandoned by their developers or sold to commercial companies.

Monitoring your systems is a required task, and it's more than a simple up/down status check. You must maintain constant vigilance over your systems' performance and capacity to minimize outages and provide business continuity to your applications and resources.

## CHAPTER 10

Scripting and Automation

Sysadmins automate what they can. But you can't automate everything. Automation is a good thing but has its limitations. In this chapter, I discuss both the pros and cons of automation. Some tasks are difficult to automate because they involve too many variables. And automation does come with some security risks because automating tasks that require elevated privileges creates security holes that can lead to system compromise. Other obstacles to automation include timing and time drift, system failure, script error conditions, and human interactions.

Creating scripts and automating tasks is challenging and fun. Watching a series of scripts and schedules work as planned to mimic human keystrokes, decisions, and activities is rewarding. Every sysadmin must know how to create basic shell scripts and should automate every possible nonprivileged, repetitive task. This chapter covers the concepts of scripting and automation but not the low-level mechanics of scripting (loops, file I/O, etc.), which are well-documented on the web.

Answering the Question: Why Automate?

I've had a few sysadmins ask me why they should automate anything. The answer is simple: so you can focus on higher-level tasks while your computer systems handle the mundane, daily jobs that you must perform but that a CPU and some memory can address without making mistakes. Do you want your day filled with the drudgery of manually creating backups, copying backups to an archive location, checking capacity on every system, installing updates, checking log files for errors, and checking uptimes, or would you rather focus on system security, testing new software, and sharpening your scripting skills?

You have only a limited number of hours to perform the work that must be done. And you probably have an almost inexhaustible supply of computing power at your fingertips. Use it. The tasks that require hours of your time can be handed off to systems that complete those repetitive tasks flawlessly, without getting tired or frustrated, and with almost no overhead. And those are the reasons to automate every task that you possibly can.

Automating Yourself Out of a Job

Spoiler alert: you're never going to automate yourself out of a job, but you should try. Seriously, you can automate every repetitive, mundane task you face, but you'll never succeed in losing your job because you've automated it. Too many variables and things can go wrong with the hardware, software, networks, and, most of all, users to end your employment because you've successfully automated too much.

Here are answers to five common questions about automation that I'm confident will clear things up for you:

Which tasks should I automate?
> Anything that can be scripted reliably, even if it requires user input.

Are there tasks that cannot be automated?
> Yes, plenty of them. Most things requiring a complex, multistep decision can't be automated (although some can). You can use various techniques to automate them, including `expect`, shell scripts, Perl, PHP, and other scripting and compiled languages.

Are there tasks that should never be automated?
> Yes. You should not automate tasks such as those that require you to store an unencrypted password in a text file. There are multiple methods of automating tasks where you can use encrypted passwords, key files, limited `sudo`, or nonprivileged accounts.

Which task should I automate first?
> Backups. For example, create a backup of your */etc* directory and use secure copy (SCP) to archive it onto another system.

Should I purchase a commercial automation solution?
> You can, but you should begin by using your own scripts and exhausting your options before spending money on something you can do just as efficiently and free of charge. But certainly, purchase a commercial solution if the number of hosts makes it reasonable.

Basic automation is easy to do, it saves money and time, and it prevents mistakes made by human hands.

There is also a psychological aspect of automation—sysadmins who automate experience less burnout than those who perform every task manually. Think about the repetitive nature of making backups, transferring them to an archive location, checking backups, and removing old archives. If you manage more than a handful of systems, it will take a significant portion of your day (or evening) to type every command manually. This kind of labor wears on a person's psyche and causes burnout and job dissatisfaction. Multiple studies show that automation does increase job satisfaction. Alex Edelstein's blog post "89% of Your Employees Could Benefit with This One Change" (*https://oreil.ly/5-iR9*) explains this concept further.

Creating Scripts

If you need a script to perform a particular task, chances are excellent that you can find one with a simple online search. You don't have to write one from scratch. Adapt scripts to your needs and use them without guilt. Other system administrators place their scripts online for you to use. You should, however, learn the basics of scripting, such as reading from a file, writing to a file, grepping, piping, redirecting, looping, and calling other scripts from within a script. You don't have to become a scripting expert but learning the basics helps you find what you need and allows you to adapt what you find to your circumstances.

Writing backup scripts is a good place to start. Backups are required, and you'll be a hero in case of a failure or human error, which could be your own. I've known sysadmins with more than ten years of experience who have removed entire */etc* directories by accident, so a good backup is essential to a happy life as a sysadmin. The following sections teach you scriptwriting concepts. The most important of these is outlining your script.

Outlining Your Scripts

Before you write a script, outline what you want the script to do. No, you don't have to create a flowchart, but you should list the steps that you want to occur during the script's run. Here's an example of a script that I'll call *backup_server1.sh*:

- Create a `tar` file of the */etc* directory.
- Compress the `tar` file.
- Transfer the file to server *archive1*.

That's simple enough. The script is a simple, top-down procedure with no decision tree or branching.

Writing a Script from an Outline

And now that you have your script outline, you also have the documentation for your script. You must document your scripts because, in six months or a year, you might not remember the script's purpose or even that you wrote it.

The contents of *backup_server1.sh* are as follows:

```
#!/bin/bash

# Create a tar file of /etc.
sudo tar cvf server1_etc.tar /etc

# Compress the tar file
gzip -9 server1_etc.tar

# Transfer the file to archive1 into the /server1/backups directory
scp server1_etc.tar.gz archive1:/server1/backups
```

Save the file, give it execute permission, and it's ready to use. The */server1/backups* directory on the *archive1* system should be executable and writeable by the user placing the backups into it. For better security, you should designate a backup user and create backup directories with permissions restricted to that user.

Create a Backup and Restore (bur) user on all systems and set up passwordless SSH key files for the bur user. Set up cron jobs for backups as the bur user on all systems:

```
drwx------   2 bur  bur        64 Oct  4 08:01 backups
```

Here is the crontab for the bur user on *server1*:

```
0 2 * * * /home/bur/backup_server1.sh
```

The bur user's crontab will back up *server1*'s */etc* directory every day at 2 a.m. The backups will transfer to *archive1* into the */server1/backup* directory. You need to set up this scenario on every system. The backup for *archive1* should be sent to a different system.

The */etc* directory isn't the only directory you need to back up. This is just an example. You might need to back up */home*, */var/www/html*, */opt*, and others to restore a system to its previous state before a security incident or failure. The crontab (scheduled task) will be explained in detail in the next section.

Scheduling Tasks

The cron utility schedules commands to run at a specific time. It helps to automate repetitive tasks that must be performed at a specific time, multiple times, or at inconvenient times for humans.

Over the years, developers have attempted to replace the cron utility with little success. cron is difficult to replace because it works well and is versatile enough to handle most scheduled activities. cron is reliable because it uses the computer's system clock to act on scheduled activities. The one flaw with cron, if you can call it that, is that you will encounter problems if your automated tasks involve multiple systems and their times drift out of sync. The solution is to reference a central time server. I will cover the network time protocol later in this section.

Using cron to Schedule Tasks

The cron utility is available on all Linux systems, and it just works. There's no tweaking or configuration required. It's a time-tested application built to do one job: run commands at a specific time—and it does that job very well. The best way to learn cron is by example because the syntax isn't necessarily intuitive.

cron has a simple "syntax" or format:

```
# ┌─────────────── minute (0 - 59)
# │ ┌───────────── hour (0 - 23)
# │ │ ┌─────────── day of the month (1 - 31)
# │ │ │ ┌───────── month (1 - 12)
# │ │ │ │ ┌─────── day of the week (0 - 6) (Sunday to Saturday;
# │ │ │ │ │                        7 is also Sunday on some systems)
# │ │ │ │ │
# │ │ │ │ │
# * * * * * command to execute
```

What isn't shown here is that you can run scripts or commands multiple times using only one schedule or cron "job." For example, you need to run a script that checks for the existence of a file every 5 minutes every day. The format for that entry is as follows:

```
0,5,10,15,20,25,30,35,40,45,50,55 * * * * /path/to/script.sh
```

If you want a script to run every Monday, Wednesday, and Friday at 2:00 p.m., the cron schedule takes the following form:

```
0 14 * * 1,3,5 /path/to/script.sh
```

If you want your script to run at 6 a.m. on the 15th of every month:

```
0 6 15 * * /path/to/script.sh
```

You have a full range of possibilities with cron schedules.

 Do not set a schedule in cron for * * * * * */path/to/script.sh* unless you want your script to run every minute of every day. For most monitoring scenarios, once every five minutes is sufficient to catch any process, error, or file you're trying to capture or track.

Preventing Time Drift with the Network Time Protocol

One of the problems with writing scripts that operate on multiple systems is synchronizing system time among them. For example, imagine you have a script that gathers files from *Server A* and copies them to *Server B*, and once those files are copied, *Server B* checks for them and then creates a tarball and copies them onto NAS for archiving. If this needs to happen multiple times per day and in a timed sequence, you can see how synchronized time among server systems is essential.

The way to keep time synced among all your systems is to reference an internet time server plus a time server inside your network (in case you experience an internet connectivity outage).

Install ntp or chrony to allow your systems to synchronize with an external (internet) time server. Installing chrony is easy and requires no configuration as a client. Here, I demonstrate how to install and configure chrony. It works similarly on Debian distributions except that your chrony configuration file is located in */etc/chrony/* rather than simply in */etc*:

```
$ sudo yum -y install chrony

$ sudo apt install chrony

$ sudo systemctl enable chronyd
Created symlink /etc/systemd/system/multi-user.target.wants/chronyd.service
→ /usr/lib/systemd/system/chronyd.service.

$ sudo systemctl start chronyd
```

The chrony package provides you with the chrony daemon, chronyd, and a command-line interface utility that has dozens of options, which you can find in its man page. To perform a quick check, use the following command:

```
$ chronyc activity
200 OK
4 sources online
0 sources offline
0 sources doing burst (return to online)
0 sources doing burst (return to offline)
0 sources with unknown address
```

You can also configure chrony as a time server for your local network. To do so, uncomment the following two lines in the */etc/chrony.conf* file on the system you wish to set up as the time server:

```
# Allow NTP client access from local network.
#allow 192.168.0.0/16

# Serve time even if not synchronized to a time source.
#local stratum 10
```

Change the Allow line to cover your subnet(s) and restart the chronyd:

```
$ sudo systemctl restart chronyd
```

To set up other Linux systems to use your chrony server, enter the following line into your */etc/chrony.conf* file:

```
server  192.168.1.80 prefer iburst
```

The prefer designation tells chrony that this local system should be consulted first for the correct time. Restart the chronyd to accept the new setting and check your chronyd sources with the following command:

```
$ chronyc sources
MS Name/IP address         Stratum Poll Reach LastRx Last sample
===============================================================================
^? server1                    0   6    0     -    +0ns[   +0ns] +/-    0ns
^- mon2.hostin.cc             2   6    7     1   +37ms[  +31ms] +/-  138ms
^+ ntp.netnod.se              1   6    7     1  +9151us[+2267us] +/-   81ms
^? nobody.yourvserver.net     2   6    1     4  -2309us[-9194us] +/-   65ms
^* nettuno.ntp.irh.it         2   6    7     1  -4454us[  -11ms] +/-   67ms
```

You could also configure all your client systems to use only the local server by commenting out the "pool" line(s) in */etc/chrony.conf*. You may also edit the *chrony.conf* file to set up more specific settings. What I've shown here is a minimal but working configuration.

Although `cron` and `chrony` sound similar, deal with timing, and work together, they are quite different. The `cron` utility schedules jobs to be executed at a specific day and time, whereas `chrony` synchronizes the system clock with an external time server. `chrony` keeps system time stable so that `cron` jobs run at the correct time, which is especially important when timing jobs across multiple systems.

Summary

Timing is everything. Scheduling jobs, synchronizing time among local systems, timing automated scripts among systems, and synchronizing time with an external "source of truth" is essential. Automation is but one reason to keep your systems' times synchronized. Security is another. Consider the scenario where you're attempting to isolate a security incident, and your systems are not time synchronized. It would be difficult to pinpoint a timeframe for the incident to determine when it occurred and its length.

Automation is an important part of your work as a system administrator. There aren't enough hours available to manually complete every required task. You must hand off your repetitive, mundane tasks to your systems. They won't complain, tire, or mistype a command. Automation is a good thing, and you should embrace it. Try to automate yourself out of a job.

## CHAPTER 11

Deploying Samba for Windows Compatibility

Interoperability is the capability for disparate systems such as Windows, Linux, Unix, and macOS to coexist and work together. Interoperability is now a standard and accepted feature of all data center operating systems, although some functionality requires third-party software. Hardware, software, and operating systems can no longer exist in a proprietary vacuum. In other words, vendors must ensure that their products are cross-platform capable. Contemporary data centers are heterogenous—meaning that Windows, Linux, and Unix systems occupy racks.

Both native and third-party utilities make interoperability possible. From Active Directory (AD) and LDAP to Samba/SMB to *nix utilities and applications, systems can work together toward a common goal: serving customers.

 The generic wildcard designation "*nix" represents all Unix, Linux, and similar operating systems and distributions.

Samba is a suite of utilities that enable Windows interoperability for Linux and Unix. Samba provides secure, stable, file and print services for non-Windows systems using the Server Message Block/Common Internet File System (SMB/CIFS) protocol. Samba has its own authentication structure consisting of permissions and passwords.

Using Samba, Linux systems may do the following:

- Share directories, filesystems, and printers with Windows computers
- Mount Windows shares
- Browse the network for shares provided by Windows and other Linux computers
- Participate in Windows domain authentication and authorization
- Use Windows name resolution services
- Use shared printers

With Samba installed on Linux servers, Windows computers may do the following:

- Browse Linux shares
- Use shared printers
- Map network drives to Linux shares

This chapter explores some utilities and applications that enable Linux systems to interoperate with Windows. The following section discusses the challenges of interacting with Windows systems, and tools and configurations to make it work.

Planning Your Samba Environment

Requests for new file shares are commonplace in any business. Coworkers, often separated by hundreds or thousands of miles, want a shared space to place files such as documents, spreadsheets, text files, scripts, and images. As a system administrator, there are some questions you must ask of your groups who want this shared space.

For this scenario, the Facilities department has requested the shared file space. So, you will set up their Linux system as a Windows file server. The following is a list of five important questions to ask:

1. Should this space be restricted to your group only?
2. Do you want everyone in your group to be able to copy and create files in the shared space?
3. Are there any default permissions you want to set on uploaded files?
4. Do you need any read-only folders for documents?
5. Is this a permanent or a temporary shared space?

For this scenario, the facilities manager gave the following answers:

1. Yes, restrict to facilities employees only.
2. Everyone needs to be able to copy and create files.
3. Everyone in the group needs read and write access to all files.
4. Yes, we need a *Policies* folder from which no one can edit or remove files.
5. This is a permanent space.

The answers give you a starting place for the new shared space for the facilities team. If a facilities group doesn't exist, create one now and add facilities team members as their primary group. The group member accounts are atran, areed, and akumar.

 Samba usernames and passwords must match exactly with those configured on Windows systems.

To demonstrate Samba's functionality, perform the following tasks:

```
$ sudo groupadd -g 9001 facilities
$ sudo usermod -g facilities atran
$ sudo usermod -g facilities areed
$ sudo usermod -g facilities akumar
```

Create a directory such as */opt/facilities* that will be shared via Samba:

```
$ sudo mkdir /opt/facilities
```

Change the group ownership and permissions of the */opt/facilities* directory to reflect the requested permissions:

```
$ sudo chgrp facilities /opt/facilities
$ sudo chmod 770 /opt/facilities
```

Create a subdirectory under */opt/facilities* and name it *Policies*. Make the *Policies* directory read-only for the facilities group:

```
$ sudo mkdir /opt/facilities/Policies
$ sudo chmod 740 /opt/facilities/Policies
```

Now the shared space setup is complete and ready for Samba configuration.

Installing Samba and Its Dependencies

Before configuring anything related to Samba, you must install it and its dependent software:

```
$ sudo yum install samba

Last metadata expiration check: 2:55:52 ago on Sat 08 Oct 2022 11:42:12 AM EDT.
Dependencies resolved.
================================================================================
 Package               Architecture   Version            Repository       Size
================================================================================
Installing:
 samba                 x86_64         4.14.5-7.el8_5     baseos          848 k
Installing dependencies:
 libwbclient           x86_64         4.14.5-7.el8_5     baseos          121 k
 Samba-client-libs     x86_64         4.14.5-7.el8_5     baseos          5.4 M
 samba-common          noarch         4.14.5-7.el8_5     baseos          221 k
 Samba-common-libs     x86_64         4.14.5-7.el8_5     baseos          173 k
 samba-common-tools    x86_64         4.14.5-7.el8_5     baseos          500 k
 samba-libs            x86_64         4.14.5-7.el8_5     baseos

Transaction Summary
================================================================================
Install  7 Packages

Total download size: 7.4 M
Installed size: 25 M
Is this ok [y/N]: y
```

The process works similarly on other distributions. This transaction installs everything you need to set up your Linux system as a Windows file server.

Enable and start the Samba services (smb and nmb):

```
$ sudo systemctl enable smb
Created symlink /etc/systemd/system/multi-user.target.wants/smb.service
→ /usr/lib/systemd/system/smb.service.

$ sudo systemctl enable nmb
Created symlink /etc/systemd/system/multi-user.target.wants/nmb.service
→ /usr/lib/systemd/system/nmb.service.

$ sudo systemctl start smb
$ sudo systemctl start nmb
```

Samba services are now started and will start at boot time.

Adding Samba Users to Your System

Because Samba manages its own user list, you must add each user to the Samba User Database. For demonstration purposes, I use `PaSSw0rd` for the Samba password:

```
$ sudo smbpasswd -a atran
New SMB password:
Retype new SMB password:
Added user atran.
```

A configuration is available to sync Samba and Linux passwords. I cover this later in the chapter.

Managing Samba Users as a Group

Groups make it easier to manage large numbers of users. Groups are easier to manage because you can apply security to multiple users at once without the overhead of tracking the security settings for each user. In other words, managing security for 10 groups is much easier than managing it for 100 individual users.

You can create new Linux groups or use existing ones for Samba users and grant group access to a share. You can also grant individual users access to a share, but it's much more labor-intensive.

Continuing with the example scenario where you have a facilities Linux group containing three members, you can manage directory and file permissions for all three group members for a particular directory (*/opt/facilities*). This is standard Linux administration practice.

If you then share that same directory (*/opt/facilities*) via Samba, add `valid users = @facilities` in the configuration file to allow the entire group access to the shared directory. The `@facilities` declaration refers to the facilities Linux group, and its group members are valid users of that share.

Linux file and directory permissions are different from Samba permissions. A Linux user might have write access permission to a directory, but the share might be read-only for the same user. If you don't add valid users to a share, it doesn't matter that the Linux file permissions allow the group to write to the directory; group members won't be able to access that directory via the share.

One of the primary reasons for enabling Samba shares is to create compatibility between Windows and Mac clients and Linux servers. The rest of this chapter deals with configuring and supporting that interoperability.

Providing Services to Mac and Windows Clients

As a Linux system administrator, you must realize that Linux is a great *server* operating system. Some believe massive Linux desktop adoption is "just around the corner." However, realistically, Windows and Mac workstations are the corporate standards, while Linux is still the outlier. Because Linux is a great server operating system, sysadmins must provide services compatible with Windows and Mac clients. macOS, having *nix roots, is generally Linux compatible, so less effort is required to make Mac systems and Linux work together.

Windows, however, is not so easy to integrate with Linux—at least, not right out of the box. Windows systems require third-party tools and utilities, and Linux systems require extra software packages and special configurations. But it's possible to make the two systems work together seamlessly, and the solutions are also quite elegant and stable.

Serving Network Storage to Desktop Clients

Administrators provide network storage to Windows systems via mapped drives and to Mac clients via mounted shares. A mapped drive, in Linux terms, is a mounted remote shared directory. Windows labels these remote shares as drive letters, such as *F:* through *Z:*. From the Linux system, sysadmins share directories through Samba, which is somewhat analogous to *nix Network File System (NFS) shares. macOS systems can also mount Samba shares by browsing the network using the Samba protocol or by direct connection.

Samba shares are handy because users can drag and drop files onto a shared directory without using file transfer software such as FTP, SFTP, SCP, or others. Samba shares appear to be shared from a Windows server system, which further integrates Linux into a Windows and Mac desktop environment.

Exploring global Samba settings

You can set dozens of "directives" in the [global] portion of your */etc/samba/smb.conf* file. Still, in my opinion, the following directives are the ones you should set, regardless of your use of domain controllers and AD, but they are best used as a standalone Samba server. Many of the directives shown are defaults:

```
[global]
    load printers = yes
    passdb backend = tdbsam
    security = user
    cups options = raw
    workgroup = YOUR_DOMAIN_NAME
    printcap name = cups
    printing = cups
    os level = 20
```

```
netbios name = SERVER1
browseable = yes

interfaces = lo eth0 192.168.1.0/24
hosts allow = 127. 192.168.1.
```

Change the settings to match your network and needs. The workgroup is usually set to the same as your domain name or workgroup if you aren't using a domain. The NetBIOS name is the name of the Samba server that you'll see in a network browse list.

Printing via Samba

You can also share printers, but because most systems print directly to printers via their IP addresses, printer sharing isn't covered here. There is a sample configuration for sharing printers in the */etc/samba/smb.conf* file:

```
[printers]
        comment = All Printers
        path = /var/tmp
        printable = yes
        create mask = 0600
        browseable = no

[print$]
        comment = Printer Drivers
        path = /var/lib/samba/drivers
        write list = @printadmin root
        force group = @printadmin
        create mask = 0664
        directory mask = 0775
```

These configurations will get you started. I suggest that you change `browseable = no` to `browseable = yes`. Remember to restart the `samba` service every time you make a configuration change. The next two sections step you through sharing a directory for user access.

Deploying the lmhosts file

Just as you have in Windows systems, Samba supports the *lmhosts* file. The *lmhosts* file lists NetBIOS names and IP addresses of systems on your network. I suggest you copy and paste the contents of a Windows *lmhosts* file to your Linux systems that provide Samba services. Do not transfer the Windows *lmhosts* file to your Linux servers because of text formatting differences between Windows and Linux systems. The default *lmhosts* file in */etc/samba* only contains localhost information:

```
127.0.0.1 localhost
```

Think of the *lmhosts* file the same way you consider the */etc/hosts* file. You can also set other directives in the *lmhosts* file shown in the following list. Directives follow entries and use the #:

#PRE

Entries loaded into cache for name lookup and resolution:

```
192.168.1.50    testserv1    #PRE
```

#DOM:*domain*

Domain server entries. Use this directive with the #PRE directive:

```
192.168.1.100  DC1  #PRE #DOM:WEST  #The West Domain Controller DC1
```

#INCLUDE *UNC Path\To File*

Includes a file from another system. This is often used to integrate *lmhosts* files from frequently updated Windows systems:

```
#INCLUDE \\server1\public\lmhosts
```

#BEGIN_ALTERNATE/#END_ALTERNATE

Groups multiple #INCLUDE directives together:

```
#BEGIN_ALTERNATE

#INCLUDE \\server1\public\lmhosts
#INCLUDE \\server2\public\lmhosts
#INCLUDE \\server3\public\lmhosts

#END_ALTERNATE
```

I always use *lmhosts* files on my Samba servers. I set up an automated script to keep the local *lmhosts* file in sync with a single source of truth. However, the #INCLUDE directive that points to another system's *lmhosts* file is a good alternative.

The next few sections demonstrate how to set up and use a Samba share.

Configuring a Shared Directory

The */etc/samba/smb.conf* file is the Samba configuration file where you set up shared directories. The homes share is a good place to start for your custom shared directory configuration.

The following sample shared directory is from an */etc/samba/smb.conf.example* file:

```
[homes]
    comment = Home Directories
    browseable = no
    writeable = yes
;   valid users = %S
;   valid users = MYDOMAIN\%S
```

The following is the facilities share configuration in my */etc/samba/smb.conf* file. The bracketed portion, [`Facilities`], is the share name. Remember to keep share names to 15 characters or less, and avoid nonalphanumeric characters and spaces.

The `create mode` and `directory mode` are set according to the facilities manager's needs from the previously mentioned five questions:

```
[Facilities]
    create mode = 0660
    writeable = yes
    path = /opt/facilities
    comment = Facilities Group Share
    directory mode = 0770
    only user = yes
    valid users = @facilities
    browseable = yes
```

The `valid users` entry limits access to users listed in the facilities Linux group. `browseable` means that if you perform a network browse, the system and this share appear in the list of available shares. The `create mode` directive (`0660`) is the default file creation permission for files in the share. When you create a new file in the shared directory via the share, its permissions will be `0660`. The directory mode is the permissions given to the share.

Browsing for Shared Directories

This section covers browsing for and connecting to Linux Samba shares from Mac, Windows, and Linux computers. Refer to Figures 11-1 and 11-2 to see how a Mac system views Samba shares on Linux systems. *server1* is the CentOS system I've used in the examples, and *server2* is an Ubuntu system also used in this book.

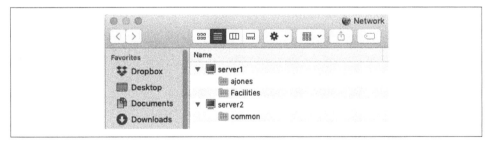

Figure 11-1. A Samba network browse on a macOS system

Once connected, the mounted shares appear as resources in the macOS Finder application.

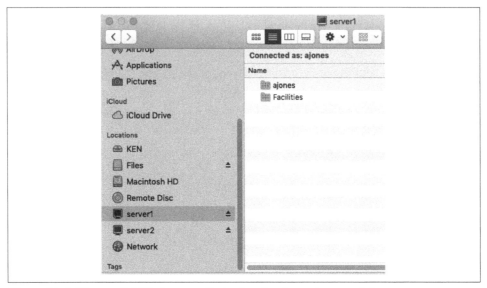

Figure 11-2. The macOS Finder app displaying Samba systems and shares

On Windows systems, the view is similar, but to connect to a remote share, you must map a drive. Mapping a drive means mounting the remote share and using it as if it were local to the system. Recall the NFS reference from earlier. See Figures 11-3 and 11-4.

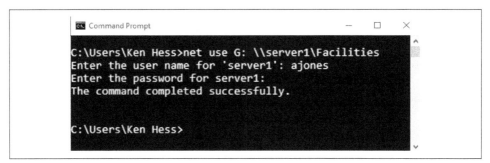

Figure 11-3. Mapping a drive (G:) to the remote share \\server1\Facilities

Mapping the share makes it available as a drive letter on the client system.

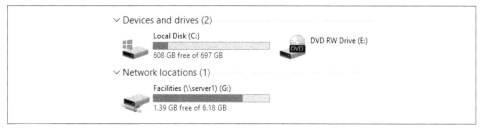

Figure 11-4. The mapped drive in Windows File Explorer

With the drive mapped, the user, ajones, can freely access the *Facilities* share, and this user can create, edit, and copy files to the shared directory. The following section deals with how Linux systems view and connect to Windows shares.

Mounting Windows System's Shares

You can also browse shares on a remote Windows (or other Linux) system from a Linux computer using the Samba protocol:

```
$ smbclient -U "Ken Hess" -L WIN10
Enter WORKGROUP\Ken Hess's password:

    Sharename       Type        Comment
    ---------       ----        -------
    ADMIN$          Disk        Remote Admin
    C$              Disk        Default share
    Files           Disk
    IPC$            IPC         Remote IPC
Reconnecting with SMB1 for workgroup listing.
do_connect: Connection to WIN10 failed (Error NT_STATUS_RESOURCE_NAME_NOT_FOUND)
Unable to connect with SMB1 -- no workgroup available
```

The message concerning SMB1 can be ignored. It doesn't affect functionality. Depending on your Samba client and server versions on the systems you're browsing, you can receive different messages referring to SMB versions. All can be ignored.

mount the remote Windows share (Files) on the WIN10 computer:

```
$ sudo mount -t cifs \\\\WIN10\\Files /mnt
Password for Ken Hess@\WIN10\Files:  ********
[khess@server1 facilities]$ ls /mnt
abi.mp4  new.txt  untitled.mp3
```

If you don't use the filesystem type `cifs` as part of the `mount` command, you'll receive the following message:

```
mount: /mnt: special device \\WIN10\Files does not exist.
Use four backslashes (\\\\) and two for the UNC mapping command's share name
(\\). For example, \\\\WIN10\\Files. You may also use single-quoted backs...
('\\'WIN10'\'Files). Remember that in Linux, you escape a character with ...
(\), so you must escape (or quote) the backslash character with a backsla...
to tell the shell that this is a literal backslash. A regular UNC mapping...
looks like this: \\WIN10\Files.
```

Summary

Linux interoperability everywhere from contemporary enterprise data centers to small server rooms provides increased functionality, lowers costs, and offers greater freedom of software choice. Regardless of which distribution you choose to integrate into your business, providing services to Windows and Mac clients is essential to Linux adoption and success. You must seamlessly duplicate standard Windows Server services and demonstrate to users and management that Linux can dispel skepticism with higher stability and lower maintenance than its costly alternatives.

## CHAPTER 12

Troubleshooting Linux

Some have compared Linux troubleshooting to an "exercise in futility," but trouble-shooting Linux is neither so dramatic nor difficult if you simply take time to investigate what's going on with your system. All too often, rather than perform any relevant troubleshooting, sysadmins will make a quick backup and then reimage (wipe the disk and reinstall) the system. I'm not a fan of this practice, though in cases of significant security breaches, it's the best option.

This chapter teaches you general troubleshooting concepts and tools rather than how to troubleshoot a specific issue (such as how to fix a website that's not working correctly). Troubleshooting individual problems could fill a very thick book or series of books. I discuss operating system troubleshooting, software, hardware, and security in the chapter.

This chapter aims to give you some basic troubleshooting skills, introduce you to essential tools, and show you how to find a solution should other options fail. Troubleshooting is a personal process; not everyone approaches it the same way. These procedures and tools have carried me through my career, but your results may vary and, eventually, you'll find steps and guidelines that work best for you.

Let's begin your lessons in troubleshooting with the operating system itself.

Reviving the Operating System

Troubleshooting the operating system is either very easy or next to impossible. There seems to be no middle ground. System errors are often, but not invariably, fatal. When I use the word *fatal* in this chapter, I mean unrecoverable errors that require you to reimage the system. Operating system problems can be as simple as running a filesystem check (`fsck`) and repairing a few files. It can be as complex as a multiday troubleshooting session ending in a full system reimage. For example, if you experience a kernel panic, your first thought might be to reimage the system, but this is only sometimes necessary.

The following section demonstrates how to resolve a kernel panic.

De-escalating a Kernel Panic

There are multiple reasons systems boot with a kernel panic. Most of the time, it's either a corrupted *initramfs* file or an improperly created *initramfs* file. The *initramfs* file is specific for each kernel, so if you've recently upgraded your kernel, it's possible that the *initramfs* didn't get created in the install process or that the *initramfs* creation process didn't go well. Kernel panics can also result from a recent bad patch. Other issues may still cause kernel panics, such as hardware failure, but those listed here are the most common and easily remedied. A relatively simple procedure (discussed next) might make your system bootable again and save the pain of reinstalling everything.

Imagine you've received a message similar to the example in Figure 12-1.

```
[    1.076702] Kernel panic - not syncing: UFS: Unable to mount root fs on unkno
wn-block(0,0)
[    1.077718] CPU: 0 PID: 1 Comm: swapper/0 Not tainted 3.10.0-327.el7.x86_64 #
1
[    1.078657] Hardware name: VMware, Inc. VMware Virtual Platform/440BX Desktop
 Reference Platform, BIOS 6.00 07/31/2013
[    1.079594]  ffffffff8184e920 000000001e6559f5 ffff880139387d60 ffffffff81635
1f1
[    1.080528]  ffff880139387de0 ffffffff8162ea6c ffffffff00000010 ffff880139387
df0
[    1.081446]  ffff880139387d90 000000001e6559f5 000000001e6559f5 ffff880139387
e00
[    1.082371] Call Trace:
[    1.082616]  [<ffffffff816351f1>] dump_stack+0x19/0x1b
[    1.083005]  [<ffffffff8162ea6c>] panic+0xd8/0x1e7
[    1.083382]  [<ffffffff81a8d5fa>] mount_block_root+0x2a1/0x2b0
[    1.083826]  [<ffffffff81a8d65c>] mount_root+0x53/0x56
[    1.084223]  [<ffffffff81a8d79b>] prepare_namespace+0x13c/0x174
[    1.084667]  [<ffffffff81a8d268>] kernel_init_freeable+0x1f0/0x217
[    1.085125]  [<ffffffff81a8c9db>] ? initcall_blacklist+0xb0/0xb0
[    1.085570]  [<ffffffff81624e10>] ? rest_init+0x80/0x80
[    1.085961]  [<ffffffff81624e1e>] kernel_init+0xe/0xf0
[    1.087300]  [<ffffffff81645858>] ret_from_fork+0x58/0x90
[    1.088660]  [<ffffffff81624e10>] ? rest_init+0x80/0x80
_
```

Figure 12-1. Linux kernel panic

The screen *freezes* here. There is no "press any key to continue" message. You must power off the system and power it back on to begin a new boot process. At this point, reboot your system and either start from a bootable ISO, or restart and enter the rescue process from the Grub menu. You will be the root user when you boot into rescue mode or use a bootable ISO, so be careful.

Display your kernel version:

```
# uname -r
3.10.0-327.el7.x86_64
```

Run the following command to re-create the correct *initramfs* from your kernel:

```
# dracut -f /boot/initramfs-3.10.0-327.el7.x86_64.img 3.10.0-327.el7.x86_64
```

You might receive a message similar to the following:

```
dracut: Will not override existing initramfs (/boot/initramfs...) without --force
```

You must create the *initramfs* file using a different command:

```
# mkinitrd --force \
/boot/initramfs-3.10.0-327.el7.x86_64.img 3.10.0-327.el7.x86_64
```

Reboot your system. Hopefully, it will boot without issue. If you experience another kernel panic after this repair procedure, you could have a bad hard disk, another corrupted boot-related file, or a buggy kernel. Retry the rescue process and install a different kernel. Be sure to have your ISO image handy for the process.

Boot to the root rescue shell, mount your ISO image, and install the kernel that's available in the ISO image.

For this example, your root filesystem is mounted on */mnt/sysimage* and you mounted your ISO under */opt/mnt*:

```
# cd /opt/mnt/install/repo/Packages
```

```
# rpm -Uvh --root=/mnt/sysimage kernel-3.10.0-1127.10.1.el7.x86_64
```

Use the kernel package that's in the ISO image. Now, reboot your system; if everything goes well, you should have a functioning system. If not, you should consider booting to the rescue environment again—creating a backup of critical files, if necessary—and then reimaging the system. Of course, this process may also result in kernel panic if you have a hardware problem, such as a bad disk or controller.

There are other sources of operating system problems, but they're so varied that it's impossible to cover them here. Instead, you should check the system's logs, which the next section covers.

Scraping System Logs

Scraping system logs means searching through logs for errors or other relevant messages. However, sysadmins live a good part of their lives in */var/log*; sometimes, log files are all you have to rely on for troubleshooting system problems.

My starting point is to issue a filtered dmesg command such as the following:

```
$ dmesg | grep -i error
[ 2.229324] RAS: Correctable Errors collector initialized.
[ 3.820963] [drm:vmw_host_log [vmwgfx]] *ERROR* Failed to send host log message.
[ 3.829724] [drm:vmw_host_log [vmwgfx]] *ERROR* Failed to send host log message.
```

This often narrows the possibilities of where to look for a problem with the operating system and hardware. If you don't find any relevant errors via dmesg, you can investigate further using other filters such as fault, failed, undefined, or unknown:

```
$ dmesg | grep -i failed
[ 3.820963] [drm:vmw_host_log [vmwgfx]] *ERROR* Failed to send host log message.
[ 3.829724] [drm:vmw_host_log [vmwgfx]] *ERROR* Failed to send host log message.

$ dmesg | grep -i fault
[ 0.004466] MTRR default type: uncachable
[ 0.362760] pid_max: default: 32768 minimum: 301
[ 0.710356] iommu: Default domain type: Translated
[ 0.728057] NetLabel:  unlabeled traffic allowed by default
[ 0.802045] PCI: CLS 0 bytes, default 64
[ 5.766858] systemd[1]: systemd 245.4-4ubuntu3.17 running in system mode. (+PA...
[333390.696268] systemd[1]: systemd 245.4-4ubuntu3.18 running in system mode. ...

$ dmesg | grep -i undefined

$ dmesg | grep -i unknown
[ 0.374321] SRBDS: Unknown: Dependent on hypervisor status
```

Use your system's log files if previous searches reveal nothing of value:

```
$ cd /var/log
$ sudo grep -ir error *
```

This might produce a very long list. If it does, I suggest redirecting the output to a file so that you can scrape these results:

```
$ sudo grep -ir error * > ~/errors.txt
```

Then you can search for something more specific in this text file:

```
$ cd
$ grep host errors.txt
```

I grepped for host here, but you should grep for whatever term you need to search for in these results. Refine this process until you find the relevant error that fits your problem. It can take time. This is my process, but it usually yields valuable information and provides me with a few next steps for further investigation.

The next section deals with software troubleshooting and my process for finding errors and problems.

Unraveling Software Problems

Software troubleshooting can be tricky. The root cause of software problems might not be the software. Still, the problem can manifest itself as a software issue until you investigate further. As any experienced sysadmin will tell you, software problems can have root causes in hardware, other software, file corruption or deletion, software dependency issues, network problems, duplicated ports, duplicated IP addresses, and dozens of possible configuration or misconfiguration problems anywhere on the system. Software error messages won't necessarily pinpoint a solution, but they're a first step. However, error codes and logs are a good starting place for troubleshooting.

In this section, I direct you to locate and sift through system and application logs and to perform any built-in or vendor-supplied status and configuration checks.

Inspecting System Logs

System logs are a great starting place to find errors, failures, and successes. Yes, successes are not necessarily benign. Think about the scenario where someone has breached your network, logs into a system with a legitimate account, becomes root, and then exfiltrates confidential data or encrypts your data. It's only the acting party—the person fraudulently accessing the system—that isn't legitimate. The system sees every login and action from this malicious actor as normal, legitimate, and successful. These actions probably wouldn't set off any alarms at all.

Your system logs show what's happening, so don't discount checking for successful logins. In a later section of this chapter, I give you an example security script that shows you logins at a glance for your inspection.

System logs are located in *root privileges.

Although the output is too long and too wide for the text of this book, here are the two troubleshooting filters I use on system logs:

```
$ sudo grep -i error *.log
$ sudo grep -i fail *.log
```

I always use the `-i` option to ignore case so that I'm sure to catch every instance of error and fail regardless of how the log captures them. The next section deals with checking application-specific logs, often more helpful than relying on system logs alone.

Checking Application Logs

Fortunately, application logs provide specific errors or error codes that help you troubleshoot software problems. These logs may be located in *var/log/httpd*, but on Red

---

Hat Enterprise Linux–based systems, there is also a symbolic link from */etc/httpd/logs* to */var/log/httpd*. Often these links exist to be backward compatible with other applications.

Leveraging Internal Application Checks

Some developers include configuration checkers and specific tools with their software to help you identify, isolate, and troubleshoot problems. These utilities are your best option when facing application-specific configuration issues and failures. Some configuration files have a rather complex syntax, and missing a single parenthesis or semicolon can be extremely difficult to isolate.

For example, the following command provides excellent feedback to check your Apache HTTP Server configuration syntax. When everything in the *httpd.conf* is configured correctly, you receive a Syntax OK message:

```
$ apachectl configtest
Syntax OK
```

However, if a configuration directive is incorrect, your configtest results isolate the problem:

```
$ apachectl configtest
AH00526: Syntax error on line 34 of /etc/httpd/conf/httpd.conf:
Invalid command 'ServerBoot', perhaps misspelled or defined by a module not
included in the server configuration
```

The configuration is also checked on the start or restart of the application:

```
$ sudo apachectl restart
Job for httpd.service failed because the control process exited with error code.
See "systemctl status httpd.service" and "journalctl -xe" for details.

$ systemctl status httpd.service
httpd.service - The Apache HTTP Server
   Loaded: loaded (/usr/lib/systemd/system/httpd.service; enabled; vendor prese...
   Active: failed (Result: exit-code) since Sun 2022-10-16 08:49:44 EDT; 17s ago
     Docs: man:httpd.service(8)
  Process: 58661 ExecReload=/usr/sbin/httpd $OPTIONS -k graceful (code=exited,...
  Process: 59189 ExecStart=/usr/sbin/httpd $OPTIONS -DFOREGROUND (code=exited,...
 Main PID: 59189 (code=exited, status=1/FAILURE)
   Status: "Reading configuration..."

Oct 16 08:49:44 server1 systemd[1]: httpd.service: Succeeded.
Oct 16 08:49:44 server1 systemd[1]: Stopped The Apache HTTP Server.
Oct 16 08:49:44 server1 systemd[1]: Starting The Apache HTTP Server...
Oct 16 08:49:44 server1 httpd[59189]: AH00526: Syntax error on line 34 of /etc...
Oct 16 08:49:44 server1 httpd[59189]: Invalid command 'ServerBoot', perhaps mi...
Oct 16 08:49:44 server1 systemd[1]: httpd.service: Main process exited, code=e...
Oct 16 08:49:44 server1 systemd[1]: httpd.service: Failed with result 'exit-co...
Oct 16 08:49:44 server1 systemd[1]: Failed to start The Apache HTTP Server.
```

In the preceding error message, the line `Oct 16 08:49:44 server1 httpd[59189]:` `AH00526: Syntax error on line 34 of /etc/httpd/conf/httpd.conf:` (part of which has been elided in the preceding code listing) informs me there is a syntax error in my configuration file and I need to investigate further:

```
$ cd /var/log
$ sudo grep -ir "Syntax error" *
Binary file journal/027dd8a8c9624671b26d07e94eae8f1d/system.journal matches
```

The results of my search don't help troubleshoot the syntax error, so I use the other recommended system tool, `journalctl`, from the preceding `apachectl restart` command (See `"systemctl status httpd.service" and "journalctl -xe" for details.`), the results are just as vague:

```
$ sudo journalctl -xe
-- Support: https://access.redhat.com/support
--
-- The unit httpd.service has entered the 'failed' state with result 'exit-code'.
Oct 16 08:49:44 server1 systemd[1]: Failed to start The Apache HTTP Server.
-- Subject: Unit httpd.service has failed
-- Defined-By: systemd
-- Support: https://access.redhat.com/support
--
-- Unit httpd.service has failed.
--
-- The result is failed.
```

Your best course of action is to examine lines in the *httpd.conf* file you changed that caused the error. Common problems such as misspelling or using an incorrect directive are typical reasons for syntax errors.

Managing Firewalls and Their Rules

Firewalls are great for slowing down intruders, but they can also interfere with troubleshooting. Avoid the temptation to disable your firewall during troubleshooting. Instead, add new rules to accommodate what you need to do. You might forget to re-enable the firewall, which can lead to disastrous consequences.

The firewall isn't 100% foolproof, but it has value in slowing down a would-be intruder. Sometimes its existence is enough to deter a malicious actor and encourage them to seek out easier prey. It's frustrating to troubleshoot a new service for hours to eventually remember that it could be your firewall causing the problem.

Removing and Reinstalling Software

Endless troubleshooting is often an exercise in patience-testing and isn't recommended. There's no set standard for how long you should spend troubleshooting a software problem, but at some point, you must determine that further troubleshooting is a waste of your valuable time. You should back up the application's configuration files and data at that time and then remove and reinstall it.

Before reinstalling an application, be sure you have installed the latest stable package available or downloaded the latest stable source code. If you were on the latest version, try returning to an earlier stable version. Also, be sure that your system is updated and has the latest compatible tools and utilities for your application. The *README* or *INSTALL* text files, included with source code packages, often list compatible compiler versions and versions of other required supporting software.

Rebooting Your System

The concept of regular system rebooting is not only foreign to many Linux system administrators; it's downright unheard of. However, rebooting should be a part of regular system maintenance. Rebooting refreshes both hardware and software configurations, but it also informs you of any failures or problems. For example, you might find that some applications don't start automatically after a reboot. Perhaps you didn't enable them with a `systemctl enable` *service_name* command. Starting a service places it into memory, sets up listening ports, and allows connectivity. Still, that service, unless enabled, will not start on the next reboot, whether human-initiated or one resulting from a crash.

The `dmesg` command informs you of any problems from your latest reboot. You can discover both software and hardware errors by filtering the results. Here are two such examples:

```
$ dmesg | grep -i error
[ 8.741308] [drm:vmw_host_log [vmwgfx]] *ERROR* Failed to send host log message.
[ 8.741321] [drm:vmw_host_log [vmwgfx]] *ERROR* Failed to send host log message.

$ dmesg | grep -i fail
[ 0.063026] acpi PNP0A03:00: fail to add MMCONFIG information, can't access ...
[ 8.741308] [drm:vmw_host_log [vmwgfx]] *ERROR* Failed to send host log message.
[ 8.741321] [drm:vmw_host_log [vmwgfx]] *ERROR* Failed to send host log message.
```

Rebooting your systems shouldn't be controversial. Monthly warm booting (restart) and quarterly cold booting (power off/on) is a standard part of many enterprise maintenance cycles, as is patching, security auditing, and port scanning. The next section is a discussion of hardware troubleshooting.

Dealing with Hardware Failures

Troubleshooting hardware is generally very easy; hardware either works or doesn't. There are times when hardware begins to fail, and you experience erratic behavior, such as intermittent functionality of a network interface card (NIC) or file corruption on a failing hard disk. But often a hardware device fails and you must replace it. Data center server systems have built-in redundancy of several subsystems so that failures aren't catastrophic. Always purchase server systems with redundant power supplies, multiple NICs, and plenty of RAM. Set up disks in arrays such as RAID 10 so that failures don't ruin your evenings and weekends.

Even if you have a multidisk array, please note that if one of the drives fails, there will be a performance impact. You'll receive a warning that a disk has failed, and if you have physical access to the system, it's easy to determine, via status lights, which disk has failed. And, although there's an expense involved, you should have multiple new disks on hand to swap out when failures occur. The other option is to migrate to solid-state drives (SSDs) that run cooler and have a longer lifespan than mechanical drives. Remember that heat is the enemy of electronics, which is why data centers seem windy and chilly. Heat dissipation is one of the big problems and major design features of any good data center.

The following sections cover preemptive troubleshooting, diagnostics, and hardware replacement and a discussion of system design.

Preemptively Troubleshooting Hardware

Unless you have some very smart hardware diagnostics from a blade server system chassis or a third-party software suite, preemptive hardware failure prediction isn't possible. Native Linux commands provide you with a general listing or status. Still, if your hardware components are operating, it's rare to find a "flagged" device or to receive a warning about an imminent failure.

Hardware failures are difficult to predict because, as I mentioned earlier, hardware either works or doesn't. Some hardware components *can* partially fail. Network interface cards (NICs) can begin to fail and "jabber" or send malformed packets. Jabbering network cards are failing and should be replaced.

Mechanical hard disks can partially fail by corrupting files or by booting incorrectly, randomly, or not at all. Sometimes a failing hard drive will temporarily repair itself after a cold boot. Sometimes you can hear a mechanical hard disk spinning up, spinning down, clicking, or *clunking* when they fail. Use a recent backup and replace the drive. Use solid-state drives whenever possible. Mirror your drives whenever possible too. Solid-state drives will fail on a general or all-or-nothing basis. I've never seen a solid-state drive partially fail.

Memory "sticks" will generally fail on an all-or-nothing basis. I've never seen one partially fail. The RAM doesn't count up completely during the boot process when a memory stick fails. For example, if a system contains 64 GB of RAM, it might only recognize 48 GB. Although memory sticks may fail individually, they are read in pairs. So if you have eight 8 GB memory sticks in a system to add up to a total of 64 GB, and you have a single stick failure, the RAM count fails in pairs. To clarify, if your system has four banks of two memory sticks (8 GB each × 8 sticks = 64 GB), and one memory stick fails, then its paired memory stick will also appear to have failed, and you will see only 48 GB of RAM count up on boot.

The next section introduces you to a handful of useful hardware commands.

Gathering System Hardware Information

I don't have any bare metal systems with Linux on them. I only have virtual machines to work with. I suggest using the commands discussed in this section to collect hardware data for every unique physical system you manage and keeping this information where you can easily refer to it later. Gather hardware information for each bare-metal system and then collect the same information for a single virtual machine from each virtualization platform. Virtual hardware is very consistent per platform and even between virtual hosts. In other words, if you have all VMware hosts and your host software version is consistent, then your virtual machine hardware should all be the same. Virtual machines may move among hosts without issue because their virtual hardware is generic and consistent regardless of what the underlying hardware looks like.

The commands presented in this section gather information about your hardware, and while some of the information might overlap, it's still good to gather information from multiple commands. As you'll see, some commands gather specific details about your hardware, while others gather only product names and functions. You can execute the commands as a regular user, but some warn you to use the root account, or the information might be incomplete or inaccurate. All commands in this section are run as the root user. The output from these commands is generally too long to fully reproduce in this book, but I'll provide excerpts for each to give you an idea of what the commands report. There are multiple options available for each command that offer custom output and reports. Refer to each command's man page to learn more about their options. Finally, note that depending on your specific Linux distro, some of the tools discussed might be present and other tools might need to be installed.

hwinfo

The `hwinfo` utility probes your system's hardware and reports on its findings. The report is very long but very thorough. You can use the `--short` option to create an abbreviated summary report. The following listing is the complete short report:

```
# hwinfo --short
cpu:
                        Intel(R) Core(TM) i5-5350U CPU @ 1.80GHz, 1800 MHz
keyboard:
  /dev/input/event2    AT Translated Set 2 keyboard
```

```
mouse:
  /dev/input/mice      Mouse
graphics card:
                       VMware VMWARE0405
sound:
                       Intel 82801AA AC'97 Audio Controller
storage:
                       Intel 82801HM/HEM (ICH8M/ICH8M-E) SATA Controller [AHCI...
                       Intel 82371AB/EB/MB PIIX4 IDE
network:
  enp0s3               Intel PRO/1000 MT Desktop Adapter
network interface:
  lo                   Loopback network interface
  enp0s3               Ethernet network interface
disk:
  /dev/sdb             VBOX HARDDISK
  /dev/sdc             VBOX HARDDISK
  /dev/sda             VBOX HARDDISK
partition:
  /dev/sdc1            Partition
  /dev/sda1            Partition
  /dev/sda2            Partition
cdrom:
  /dev/sr0             VBOX CD-ROM
usb controller:
                       Apple KeyLargo/Intrepid USB
bios:
                       BIOS
bridge:
                       Intel 82371SB PIIX3 ISA [Natoma/Triton II]
                       Intel 82371AB/EB/MB PIIX4 ACPI
                       Intel 440FX - 82441FX PMC [Natoma]
hub:
                       Linux Foundation 1.1 root hub
memory:
                       Main Memory
unknown:
                       FPU
                       DMA controller
                       PIC
                       Keyboard controller
                       InnoTek Systemberatung VirtualBox Guest Service
```

The entire report is very long, but the short version is complete without all the details. Creating both reports for each system you manage is a good strategy.

Next, we'll cover the so-called "ls commands" for hardware. Each one begins with the letters ls and lists various pieces of a system's hardware complement.

lshw

The `lshw` utility provides detailed hardware information, including CPU, mainboard, memory, firmware, cache configuration, and bus speeds. You can optionally create an HTML report version with the `-html` option. The following is a partial output from the `lshw` command with no options:

```
# lshw
server1
    description: Computer
    product: VirtualBox
    vendor: innotek GmbH
    version: 1.2
    serial: 0
    width: 64 bits
    capabilities: smbios-2.5 dmi-2.5 vsyscall32
    configuration: family=Virtual Machine uuid=1f88c169-07a7-024b-8d54-6dc9070...
```

The `lshw` utility is a comprehensive hardware snapshot of your system. The remainder of this section's `ls` commands are specific to subsystems.

lspci

The `lspci` utility lists all PCI devices, their manufacturer, and version information:

```
# lspci
00:00.0 Host bridge: Intel Corporation 440FX - 82441FX PMC [Natoma] (rev 02)
00:01.0 ISA bridge: Intel Corporation 82371SB PIIX3 ISA [Natoma/Triton II]
00:01.1 IDE interface: Intel Corporation 82371AB/EB/MB PIIX4 IDE (rev 01)
00:02.0 VGA compatible controller: VMware SVGA II Adapter
00:03.0 Ethernet controller: Intel Corporation 82540EM Gigabit Ethernet Contro...
00:04.0 System peripheral: InnoTek Systemberatung GmbH VirtualBox Guest Service
00:05.0 Multimedia audio controller: Intel Corporation 82801AA AC'97 Audio Con...
00:06.0 USB controller: Apple Inc. KeyLargo/Intrepid USB
00:07.0 Bridge: Intel Corporation 82371AB/EB/MB PIIX4 ACPI (rev 08)
00:0d.0 SATA controller: Intel Corporation 82801HM/HEM (ICH8M/ICH8M-E) SATA Co...
```

One of the most interesting options for `lshw` is `-sanitize`, which removes any sensitive information from the report.

lsblk

The `lsblk` utility lists all block devices, their mount points, sizes, and other information. To view a complete report available from `lsblk`, you must execute it as root because of how it queries information from *sysfs* and the *udev db* (if available):

```
# lsblk
NAME            MAJ:MIN RM  SIZE RO TYPE MOUNTPOINT
sda              8:0     0    8G  0 disk
├─sda1           8:1     0    1G  0 part /boot
└─sda2           8:2     0    7G  0 part
  ├─cl-root    253:0     0  6.2G  0 lvm  /
```

```
└─cl-swap            253:1    0  820M  0 lvm  [SWAP]
sdb                   8:16    0  1.5G  0 disk
└─vgsw-software--lv 253:2    0  1.5G  0 lvm  /sw
sdc                   8:32    0    1G  0 disk
└─sdc1                8:33    0 1023M  0 part /home
sr0                  11:0     1 1024M  0 rom
```

You can use other options to extract more information, such as device owner, permissions, and UUID. The output isn't formatted correctly for this text, but you can enter the following command to see extended block device information:

```
# lsblk -fm
```

The lsblk utility does not report on RAM disk devices.

lscpu

The lscpu utility reports architecture information about a system's CPUs. It has a lot of options, and some must be stacked, or used together, so refer to the man page to review specific requirements for the report you need:

```
# lscpu
Architecture:        x86_64
CPU op-mode(s):      32-bit, 64-bit
Byte Order:          Little Endian
CPU(s):              1
On-line CPU(s) list: 0
Thread(s) per core:  1
Core(s) per socket:  1
Socket(s):           1
NUMA node(s):        1
Vendor ID:           GenuineIntel
CPU family:          6
Model:               61
Model name:          Intel(R) Core(TM) i5-5350U CPU @ 1.80GHz
Stepping:            4
CPU MHz:             1799.999
BogoMIPS:            3599.99
Hypervisor vendor:   KVM
Virtualization type: full
L1d cache:           32K
L1i cache:           32K
L2 cache:            256K
L3 cache:            3072K
NUMA node0 CPU(s):   0
Flags:               fpu vme de pse tsc msr pae mce cx8 apic sep mtrr pge mca ...
```

CPUs rarely fail, but the information is valuable if you need to check for compatibility or when upgrading to a new CPU generation.

Using these utilities for troubleshooting a system requires gathering pre-failure information as a hardware audit and then comparing those initial reports with those after a suspected failure. A simple `diff` between the pre- and post-failure reports will inform you of any differences. Remember that this works because many of these utilities probe your hardware when you execute them rather than only reading a configuration from a static system text file.

The next section covers security troubleshooting and tools you use to assess your security.

Creating Automated Security Checks

Before troubleshooting a problem, you must know it exists. The way to find out if you have a problem is through observation via logs, reports, failed processes, removed or damaged files, compromised accounts, and so on. Detecting and fixing security issues is a full-time job for software and personnel. In other words, if you manage more than a handful of server systems, and depending on their criticality, you need to purchase security software with monitoring, automatic updating, notification, and some security tools and utilities for system scanning, auditing, and mitigation. Furthermore, a single tool isn't sufficient. You need an intrusion detection/prevention system, firewalls, SELinux, anti-malware, and numerous secure system configurations to improve your systems' overall security profile.

In this section, I cover creating a daily security report that you can automate for reporting on system security. It's impossible to watch every system 24 hours per day unless you have some automated processes taking care of it for you. Malicious actors and applications often stop, disrupt, or erase logs to cover their covert operations, so sometimes, the lack of information tells you that you have a problem.

As I start my day, I prefer to view an automated security report as an HTML page to determine if any problems require further investigation. The following is an example of a daily security script (*daily_report.sh*) that I've used in the past. The */opt/note* directory is a web-enabled directory aliased as *reports* in my Apache config. I've spaced it so that it's easier to read:

```
#!/bin/bash

#Daily Report Script

today=`date +%m-%d-%Y`

touch /opt/note/$today.html

echo "<pre>" >> /opt/note/$today.html

echo "Last Log " >> /opt/note/$today.html
last | grep root >> /opt/note/$today.html

echo "Non-privileged accounts in the Last Log " >> /opt/note/$today.html
```

```
last | grep -v root >> /opt/note/$today.html

echo " " >> /opt/note/$today.html

echo "Root Accounts " >> /opt/note/$today.html
grep :0 /etc/passwd >> /opt/note/$today.html

echo " " >> /opt/note/$today.html

echo "Files modified since yesterday " >> /opt/note/$today.html
find /etc -mtime -1 >> /opt/note/$today.html

echo "</pre>" >> /opt/note/$today.html
```

Creating the report file as *today'sdate.html* ensures you can keep a list of these files for comparison. For example, if you believe you have a possible breach, you can perform a diff on two files to see if there are differences you should be aware of:

```
# diff 10-20-2022.html 10-21-2022.html
```

No response means the files are the same. However, if you perform a diff and receive something similar to the following, you need to begin investigating further:

```
# diff 10-20-2022.html 10-21-2022.html

4a5
> jamd:x:0:0:root:/root:/bin/sh
```

This diff shows that someone has created a new root-level account, jamd, on 10-21-2022. Unfortunately, the way the intruder created this account, any file that jamd touches, modifies, or creates will have root ownership and will look as if the root account created or modified it. And, now that jamd has a root account, they can change the root password, remove accounts from */etc/passwd*, and remove the */etc/ sudoers* file, essentially excluding system administrators from accessing the system except for through the console.

 Intruders rarely lock out system administrators because doing so will cause action and remediation. Instead, intruders try to cover their actions and use the systems for data exfiltration or attack other systems inside or outside the current network.

You can filter logs by specific errors or redirect output from other commands to the file, such as a firewall status check. Place the commands in this script that you use to check on your systems' security and then set up a cron job as www-data to run the script daily and check it as soon as you get to work to begin some forensic investigation or breathe easy and continue your day. Ensure that the www-data user has read, write, and execute permissions on the */opt/note* directory.

Summary

Troubleshooting is a learned skill that takes time and experience to sharpen, but remember to rely on your coworkers, knowledge bases, logs, and your favorite internet search engine to help you navigate difficult problems. There's no shame in looking for help from a variety of sources. And remember, sometimes the best solution is to abandon a lengthy troubleshooting session and start with a clean installation.

Chapter 13 deals with securing your system, an ongoing task requiring focus, skill, and multiple layers of action.

Securing Your System

System security is the application of configurations, software, policies, rules, and best practices to a system (whether it's new or years old) so that the system operates without significant downtime due to security breaches and compromises. As a system administrator, security is your most important and time-consuming task.

This chapter concentrates on the prevention of security problems. Discovery and mitigation are briefly covered. You will learn how to secure both newly deployed systems and systems that have been in operation for years. No single treatment is comprehensive because new threats and vulnerabilities arise on what seems like a daily basis. You will learn how to apply basic security settings to your Linux systems. Because many larger companies have their own standards, the security settings I recommend are a good place to start, but you should always comply with corporate security protocols and policies.

Protecting the Root Account

The root user account is the all-powerful account on every Linux system, and you must protect access to it. If someone compromises this account, they can lock you out, destroy the system, steal data, or maintain control of it and use it to pivot to and compromise other systems within your network. Never write down or share the root password with anyone outside the system administrators group. If you use a database or other secure password manager to generate and store passwords, ensure that you exercise extreme security measures around those applications.

Beyond the protection of regular user accounts (with password complexity, length, and expiration), you have the ultimate responsibility of protecting the root account as a system administrator. System user account passwords can be shared, written down, stolen via phishing, or given verbally to someone attempting to exploit a user via social engineering tactics. For these reasons, passwords, no matter how complex, are still vulnerable to many different types of attacks and should be replaced with passwordless key files, whose creation and use are covered later in this chapter.

The next section helps you understand the balance you must find and maintain between securing a system and locking it down so tightly that users will be tempted to circumvent security altogether by creating rogue systems or local virtual machines that likely have little to no security measures in place.

Finding the Balance Between Security and Usability

As we've established, security is your greatest responsibility. However, you must also support usable systems. The most secure system is powered off and locked away, but it's also not usable. Therefore, you have to strike a balance between a system that is secure for everyone and one that's also usable.

Systems must have users, software, files, and network connections to be useful. All of these make your system less secure but more usable.

Your job is to do the following:

- Maintain systems so they're secure from over-the-network attacks
- Protect the system from careless users
- Protect users from one another
- Protect the system's configurations and data from everyone except those with appropriate access granted to them.

In the following sections, you'll learn how to perform these functions.

Minimizing Your System's Attack Surface

Have you ever seen a reenactment of a duel on television or in a movie? Notice that the participants turn sideways to each another with one arm outstretched and holding the dueling pistol while holding the other hand behind them. This "dueling" stance minimizes their exposed shootable surface, making them harder to hit. By decreasing the target size, you also decrease the chances of a fatal strike. You should protect your systems by decreasing their attackable surface in the same way, exposing only what you must to support normal user operation.

You must carefully select which services to install when installing a new system. For example, when I install a Red Hat–based server system, I use a minimal installation option that usually includes only the SSH service. I add services and packages as required to keep my systems' footprints purposely small and focused on a single task. I never install a graphical user interface (GUI) or graphical display manager onto a server system because of the security vulnerabilities inherent in these user-friendly interfaces.

Checking for and removing a GUI

To check if your system has a graphical display manager, issue the following command:

```
$ systemctl get-default
multi-user.target
```

If the response is anything but `multi-user.target`, run the following command to correct it:

```
$ sudo systemctl set-default multi-user.target
```

Check for the installation of a GUI or graphical display manager:

```
$ rpm -qa | grep xorg | grep server
```

If you receive any response, it might look similar to the following:

```
xorg-x11-server-utils-7.7-27.el8.x86_64
```

You might also see packages similar to `xorg-x11-server-common` and `xorg-x11-server-utils`. If you see any of these packages, issue the following command to remove them. Use the specific package name corresponding to your system's installed package:

```
$ sudo yum remove xorg-x11-server-Xorg \
xorg-x11-server-common xorg-x11-server-utils
```

Creating single-purpose systems

At a minimum, each of your systems needs an SSH server. It's a secure method of connecting and managing systems. Unused services make your system vulnerable and are entry points for system- and network-wide compromise. You should install your systems using a server or a minimal install option and add services as required after installation and setup.

If your distribution doesn't have a server or minimal install option, then you must selectively uninstall any service or software package that isn't explicitly required for the system's prescribed purpose. Let's examine how to create systems with a single purpose.

Virtualization and cloud computing have allowed businesses to focus on a single service per system. Because of hardware costs, we used physical systems as servers rather than virtualization hosts and had to stack multiple services on a single system. Virtualization host systems can serve dozens of virtual machines or hundreds of container systems, each performing a single business task, such as a web server, database server, or application server.

Building a system that hosts a single service is much easier than paring down one that has existed for some time. However, as part of your system administrator duties, you should perform security "sweeps" of any system under your management. And a security sweep or audit includes examining the system for unused and outdated services that cause it to be vulnerable to attack. A security sweep consists of checking listening ports on the local machine using the following commands:

```
$ netstat -an | grep LISTEN | grep tcp
tcp        0      0 0.0.0.0:22              0.0.0.0:*              LISTEN

$ netstat -an | grep LISTEN | grep udp
```

These two commands provide a list of listening daemons (services). The interface 0.0.0.0 is all interfaces. Services accessible only on the local system listen on 127.0.0.1 (localhost or loopback). Malicious actors often set up an exfiltration service disguised as a web service, DNS service, or other legitimate service to fool system administrators and port scanners. You should check the legitimacy of all listening processes on your systems:

```
$ netstat -an | grep LISTEN | grep tcp
tcp        0      0 127.0.0.1:80            0.0.0.0:*              LISTEN
tcp        0      0 0.0.0.0:22              0.0.0.0:*              LISTEN
```

For example in the */etc/httpd/conf/httpd.conf* file (or your specific Apache configuration file), there are two possible configurations, but you may only use one or the other. You must comment the one you don't wish to use. Here is the excerpt from *httpd.conf*:

```
# Listen: Allows you to bind Apache to specific IP addresses and/or
# ports, instead of the default. See also the <VirtualHost>
# directive.
#
# Change this to Listen on specific IP addresses as shown below to
# prevent Apache from glomming onto all bound IP addresses.
#
Listen 127.0.0.1:80
#Listen 80
```

You may specify a particular network interface and port (Listen 127.0.0.1:80) or a port to listen on all interfaces (Listen 80). The former configuration ensures that only local system users may use the web service. While a local-only web server isn't very practical, it illustrates how to limit access to a network service.

You should perform an autoremove to remove unused software from your system:

```
$ sudo yum autoremove
$ sudo apt autoremove
```

This command removes any leftover software package dependencies from an incomplete uninstall or insufficient package removal cleanup.

Remember that enabling any over-the-network listening daemon or service puts your system at potential risk. Protect all services with secure protocols, firewalls, access control lists, and IP restrictions as necessary.

The next section discusses security for user accounts.

Creating and Securing User Accounts

As soon as you create a user account on your system, your system's security is weakened. However, as you know, user accounts are a requirement. It is a rare system with no user accounts other than the root account. Service accounts are common user accounts, even with no interactive shell. Having no shell means no one may interactively log in as that user and issue shell commands. Most systems have interactive shell user accounts so that regular users may log in and issue commands, compile software, connect to other systems, and use resources such as storage and data.

The biggest problem with interactive user accounts is weak passwords. Weak passwords threaten your system's security. There are at least two methods of mitigating this problem. One is to set up your system to require strong passwords by creating and enforcing a strong password policy. Another is to disable password use in favor of SSH key files so that users can connect to other systems without a password. You can also configure multifactor authentication (MFA) using various free or commercial tools. MFA implementation is beyond the scope of this book.

Creating and enforcing a strong password policy

On Red Hat Enterprise Linux–based systems, the */etc/security/pwquality.conf* file is the configuration file that allows system administrators to set and enforce corporate password policies. The following is a complete listing of that file:

```
# Configuration for systemwide password quality limits
# Defaults:
#
# Number of characters in the new password that must not be present in the
# old password.
# difok = 1
#
# Minimum acceptable size for the new password (plus one if
# credits are not disabled which is the default). (See pam_cracklib manual.)
# Cannot be set to lower value than 6.
# minlen = 8
#
# The maximum credit for having digits in the new password. If less than 0
# it is the minimum number of digits in the new password.
# dcredit = 0
```

```
#
# The maximum credit for having uppercase characters in the new password.
# If less than 0 it is the minimum number of uppercase characters in the new
# password.
# ucredit = 0
#
# The maximum credit for having lowercase characters in the new password.
# If less than 0 it is the minimum number of lowercase characters in the new
# password.
# lcredit = 0
#
# The maximum credit for having other characters in the new password.
# If less than 0 it is the minimum number of other characters in the new
# password.
# ocredit = 0
#
# The minimum number of required classes of characters for the new
# password (digits, uppercase, lowercase, others).
# minclass = 0
#
# The maximum number of allowed consecutive same characters in the new password.
# The check is disabled if the value is 0.
# maxrepeat = 0
#
# The maximum number of allowed consecutive characters of the same class in the
# new password.
# The check is disabled if the value is 0.
# maxclassrepeat = 0
#
# Whether to check for the words from the passwd entry GECOS string of the user.
# The check is enabled if the value is not 0.
# gecoscheck = 0
#
# Whether to check for the words from the cracklib dictionary.
# The check is enabled if the value is not 0.
# dictcheck = 1
#
# Whether to check if it contains the user name in some form.
# The check is enabled if the value is not 0.
# usercheck = 1
#
# Length of substrings from the username to check for in the password
# The check is enabled if the value is greater than 0 and usercheck is enabled.
# usersubstr = 0
#
# Whether the check is enforced by the PAM module and possibly other
# applications.
# The new password is rejected if it fails the check and the value is not 0.
# enforcing = 1
#
```

```
# Path to the cracklib dictionaries. Default is to use the cracklib default.
# dictpath =
#
# Prompt user at most N times before returning with error. The default is 1.
# retry = 3
#
# Enforces pwquality checks on the root user password.
# Enabled if the option is present.
# enforce_for_root
#
# Skip testing the password quality for users that are not present in the
# /etc/passwd file.
# Enabled if the option is present.
# local_users_only
```

Connecting to other systems via passwordless key files

Capturing passwords through packet sniffing or keylogger programs is a common method of compromising systems when unsuspecting users connect from one system to another using passwords. One of the best methods of password capture prevention is to discontinue the use of passwords altogether. Using key files, users may connect from one system to another without the need to interactively enter a password.

Setting up key files between systems is trivial but a little time-consuming. Ultimately, it increases security because no passwords are traveling across networks, written on sticky notes, or so simple that anyone can guess them.

Creating the key file.   Remote login via key files provides you with a more secure connection between remote systems than using passwords. Without going into great detail about how private/public key authentication works, which you can certainly research on your own, realize that using key files doesn't pass an encrypted or unencrypted password to another system. There is no usable data (passwords) for an attacker to capture, so brute-force attacks against encrypted information aren't possible. Creating a private/public key pair is easy.

The following example uses two Linux systems, server1 and server2. You can see in the following code that you haven't configured remote login via key files between these two systems:

```
[khess@server1 ~]$ ssh server2
The authenticity of host 'server2 (192.168.1.20)' can't be established.
ECDSA key fingerprint is SHA256:dh2YOMWKu2pF/SivS++Y1u1FaE9LcadCKIl6shlSUuc.
Are you sure you want to continue connecting (yes/no/[fingerprint])? yes
Warning: Permanently added 'server2' (ECDSA) to the list of known hosts.
khess@server2's password:
Last login: Thu Aug 11 08:12:06 2022 from 192.168.1.234
[khess@server2 ~]$
```

Run the following commands on both systems to set up your private/public key pair between these two:

```
[khess@server1 ~]$ ssh-keygen -t ecdsa -b 521
Generating public/private ecdsa key pair.
Enter file in which to save the key (/home/khess/.ssh/id_ecdsa):
Enter passphrase (empty for no passphrase):
Enter same passphrase again:
Your identification has been saved in /home/khess/.ssh/id_ecdsa.
Your public key has been saved in /home/khess/.ssh/id_ecdsa.pub.
The key fingerprint is:
SHA256:KGNaYYxQXO46dm2J7/8960FLAYQ5mb3e+wgRghX4BUk khess@server1
The key's randomart image is:
+---[ECDSA 521]---+
|.o...  oE@o       |
| ..+  .oB o.      |
| . = ...o...      |
|  o . ...... .    |
|   * . S...o      |
|   = = . .+..     |
|   = o +  . o.    |
| . o o     ooo    |
|    .o.....=+.    |
+----[SHA256]-----+
```

The default encryption algorithm is RSA, but both RSA and DSA algorithms are old, and you shouldn't use them. The newer elliptical curve digital signature algorithm (ECDSA) is currently the best option. And while this algorithm accepts 256- and 384-bit encryption, use 521 for maximum protection. You may optionally provide a passphrase to protect your key file pair further. Providing a passphrase ensures that even if your private key is stolen, it can't be used without the passphrase.

The three available key sizes are 256, 384, and 521. No, the 521 you see in the command isn't an error. One would think the next available key size would be 512, but for ECDSA, it is 521.

Copy the ID from one server to another using the following command:

```
[khess@server1 ~]$ ssh-copy-id server2
/usr/bin/ssh-copy-id: INFO: Source of key(s) to be installed: "/home/khess/.ss...
/usr/bin/ssh-copy-id: INFO: attempting to log in with the new key(s), to filte...
/usr/bin/ssh-copy-id: INFO: 1 key(s) remain to be installed -- if you are prom...
khess@server2's password:

Number of key(s) added: 1

Now try logging into the machine, with:   "ssh 'server2'"
and check to ensure that only the key(s) you wanted were added.
```

As the message suggests, try to log into `server2`:

```
[khess@server1 ~]$ ssh server2
Last login: Fri Aug 12 14:10:46 2022 from 192.168.1.80
[khess@server2 ~]$
```

You have successfully created the key pair and may now log in from `server1` to `server2` without a password. Your next question should be, "Is this passwordless login only valid from `server1` to `server2` (unidirectional), or is it bidirectional (`server2` to `server1`)?"

To answer the question, try to log in from `server2` to `server1`:

```
[khess@server2 ~]$ ssh server1
The authenticity of host 'server1 (192.168.1.80)' can't be established.
ECDSA key fingerprint is SHA256:Aim3J/cp24ZIneGzoNyZpf3kWG17ZRrMQVicvOQRyPM.
Are you sure you want to continue connecting (yes/no/[fingerprint])? yes
Warning: Permanently added '192.168.1.80' (ECDSA) to the list of known hosts.
khess@192.168.1.80's password:

Last login: Thu Aug 11 08:08:04 2022 from 192.168.1.234
[khess@server1 ~]$
```

The answer is no. The key pair is unidirectional. To set up a reciprocal login (`server2` to `server1`), you must repeat the process for `server2`:

```
[khess@server2 ~]$ ssh-keygen -t ecdsa -b 521
Generating public/private ecdsa key pair.
Enter file in which to save the key (/home/khess/.ssh/id_ecdsa):
Enter passphrase (empty for no passphrase):
Enter same passphrase again:
Your identification has been saved in /home/khess/.ssh/id_ecdsa
Your public key has been saved in /home/khess/.ssh/id_ecdsa.pub
The key fingerprint is:
SHA256:nlHb2YUMzW29H7XrZvubiP0RK8DnkB+I3bff9TBHsTo khess@server2
The key's randomart image is:
+---[ECDSA 521]---+
|           .o ..|
|           oo.=|
|        .   oo=|
|        .+o+o =o|
|        S..Bo+.+=|
|       . o  * +o=|
|        o    E++o|
|             o +BB|
|          . o+=O|
+----[SHA256]-----+

[khess@server2 ~]$ ssh-copy-id server1
/usr/bin/ssh-copy-id: INFO: Source of key(s) to be installed: "/home/khess/.ss...
/usr/bin/ssh-copy-id: INFO: attempting to log in with the new key(s), to filte...
/usr/bin/ssh-copy-id: INFO: 1 key(s) remain to be installed -- if you are prom...
```

```
khess@server1's password:

Number of key(s) added: 1

Now try logging into the machine, with:   "ssh 'server1'"
and check to make sure that only the key(s) you wanted were added.

[khess@server2 ~]$ ssh server1

Last login: Sun Aug 14 10:35:42 2022 from 192.168.1.20
[khess@server1 ~]$
```

You may now connect bidirectionally between server1 and server2 using key pair authentication. If you want to learn more about SSH, encryption protocols, and security-related topics, please visit the OpenSSH website (*https://oreil.ly/ontmn*).

Adding extra security to SSHD.   You should secure your SSHD by accepting key file authentication if it's not already set up. You can check by issuing the following command:

```
$ sudo grep -i pubkey /etc/ssh/sshd_config
#PubkeyAuthentication yes
```

Uncomment this line and restart the SSHD service. If you filter on the word "password," you will find the following line in */etc/ssh/sshd_config*:

```
$ sudo grep -i password /etc/ssh/sshd_config
PasswordAuthentication yes
```

This line allows users to connect and log in with a username and password. This line is a requirement for setting up key-based authentication. (Refer to the preceding subsection, where we saw that you must log in via username and password to copy your key to the remote system.)

 If you change PasswordAuthentication yes to Password Authentication no, you will exclude users who do not already have their key-based authentication configured, because they will not be able to log in with a username and password. You'll have to manually configure each user account unless you use some automation.

The preceding warning is one of those decision points that you must make as a system administrator—finding the balance between usability and security. On the one hand, your attempt to increase security by removing passwords from remote connectivity is admirable. Still, on the other hand, you must leave password authentication intact to enable users to create their key pairs for secure connectivity. My best advice is to disable passwords and handle the task for your users because if you leave this significant security step to your users, your systems may go unsecured for months or years. Should you decide not to disable password authentication, please increase password complexity, shorten the expiration interval to no more than 90 days, and enforce nonrepeated passwords.

Implementing Advanced Security Measures

The definition of *advanced* is certainly up for debate. For me, advanced means security measures that generally conform to the Security Technical Implementation Guide (STIG) as described in the National Institute of Standards and Technology (NIST) 800-53 (*https://oreil.ly/E1G1b*) and related documents. The so-called "STIGging" of a system protects it from over-the-network attacks and local system attacks.

Remember that even using STIG to secure a system is not a foolproof security method, but it's a great standard for setting up new systems. It would be best to use it to secure your inherited systems.

STIGs are generally used for government contractor–owned systems involved in Department of Defense projects that must comply with strict data-handling regulations. Still, they apply to any system, hosting sensitive data or not. It would help if you implemented as many of these items as practical, especially those in the high severity list. Figure 13-1 shows each guideline's number and severity for reference.

Figure 13-1. The findings and severity levels of the Red Hat Enterprise Linux 8 STIG

The next section discusses applying these controls to your systems.

Applying STIG Security Controls

Applying a list of STIG controls is a time-consuming task. However, as you read through the controls, you'll find that you can automate most configurations necessary to comply with the standard. And some STIGs provide you with downloadable scripts to make compliance easier. While the STIG shown in Figure 13-1 is Red Hat Enterprise Linux–specific, these standards apply to all Linux distributions used in businesses and government offices. Information related to an Ubuntu STIG is available on the Ubuntu DISA page (*https://oreil.ly/Bob4c*).

If you create "golden" images for your systems, which I highly recommend, you can develop a STIG image with the security controls already in place. New, revised STIGs are released when necessary and usually contain only a few new security fixes that you can place on your systems via script or some automation tool. Updating a golden image twice per year is probably enough to keep your systems updated so that new controls will be easy to distribute.

To implement STIG controls, begin with the Category I (High severity) controls and apply those first. If you have systems that you feel might be vulnerable, immediately implement all Category I security controls. Currently, for Red Hat Enterprise Linux 8, there are only 21 such controls, so the effort required is minimal. For Category II (Medium severity) controls, you should employ an audit tool because there are more than 300 Category II controls.

Installing and Using Security Tools

There are dozens of commercial and free security tools that you can use to better protect your systems. The following three tools used with STIG can greatly enhance your systems' security. As stated previously, you should install and run these tools at least once before deploying your systems onto a live network. An initial run provides you with a baseline assessment. Keep these initial reports to compare with those you run in the future.

I highly recommend the following short list of security tools. All new systems should have these tools installed and an initial run completed before system production deployment. These security tools have served me well and are well-accepted in many enterprise environments.

Lynis

Lynis is a lighter-weight vulnerability checker than the Security Content Automation Protocol (SCAP) and STIG tools. However, it is not a replacement for those tools if you must comply with the Department of Defense or other government security standards. Lynis is a security auditing tool that checks your servers' system and software configurations.

Install the Lynis package via your package manager, and then run a system audit:

```
$ sudo lynis audit system
```

Once the audit is complete, I usually grep for Suggestion, as shown here, to obtain a list of recommended security fixes. The list might be quite lengthy.

```
$ sudo grep Suggestion /var/log/lynis.log > lynis_fixes.txt
```

You can refer to this list, make corrections and fixes, and rerun the system audit. I recommend continuing to do this until there are no more recommended fixes or to get the list to a point where the recommendations (suggestions) do not apply to your system. The following is an excerpt from my suggestion list:

```
2022-10-31 13:35:53 Suggestion: Install Apache mod_evasive to guard webserver ...
DoS/brute force attempts [test:HTTP-6640] [details:-] [solution:-]
2022-10-31 13:35:53 Suggestion: Install Apache modsecurity to guard webserver ...
web application attacks [test:HTTP-6643] [details:-] [solution:-]
2022-10-31 13:35:54 Suggestion: Consider hardening SSH configuration [test:SSH...
[details:AllowTcpForwarding (set YES to NO)] [solution:-]
2022-10-31 13:35:54 Suggestion: Consider hardening SSH configuration [test:SSH...
[details:ClientAliveCountMax (set 3 to 2)] [solution:-]
2022-10-31 13:35:54 Suggestion: Consider hardening SSH configuration [test:SSH...
[details:Compression (set YES to NO)] [solution:-]
2022-10-31 13:35:55 Suggestion: Consider hardening SSH configuration [test:SSH...
[details:LogLevel (set INFO to VERBOSE)] [solution:-]
2022-10-31 13:35:55 Suggestion: Consider hardening SSH configuration [test:SSH...
[details:MaxAuthTries (set 6 to 3)] [solution:-]
2022-10-31 13:35:55 Suggestion: Consider hardening SSH configuration [test:SSH...
[details:MaxSessions (set 10 to 2)] [solution:-]
2022-10-31 13:35:55 Suggestion: Consider hardening SSH configuration [test:SSH...
[details:PermitRootLogin (set YES to (FORCED-COMMANDS-ONLY|NO|PROHIBIT-PASSWOR...
2022-10-31 13:35:55 Suggestion: Consider hardening SSH configuration [test:SSH...
[details:Port (set 22 to )] [solution:-]
2022-10-31 13:35:55 Suggestion: Consider hardening SSH configuration [test:SSH...
[details:TCPKeepAlive (set YES to NO)] [solution:-]
2022-10-31 13:35:55 Suggestion: Consider hardening SSH configuration [test:SSH...
[details:X11Forwarding (set YES to NO)] [solution:-]
2022-10-31 13:35:55 Suggestion: Consider hardening SSH configuration [test:SSH...
[details:AllowAgentForwarding (set YES to NO)] [solution:-]
2022-10-31 13:35:58 Suggestion: Enable logging to an external logging host for...
purposes and additional protection [test:LOGG-2154] [details:-] [solution:-]
2022-10-31 13:35:59 Suggestion: Check what deleted files are still in use and ...
[test:LOGG-2190] [details:-] [solution:-]
2022-10-31 13:36:13 Suggestion: Add a legal banner to /etc/issue, to warn unau...
users [test:BANN-7126] [details:-] [solution:-]
2022-10-31 13:36:13 Suggestion: Add legal banner to /etc/issue.net, to warn un...
users [test:BANN-7130] [details:-] [solution:-]
```

An example of something I can ignore is the */etc/issue* and */etc/issue.net* legal notice. My systems are private virtual machines, and I'm the only one who uses them. You will likely see a long list of SSH hardening suggestions. It would be best if you implemented these. Some sysadmins create "golden" images from systems that have passed through a Lynis "cleansing" so they can deploy a clean image. Of course, Lynis should be run regularly to maintain this status. A scheduled cron job is a good solution for creating regular reports.

Portsentry

Portsentry runs in memory and attempts to detect network port scans and then ban the offending hosts' IP address via *hosts.deny*, firewall rules, ipchains and iptables entries, or dropped routes.

The following ports defined in */etc/portsentry/portsentry.conf* are "activated." You may add custom ports or remove port numbers at will. In the Ubuntu implementation, this is the default list of ports:

```
# Use these if you just want to be aware:
TCP_PORTS="1,11,15,79,111,119,143,540,635,1080,1524,2000,5742,6667,12345,12346,20
034,27665,31337,32771,32772,32773,32774,40421,49724,54320"
UDP_PORTS="1,7,9,69,161,162,513,635,640,641,700,37444,34555,31335,32770,32771,327
72,32773,32774,31337,54321"
```

The default action is to drop the route back to the scanning host:

```
KILL_ROUTE="/sbin/route add -host $TARGET$ reject"
```

I also use the */etc/hosts.deny* entry by uncommenting the following line:

```
KILL_HOSTS_DENY="ALL: $TARGET$ : DENY"
```

This ensures that the route to the host is blocked and the IP address is blocked in */etc/hosts.deny*. The entries from */etc/hosts.deny* and *route* look like the result from a scan (the scanning host is 192.168.1.234).

From */etc/hosts.deny*:

```
ALL: 192.168.1.234 : DENY
```

From the *route* table:

```
Kernel IP routing table
Destination     Gateway         Genmask         Flags Metric Ref    Use Iface
default         Docsis-Gateway  0.0.0.0         UG    0      0        0 enp0s3
192.168.1.0     0.0.0.0         255.255.255.0   U     0      0        0 enp0s3
192.168.1.234   -               255.255.255.255 !H    0      -        0 -
```

Here are some entries from */var/log/syslog* that identify the offending system:

```
Oct 31 21:21:51 server2 portsentry[177518]: attackalert: Host: 192.168.1.234...
already blocked. Ignoring
Oct 31 21:21:51 server2 portsentry[177518]: attackalert: Connect from host: ...
to TCP port: 32772
Oct 31 21:21:51 server2 portsentry[177518]: attackalert: Host: 192.168.1.234...
already blocked. Ignoring
```

```
Oct 31 21:21:51 server2 portsentry[177518]: attackalert: Connect from host: ...
to TCP port: 32773
Oct 31 21:21:51 server2 portsentry[177518]: attackalert: Host: 192.168.1.234...
already blocked. Ignoring
Oct 31 21:21:51 server2 portsentry[177518]: attackalert: Connect from host: ...
to TCP port: 32774
Oct 31 21:21:51 server2 portsentry[177518]: attackalert: Host: 192.168.1.234...
already blocked. Ignoring
```

Portsentry is a handy little utility that's always been one of my security layers. You can see that it effectively eliminates connectivity from a particular host. If you have a DMZ host, you should use Portsentry on it because it will be scanned multiple times daily.

Advanced Intrusion and Detection Environment

Advanced Intrusion and Detection Environment (AIDE) is an intrusion-detection system for checking file integrity. Install AIDE from a repository:

```
$ sudo dnf install aide
```

If you do not use a Red Hat–based system, the installation proceeds differently. On Ubuntu (and I assume on all Debian-based systems), the installer steps you through a postfix configuration and creates multiple configuration files under */etc/aide*. The Ubuntu implementation is different from the Red Hat Enterprise Linux–based one. Differences are noted in the text. Before using AIDE, you must first initialize its database with the following command. This process takes a few minutes to complete.

```
$ sudo aide --init
Start timestamp: 2022-10-31 09:19:12 -0400 (AIDE 0.16)
AIDE initialized database at /var/lib/aide/aide.db.new.gz

Number of entries:     156566


--------------------------------------------------
The attributes of the (uncompressed) database(s):
--------------------------------------------------

/var/lib/aide/aide.db.new.gz
   MD5      : WzAN0+7wHIA5a+vZkzwQVQ==
   SHA1     : 8FisYNVBvBy3bdg1NaeJY1vm7LI=
   RMD160   : fwBCNvM7WMl7j8TN3EhB5X72ozs=
   TIGER    : 2fM2gL5j7aZ+BpjS9QOx4CjJKEZlZLSC
   SHA256   : XTBnehGnObWiSXR4qEJDQqOO0eCAQzfJ
              4viTZDfmQYI=
   SHA512   : M+1T1KBw04F/hbWE2uSEs3mEsYI7QzoM
              godalkUZAWLoG5LgsJTiFjPXdSnZ/dRE
              n4A83aQWtART7O7uVNR//A==


End timestamp: 2022-10-31 09:21:17 -0400 (run time: 2m 5s)
```

You can initialize the AIDE database on Ubuntu with a similar command (script), which executes aide -init:

```
$ sudo aideinit
Running aide --init...
Start timestamp: 2022-10-31 09:31:07 -0400 (AIDE 0.16.1)
AIDE initialized database at /var/lib/aide/aide.db.new
Verbose level: 6

Number of entries:    220642

--------------------------------------------------
The attributes of the (uncompressed) database(s):
--------------------------------------------------

/var/lib/aide/aide.db.new
  RMD160   : pxukBfZYMClQJluYftmJxyHvQ6c=
  TIGER    : aRgAX6JnizUa9yiTE29/uZ0HqMYioQcN
  SHA256   : lmV6LTtzpiLDUAw6qloEgfAT0sD7J74w
             2vqhj7nVLP0=
  SHA512   : VCfBAAxLvaA5CEtOJEPu2SeA/565gfUS
             T0BgFFwfXWG8RkksMbnHtm8pDtVlUSnc
             TqQhcebdU/qODLwPkGIzTg==
  CRC32    : 7jx94w==
  HAVAL    : vrZDJ+70DZkjj7t6BHzt3ph4UN4yoDnd
             8oxrBBy2hvA=
  GOST     : sDLorHAYPZb74dZmIpYYZjARR3znxOXI
             Sv0WSZiZV0g=


End timestamp: 2022-10-31 09:39:38 -0400 (run time: 8m 31s)
```

On Red Hat Enterprise Linux–based systems, you must perform one last task before checking your system:

```
$ sudo cp /var/lib/aide/aide.db.new.gz /var/lib/aide/aide.db.gz
$ sudo aide --check

Start timestamp: 2022-10-31 10:08:44 -0400 (AIDE 0.16)
AIDE found NO differences between database and filesystem. Looks okay!!

Number of entries:    156566

--------------------------------------------------
The attributes of the (uncompressed) database(s):
--------------------------------------------------

/var/lib/aide/aide.db.gz
  MD5      : WzAN0+7wHIA5a+vZkzwQVQ==
  SHA1     : 8FisYNVBvBy3bdg1NaeJY1vm7LI=
  RMD160   : fwBCNvM7WMl7j8TN3EhB5X72ozs=
  TIGER    : 2fM2gL5j7aZ+BpjS9QOx4CjJKEZlZLSC
  SHA256   : XTBnehGnObWiSXR4qEJDQqOO0eCAQzfJ
```

```
            4viTZDfmQYI=
   SHA512   : M+1T1KBw04F/hbWE2uSEs3mEsYI7QzoM
            godalkUZAWLoG5LgsJTiFjPXdSnZ/dRE
            n4A83aQWtART7O7uVNR//A==


 End timestamp: 2022-10-31 10:10:53 -0400 (run time: 2m 9s)
```

You can perform a check on Ubuntu systems without copying the file. The Ubuntu install completes the task for you. However, if you run `sudo aide --check`, you receive the error `Couldn't open file /var/lib/aide/please-dont-call-aide-without-parameters/aide.db for reading`.

The Ubuntu system shows a positive report for changes. It's lengthy but illustrates the type of report you'll see when AIDE detects changes. The report provides details of changes made to files:

```
$ sudo aide.wrapper --check

Start timestamp: 2022-10-31 10:09:42 -0400 (AIDE 0.16.1)
AIDE found differences between database and filesystem!!
Verbose level: 6

Summary:
  Total number of entries:     220641
  Added entries:            1
  Removed entries:          1
  Changed entries:          5


-------------------------------------------------
Added entries:
-------------------------------------------------

f++++++++++++++++: /var/lib/aide/aide.db


-------------------------------------------------
Removed entries:
-------------------------------------------------

l----------------: /run/systemd/units/invocation:packagekit.service


-------------------------------------------------
Changed entries:
-------------------------------------------------

f =.... ....C.. : /run/samba/smbXsrv_open_global.tdb
f =.... ....C.. : /run/samba/smbd_cleanupd.tdb
d <.... mc.. .. : /run/systemd/units
f =.... mc..C.. .: /var/log/journal/ae1c358b16f744999c9d4b7a80e.../system.journal
f >b... mc..C.. .: /var/log/sysstat/sa31


-------------------------------------------------
```

```
Detailed information about changes:
---------------------------------------------------

File: /run/samba/smbXsrv_open_global.tdb
    RMD160   : CCdm3M2ObTIu3vIXdx1vyH8emLc=        | AMx08YvCC7rmeUGhvjZ3OjLInKs=
    TIGER    : 814xHPLSSvskZzBYZ0xfLej405/LeQ2s    | PE/hVYgRx4i17ckNePiFjVXgPQu0wOGG
    SHA256   : Y6KJgoFPHLYXfqB0om9NlbkXIYAmXmjQ    | ahWfobXIOoIToffW0+jZjYYTg8W/JrFd
               /kRNN0Axa1o=                        | vrCgRinjC+g=
    SHA512   : kRDLUujEHcHUIyUVtv/u9BFldu+oCXFj    | ZudqhTqoc3x0Sp5RMntoJ0yUU6dkrifw
               9qbOjLft3SJK3btR0vfJtJHL1UW13LZC    | R+2UDQM1zTopREoU/+N/jo9i80AcDqD6
               bUf44NCR1OSQ6s2DIfcb7A==            | j44U/ao6HhDEjE/aqoMT4Q==
    CRC32    : j0j0sA==                            | E7N72A==
    HAVAL    : giCwkv0n5oPDwHs/9k0HfPoGcAvkntQF    | TJbUsmxe9Kt0+xK6R72Nk0R/2PT/XZVe
               39jkiW8nA3o=                        | Ml3VqYaXTGg=
    GOST     : P7uSZmTObQfp5nChg9W4svXupluCGaMS    | GHF0TxYsXQfay3ayLi/KBck1hDcor92t
               xKp5tZQoPsQ=                        | zHzSyOiNZYk=


File: /run/samba/smbd_cleanupd.tdb
    RMD160   : D8RmZx6959xPvPKuRbEGMJdl9ww=        | uOtFZoKw8zVjcGZdhJkXcyL3kEg=
    TIGER    : xCRjkykka/bv2rf06KRdPtigjByvsQJB    | r5sm3aHqZJ26jPmADp8tk1qvdPw1IfFF
    SHA256   : 7egAlq5dMozWAiYPYx3JH9r7kY1oyeOR    | FVaSrvPfA5ivujOsuVcKgCdS20TQTGrw
               0DYEU4MZohA=                        | MFTjvyUFZWk=
    SHA512   : AqzJDePQwKxivNPtdJzX4suWBQnDSJhO    | lYLskmVOAFSHs9dG2eVP9u4bEAWOcKM6
               hjUdEpFGKFaj0ODwuVumBHi/npByq2pZ    | M0Tf73IXztE5kaP/9YHaOJRGata0GCZk
               +tMh5Kc5IevDpGPvrj5lxQ==            | t5viYSFd2ZIL9Alr31kACg==
    CRC32    : V4u1vg==                            | haAC6Q==
    HAVAL    : 0Ny4G+Y4tTaGHfFu7cXgW7yV2iPaO7xL    | tR7ZgOfYNMjaKk0byAUOXAPx6/COqfVc
               ae5dMQFmNPY=                        | 4jpIEdYENd4=
    GOST     : dbrx9gce/697G9QVs4XcaoHXuS2fd3Nn    | jewBI4vx9CPF6Xof7f2vdZOrzmzAcD2c
               ZNAX4+OndrQ=                        | yimBCewy/bE=


Directory: /run/systemd/units
    Size     : 1760                                | 1740
    Mtime    : 2022-10-31 09:30:13 -0400           | 2022-10-31 09:35:18 -0400
    Ctime    : 2022-10-31 09:30:13 -0400           | 2022-10-31 09:35:18 -0400

File: /var/log/journal/ae1c358b16f744999c9d4b7a80e92d66/system.journal
    Mtime    : 2022-10-31 09:35:18 -0400           | 2022-10-31 10:17:02 -0400
    Ctime    : 2022-10-31 09:35:18 -0400           | 2022-10-31 10:17:02 -0400
    RMD160   : oUjngLN5zL6EG9FssV5/Y7RDdG4=        | EekegpOq7Vf0fR82TtrvxJAwXP4=
    TIGER    : ZH3LLiOvM8ew7O3yw+SC/wHiDvkTemCF    | N9DDL3wW44urrq0MJhwnclk4/c1jLuJW
    SHA256   : bfyPm9q1QlUlTm+JurRZnVMgAOYb0UFE    | 5vU1pGWJ2WxMLZK7/f3qZ/Ix4o+NANoB
               qIjQofT4Jfo=                        | kNN6Q+9pwCk=
    SHA512   : oLscXcjp62ezwcSZ3E1EUkTrRCilblyM    | Vd0CyIE+C+oGAOLsCfvfxdNlqKvasSC4
               9/g+mdsGNBxA681uxBJcyVZIPJZ1s/cX    | dVF0zmryyzd5lDsod8aH8WNLEfpHlSzL
               SQV6E+nnc2KiL4teg1YdKg==            | j9+yt6iOJAKTtO3bIdqmEg==
    CRC32    : pe7DMw==                            | br312w==
    HAVAL    : izYRs/Df2Ae5PAbD9m7RsTOXvO2sTOV0    | wamyIlLjRTtgFpwgfIABPhAodrHuRHe1
               qv7063B7mFI=                        | ee/pSNw9Z/I=
    GOST     : FH3fMIAa0W2eV+aLNnkY+wjxhjr+LhqA    | yYmdcHpvePslHVmsm1w2TpgqIo6Mh1QT
               CZbOX7wbKRA=                        | oFuber3PVDo=
```

```
File: /var/log/sysstat/sa31
  Size      : 131024                      | 139840
  Bcount    : 264                         | 288
  Mtime     : 2022-10-31 09:35:01 -0400   | 2022-10-31 10:15:01 -0400
  Ctime     : 2022-10-31 09:35:01 -0400   | 2022-10-31 10:15:01 -0400
  RMD160    : bFqT+RlB042AhIl9Ja0aAI/fGPE= | jO8DEa6NGNYnP6+U8BF/yUsweIs=
  TIGER     : /Pz1oVax6QHqhWivA3Cec/f0vHajjxx0 | XiMXwjskfSFf4NH8rRb4cWc6West9MQp
  SHA256    : t256G+V3hS8DvMj53EXw8W7e/MkwSAUe | T7r2xNaGWtzBp0Qab6seO1KNluyOmWa+
              9AYuduiSjVI=                | 634jjyPpVCk=
  SHA512    : KSUTRzDpgc/s2jwJkQIb0uS+5cJsFqXl | iguQ86cwvpqL3WAmFJWA0tpzy43REGKh
              yGXoVuzd65YDpE8msRaBRCcqTIB740pf | DcySXGUBCSHXvmFHAK4P7Zk0tJB4etzj
              dgo3E6K/s8UaqI1biiC2tQ==    | Vpg8/WZL+0nSk3XaKZ6UwA==
  CRC32     : 07QWcA==                    | 8X9Ixg==
  HAVAL     : WnGG1i1qhDBdNIL7TGF9euydFem/oZC9 | v6IskRb6hSnVRiB5tqUSCysPtqn3ZKQp
              u7o3lSxAl0Q=                | HPay7Epiak0=
  GOST      : vkWWBQUA+WBuEBvNAMLFerzUOkT5SWl9 | AZNTPCF3a1oSYHexxtKQoL0ksvP1Oyhx
              QTnod3FQCJQ=                | H+BXGeFVW70=


  --------------------------------------------------
  The attributes of the (uncompressed) database(s):
  --------------------------------------------------

/var/lib/aide/aide.db
  RMD160    : pxukBfZYMClQJluYftmJxyHvQ6c=
  TIGER     : aRgAX6JnizUa9yiTE29/uZ0HqMYioQcN
  SHA256    : lmV6LTtzpiLDUAw6qloEgfAT0sD7J74w
              2vqhj7nVLP0=
  SHA512    : VCfBAAxLvaA5CEtOJEPu2SeA/565gfUS
              T0BgFFwfXWG8RkksMbnHtm8pDtVlUSnc
              TqQhcebdU/qODLwPkGIzTg==
  CRC32     : 7jx94w==
  HAVAL     : vrZDJ+70DZkjj7t6BHzt3ph4UN4yoDnd
              8oxrBBy2hvA=
  GOST      : sDLorHAYPZb74dZmIpYYZjARR3znxOXI
              Sv0WSZiZV0g=


  End timestamp: 2022-10-31 10:18:52 -0400 (run time: 9m 10s)
```

You can also run an update that checks and updates the database, but the input and output databases must differ. The output from this command is also rather lengthy and is truncated because of that length. But the part I show here is the summary rather than the detailed view. This update was executed on an Ubuntu system but worked the same on Red Hat Enterprise Linux–based systems using the `sudo aide.wrapper --update` command:

```
$ sudo aide.wrapper --update
Start timestamp: 2022-10-31 10:42:00 -0400 (AIDE 0.16.1)
AIDE found differences between database and filesystem!!
New AIDE database written to /var/lib/aide/aide.db.new
Verbose level: 6
```

```
Summary:
  Total number of entries:    220641
  Added entries:          1
  Removed entries:        1
  Changed entries:        9


--------------------------------------------------
Added entries:
--------------------------------------------------


f++++++++++++++++: /var/lib/aide/aide.db


--------------------------------------------------
Removed entries:
--------------------------------------------------


l----------------: /run/systemd/units/invocation:packagekit.service


--------------------------------------------------
Changed entries:
--------------------------------------------------


f =.... ....C.. : /run/samba/smbXsrv_open_global.tdb
f =.... ....C.. : /run/samba/smbd_cleanupd.tdb
d <.... mc.. .. : /run/systemd/units
d =.... mc.. .. .: /var/lib/chrony
f =.... mci.C.. .: /var/lib/chrony/chrony.drift
d =.... mc.. .. .: /var/lib/snapd
f >.... mci.C.. .: /var/lib/snapd/state.json
f =.... mc..C.. .: /var/log/journal/ae1c358b16f744999c9d4b7a80e.../system.journal
f >b... mc..C.. .: /var/log/sysstat/sa31
```

As you can see, you might receive false positives because some files change often, but it's worth the slight annoyance to have a file integrity check that works. The next section is an overview of responding to security incidents, including internal and external system breaches.

Responding to Security Incidents

A security incident ranges from a user allowing another user access to their account, to a clever user attempting to crack the root user's password, to a full security breach by a malicious outside actor or advanced persistent threat. I've witnessed these, plus many other types of security incidents. One of the least-pleasant tasks that any sysadmin performs is responding to a security incident. Your worst day imaginable is when you discover a security breach or someone tells you, "We've been hacked." These words are going to ruin an otherwise uneventful day.

A well-written security policy is the best defense against insider threats, such as someone trying to crack the root user's passwords or sharing credentials between users. These incidents should be recorded and reported to management, and policy-driven action should be taken to prevent future occurrences of these types of security breaches. The story goes differently for external breaches because corporate policies do not bind malicious actors outside your organization.

The topics covered in this section deal with handling security incidents that occur from internal and external actors.

Creating a Written Security Policy

Writing a security policy is a manageable task. Many examples are freely available online. A quick search turns up hundreds of possibilities. Select one or more generic policy examples and adapt them to your organization. All security incidents are serious and should be handled as such. Even the simple sharing of usernames and passwords between friendly coworkers is a violation and should be dealt with immediately and sternly. Violating security policy is often grounds for reprimand, termination, and criminal prosecution.

Each employee should be given a copy of the written security policy and should sign that they've read and understood the policy and the consequences of its violation. Annual security refresher courses should reinforce corporate security policy standards, expectations, and violation consequences.

Confirming the Breach

You must confirm that a breach has occurred and to what extent the breach has compromised intellectual property, financial records, employee information, and other valuable information and data. Depending on your specific regulatory requirements from the Securities and Exchange Commission, Department of Defense, and other authorities, some breaches must be reported to law enforcement upon discovery and confirmation.

If you aren't classified under one of the many regulatory authorities, you might find that you're on your own for confirming and dealing with a breach. You should contact a third-party security firm that deals with breach discovery to assist in your efforts.

The first course of action is to remove compromised systems from the network. Unplug their network connections and disable WiFi adapters. Leave the systems powered on. Load your forensic tools offline onto the affected systems and perform a disk clone of the system before performing any mitigation. The duplicated disk may prove valuable to law enforcement in tracking the suspects.

Identifying the Malicious Actor(s)

Identifying internal actors is often far easier than identifying those from an external source. Law enforcement, including the FBI, the Department of Homeland Security, the NSA, and other agencies, might help with the investigation if the threat is thought to be from a foreign source. Attackers cover their tracks by removing log files, exfiltrating data in small amounts, and pivoting from one system to another to remain inside your network undetected for months or years.

If you suspect a malicious group or foreign government-sponsored collective has breached your network or stolen intellectual property, your best option is to contact law enforcement and the FBI. If your company is a contractor protected by the Department of Defense or another agency, the FBI or NSA might contact you about a breach before you know it has occurred. In these cases, it's best to provide those authorities with any information, data, and access they request. Identifying, stopping, and prosecuting cybercriminals is a high priority for government agencies.

Taking Corrective Actions

Once you've confirmed a breach and evaluated the damage, it's time to take corrective action, including scanning and cleaning files, enabling host-based firewalls, encrypting data, and reimaging systems. The actions you take will be dictated by the extent of the breach and actions taken by the malicious actors. Good backups, a disaster recovery plan, encrypted data, and multilayer security will help you recover from a breach.

You should report any breach to local law enforcement and take any recommended actions. If the breach is ongoing, inform law enforcement that the breach is ongoing so that they can take action or notify other agencies on your behalf.

Unfortunately, when an attack's breadth and depth aren't clear, it's recommended to reimage key systems offline and apply all security measures before bringing them back onto the corporate network.

Summary

Network and system security are ongoing efforts, not a "set it and forget it" scenario. Security requires constant vigilance, advanced training, regular software and hardware patching, automated system software, and multiple layers of security from MFA, firewalls, encryption, secure tools, secure development, and user training. It's wise to engage an external security firm to assist in the secure design and protection of your network and assets.

## CHAPTER 14

Continuing Your Education

It doesn't matter how technical you are. You must continue learning throughout your career. And if you're certified, many certifications require some continuing education units (CEUs) per year that you must document and submit to the certifying authority. But continuing your education involves more than just gathering certifications and collecting CEUs yearly to maintain those certifications. Continuing your education means expanding your horizons, learning something new, and enhancing your skills as a technologist.

This chapter focuses on educational opportunities, including internal corporate training, certification training, independent study, and community college and university classes.

Training Internally

Often, the least expensive and most accessible training is that which your company produces, conducts, or hosts. I'm not referring to those annual refresher courses we must take to satisfy regulatory requirements. I'm referring to technical résumé-building classes that enhance your skills and knowledge. Internal training is either training that your company develops and delivers to employees or training that your company purchases and delivers on-premises. The delivery method depends on many factors, such as cost, instructor availability, time, and other logistical considerations.

There is a downside to internal training, and it's that the training occurs on-site. Yes, one of the advantages is also a disadvantage. When you train at your local facility, you risk having users, colleagues, or your manager interrupt your training to have you fix something that will "only take a minute." These disruptions and interruptions, while possibly necessary, are detrimental to your learning. You miss valuable information, demonstrations, and lessons that are often difficult to go back and pick up on your own. Personally, every on-premises class I've taken has been interrupted by support calls. My managers always reminded me that "training is a privilege" and "the job comes first" when I requested dedicated time for training. Be prepared for your training to be interrupted or even discontinued due to the requirements of your job.

Seeking Certification

In the late 1990s and early 2000s, there was an industry-wide effort to get technical people certified. However, many certification classes focused so much on teaching test answers that the learning was thin, and experienced technical folks considered certifications to have little value. Certification gets a bad rap because of this trend. Professionals offended by the number of freshly certified IT people then began to seek "higher level" certifications such as Cisco's CCNA, CCNE, and others because they were perceived as legitimate, while those from other vendors weren't.

Fast-forward to present day, and IT certifications are still a thing; certain certifications are still considered more legitimate and worthy than others. A good example is the Certified Information Systems Security Professional (CISSP). This high-level certification has become so popular that an entire industry is now built around it. There are courses, study guides, boot camps, exam pass guarantees, cram sessions, hundreds of books, and more. When the industry becomes saturated with this certification, which was once very highly regarded, a new contender for everyone's attention and money will rise up to replace it as the next big certification to earn.

Certifications can be valuable, but I have reservations about jumping onto a trend that's likely to die out as quickly as it appeared. You should seek time- and job-tested certifications that offer value for your current job or the job you want.

Preparing for a Certification Exam

I've heard that "experience is the best teacher," but experienced professionals can still fail expensive certification exams. Do yourself a favor and prepare for the exam regardless of your level of expertise, experience, or job duties. Exams have a way of wording questions that can confuse or mislead the most experienced professionals. Don't take the exam lightly, and don't assume that you already know everything. Certification exams are serious business.

Hundreds of books and other preparation materials are available for free or at a reasonable cost. You should take practice exams to learn how exam question writers phrase scenarios. Most exams are scenario-based. This means that you have to be able to *apply* your knowledge and not just remember facts. Remembering facts will help you with some questions, but you must read a scenario and decide based on your options. And the scenarios and questions are rarely straightforward. My best advice is to use at least two different study sources by different authors to have a range of perspectives and practice questions written by multiple authors.

Taking the Exam

On the day of your exam, arrive at the testing center a little early so you can sign in, calm down, use the restroom, and get into a test-taking mindset. The test proctor will escort you into the exam room, which is sometimes private but can be a room where multiple people are also taking exams. Before entering the exam room, the proctor will have you empty your pockets, remove your jacket, and surrender your cell phone. Your belongings will be placed in a locker while you take the exam. If you're allowed to have any scratch paper and a pen, those will be provided to you at exam time. Proctors will advise you of exam rules and conduct during the exam. Once you're finished with the exam, instructions will appear on the screen to tell you what to do next, typically returning to the main desk to receive your exam results. Most exams are scored when you finish them, so you'll know whether you passed before leaving the exam facility. The proctor may provide you with your exam results. The proctor will also return your belongings to you from your locker.

If you fail an exam and want to retake it, resume your studies as soon as possible while the exam questions and subject matter are fresh in your mind. Your exam results will often highlight your strongest and weakest topics so that you can focus on those before you retake the exam. Do retake the exam until you pass. Once you're certified, no one will care how many times you have to take the exam. Use your new certified designation in your email signature, LinkedIn profile, professional correspondence, and online profiles. The next section covers independent study to enhance your technical skills.

Educating Yourself

There's nothing wrong with earning a certification. No one will ever view it as a negative career move, although it might not impact your current or future job success. If certifications aren't your thing, try some independent study. At one time, in IT shops, training was almost nonexistent. Companies didn't want to pay for professional development training; the alternative is to educate yourself at your own expense and time.

I have spent thousands of dollars and many, many hours educating myself. I purchased and set up multiple systems in my garage, onto which I installed various operating systems and experimented. I installed operating systems, applications, and automation software. At one time, I had a Hyper-V infrastructure, a vSphere infrastructure, dozens of virtual machines comprising multiple Linux distributions, multiple Microsoft desktop and server systems, and even a few one-offs such as FreeBSD, FreeDOS, and a few others that I can't recall. I would solve hardware, software, networking, printing, and application problems independently. Expanding my knowledge beyond my day job has kept me gainfully employed in full-time corporate jobs and a healthy freelance career for over 20 years. Part of my independent-study result is what you're currently reading in this book.

Independent study can make you stand out in a crowd. For example, a very old Solaris system in one of our computer labs had experienced a failure. Due to layoffs and attrition, no one knew how to fix the system because the version of Solaris was so old. Unfortunately, the system owners also didn't know how to fix it, but it had to be fixed because real dependencies were built around it. A company-wide email was issued to find someone who knew how to fix this computer dinosaur. I saw the email but ignored it until one of my colleagues, who knew of my independent study and history of solving weird problems, spoke up and volunteered me for the task. I successfully got the system working again that afternoon. The customer was grateful, and I received a few accolades and a gift card for a nice dinner for my efforts.

Independent study doesn't require a big investment in hardware and software. You can sign up for free or inexpensive virtual infrastructure and explore cloud solutions, N-tier database setups, peer-to-peer networking, software development, and other technologies and solutions that would cost thousands of dollars to build on your own. Through independent discovery and exploration, you can develop skills with technologies you ordinarily wouldn't have access to. I encourage you to search online to find independent-study opportunities.

The next section explores a newer aspect of training in traditional colleges and universities.

Formalizing Your Education

During my more than 25 years in the IT industry, I've found that coworkers who don't have degrees are about as common as those who do. I've had managers who never went to a day of college. I've also worked with some people who earned master's and PhD degrees in fields other than IT. Many of them, like myself, came to IT from other industries as career changers. There are multiple reasons for IT ranks being filled with people with degrees as diverse as psychology, English, and physics. Traditional colleges and universities didn't support IT training until somewhat recently. Sure, a few colleges and universities offered management information systems (MIS) and computer information systems (CIS) degrees before that time. Still, these programs were light on content and not well-respected in the industry in the early days. These days, full degree programs cover game development, data science, networking, security, and cloud technologies.

One of the best approaches to advanced IT training is that some colleges and universities offer remote, online, and self-paced study, which is optimal for working professionals who want to further their education and skills without the traditional residence requirements. But not all degree programs are created equal. Some programs are not well-received in the industry, and you should research before spending thousands of dollars on a degree that many employers will dismiss as inadequate.

For example, security is a hot topic right now, and many colleges offer security training and degree programs, some of which also have a certification component. Do your research to find out which of them your employer supports. If your employer has a tuition reimbursement program, ask the coordinator if the college you're exploring is on the approved list. If it isn't, keep looking until you find one that is.

The next section covers on-the-job training, which means gaining experience and education by doing a job.

Using Your Job as Education

Checking job descriptions might lead you to believe that some magical equation translates years on the job to years of education, and you'd be right. The magical ratio is one year of education equals two years of experience. This isn't my opinion but an accepted industry standard. A document (*https://oreil.ly/SSE3k*) provided by Coordinated Care Services, Inc. (CCSI) states it explicitly for a range of education and experience. Education is important, but job experience is the real winner for landing most industry jobs.

Multiple online sources discuss the struggle between education and experience. Search for yourself using "experience vs. education" and you'll see. The debate has raged for years. When you have no experience, the requirement for experience is a high barrier to employment.

To solve the education versus experience dilemma is to gain on-the-job experience to complement your education. But how do you gain experience when you have none? You should explore volunteer opportunities, internships, and student apprenticeships, as well as documenting your work and research.

Volunteer opportunities don't always present themselves—you must look for them. You could offer desktop and network support at churches, local theaters, volunteer organizations, schools, and even commercial businesses such as law firms, restaurants, and retail stores. Explain that you want to gain job experience and would like to volunteer your time for desktop support, network support, security, document management, website creation and maintenance, and other computer-related tasks. Many businesses either can't afford to hire IT support or don't need someone full-time and will welcome the opportunity to partner with you.

Internships and student apprenticeships are excellent ways to gain real job experience. These jobs, often subsidized by the government, colleges, or businesses, offer you employment that often is part of a degree, work-study, or scholarship program. Some internships and apprenticeships are competitive rather than based on need alone. Check with your school counselor, local employment office, or online sources to find out about such programs in your area.

You should also document your research and work. For example, if you build computers, install and administer Linux systems, build specialized hardware, or code your own applications, you can document this work and add it to your résumé. Your work has career relevance and value to a potential employer, so write it down.

Once employed, try to learn everything you can about the business. Learn its business cycles, profitable areas, weaknesses, vulnerabilities, position in the marketplace, and current outlook.

Summary

Education and training are both important to your career arc. You must maintain your technical edge by keeping up with the latest versions, updates, security issues, and improvements in your industry. You must keep your certifications up to date with continuing education units and take the latest exams. Remember to document all software and hardware vendors, versions, and special features with which you work in your job because these items are important résumé builders.

It's important to note that your value increases with everything you learn, whether from a class or on the job. Learn all you can from every possible source, and demonstrate your ability to put your learning into practice at the command line or in the data center.

The next and final chapter of this book covers making career moves. In it, I discuss starting your own business, moving into management, and a lot of general information on moving your career forward and avoiding pitfalls along the way.

## CHAPTER 15

Making Career Moves

Sure, our parents or grandparents might have started a job right out of high school or college, stayed with it for thirty or more years, and then retired, but that just isn't the way careers go these days. And by *these days*, I mean for the past thirty years. In the various technology-related careers, it's rare to find anyone in the same position with the same company for over five years.

From personal experience, I worked for EDS and HP for sixteen years, but I held several positions within each company during that time. Most of my jobs lasted from eighteen months to two-and-a-half years. It was prudent to switch roles often, although all were lateral moves, and I grew and learned in each one. I worked for the same manager three or more times during my tenure at EDS and HP. We both moved around inside the company and kept crossing paths. It seemed that managers moved around as often as regular employees. In those days of massive and continuous layoffs, it was wise to be a moving target.

These days, career moves aren't seen as unfavorable. One recruiter told me that some managers and companies view a technical person who doesn't make a move every eighteen to twenty-four months as less desirable as a potential candidate. I'm unconvinced that this is true. There's something to be said for someone stable enough to stay put for a few years and become competent in every aspect of their job. But you will, at some point, find yourself looking for a new job in system administration. This chapter explores the various ways to find employment, upgrade your job, and go after those highly desirable "dream" positions.

Starting Your Own Business

Have you ever thought of quitting your job and starting your own tech business? The desire for more money, or autonomy, leads you to conclude you can do it better, faster, or cheaper yourself. Or, maybe the thought of "being your own boss" appeals to you. For system administrators, being in business for yourself points to consulting, teaching, or freelancing. In all cases, it means directly selling your skills to companies. Not to be discouraging, but there are some things you need to know before you quit your job and embark on this new adventure.

Facing Self-Employment Realities

The primary reality you must face as an entrepreneur is that you are never your own boss. Every customer is your boss. When you work in a company, you generally have one manager to whom you report. Not so when you work for yourself. Your job now is to attract new customers and retain your current customers. You don't get to call in sick when you feel under the weather, you don't get to take a lot of time off for vacation, and your benefits are entirely your responsibility. This is to say, running a business is hard work.

If these realities of self-employment don't deter your interest, and you do decide to start your own business, one of your first steps should be to acquire insurance to protect yourself. Some insurance companies sell errors and omissions (E&O) insurance or some other indemnification policy to protect you against fraud, mistakes, and unhappy customers. Many community colleges offer business startup classes or small business management courses that you can take to test your venture's efficacy.

You should also incorporate your business either as an S corporation or a limited liability company (LLC). It's easy to do. If you need help, there is help available online, at the State Department, and from friends, consultants, attorneys, financial advisors, and accountants.

Managing Employees

If you thought being an employee was difficult, imagine managing employees. Dealing with vacations, sick leave, mistakes, customer care, and coworker interaction are all part of employee management. I advise you to state your expectations verbally and in writing before an employee begins work. You may do this via an employee handbook, one-on-one meetings, or other written and verbal communication forms. You should also have periodic meetings to give feedback on employee performance. Set up monthly or biweekly meetings to discuss expectations, performance, and employee issues. The number one complaint among employees is lack of communication. Don't let it happen on your watch if you've been there yourself.

You'll also have to manage payroll, taxes, and employee benefits. Engage a bookkeeping service, payroll service, or accountant to handle these tasks. Additionally, you must consider cost-of-living pay raises, bonuses, and compensatory (comp) time.

Hiring Contractors

You can operate your business without employees. Contract labor is more expensive than employees, but you don't manage vacations, comp time, bonuses, sick leave, or most other aspects of the employer/employee relationship. You still must deal with compensation and taxes for contractors. You must also set expectations for customer care and performance.

The primary problem with contract labor is that you have no control over their time, and control is the determining factor of whether someone is an employee or a contractor. Use caution when dictating working parameters so you don't cross the contractor/employee line. Get the advice of an attorney or tax accountant for rules governing contractors versus employees. Having contractors reclassified as employees by the Internal Revenue Service (IRS) is expensive and detrimental to your business. Always engage professional advice for this aspect of your business. The IRS or a qualified accountant will assist you in classifying resources as employees or contractors.

As you can see, operating a business isn't as simple as printing business cards and hiring yourself out as a contractor. There are many facets to running a business, even if it's a sole proprietorship. You need to seriously consider taxes, deductible expenses, profits, labor rates, medical benefits, and personal time before quitting your day job.

Many technology workers have started businesses and enjoyed challenges, successes, and failures. You've heard success stories of how a tech person started a business, sold that business, and is now retired or on to some new venture. You've also heard of those who try running their own companies only to return to corporate life as an employee. Don't worry; no negative stigmas are associated with going into business and returning to corporate life. Being in business is hard; it's not for everyone, and employers understand this.

The following section discusses moving into corporate management should you decide that being an employee is more to your liking.

Moving into Corporate Management

As a sysadmin, you've thought about moving from the bottom of the food chain to the corporate ladder. I considered it multiple times during my sysadmin years. Would I take a job in management and leave my technical life behind? That's a good question; you'll have to answer it at least once during your career.

Challenging Yourself

I believe that many sysadmins, myself included, think that managers don't understand what we do but realize that we're an essential part of the organization. We are the *doers* of the org chart. A senior manager once told me (and I'm quoting here), "I don't *do* anything, but I get things done." I'm sure he saw my eyebrows raise as if to say, "Yeah, I know. We all know." He didn't respond to my unsubtle reaction to his statement. He did have a point, though. The issue was that he wasn't employed to push buttons, pull levers, or reboot computers, but he was in a place to ensure someone pulled those levers and pushed those buttons. You see, management is a different perspective. Managers carry orders from above and get credit for their direct reports. The managers, in turn, are supposed to reward their achievers.

Being a manager isn't easy. A lot of corporate responsibility rests on your shoulders, but the real rewards are dispersed above your pay grade for your work via direct reports. Managers have to "play politics," which means they must strike a balance between the people on the front lines, such as the help desk technicians, desktop technicians, sysadmins, network admins, database administrators, and so on. These direct reports may be overworked, disgruntled, and underappreciated. At the same time, your manager's managers have no clue what the people at the bottom of the food chain do to keep the wheels of business turning.

Perhaps, like the captain of a ship, the upper-level managers don't need to row the boat nor care how you do it, but they need to ensure that it happens on demand and at the required pace. I don't like it, but I understand it.

Before you move into management or entertain the idea of moving into management, you'll have to weigh the costs against the benefits. One of the costs is your relationship with your former coworkers. It might not matter how long you spent in the trenches, because once you put on your management cap, your former colleagues might perceive you differently.

Managing Your New Role

If your company offers management courses, take them. These courses will teach you some generic management rules, but what you're looking for are *corporate culture* items. No matter the size, every company has its own corporate culture, and you must learn to navigate it. Training classes will help prepare you for your new role.

The next step in managing your new role is to request mentorship from a senior-level manager. Asking for mentorship will do multiple things for you. The first is that it puts you in the spotlight as someone who realizes the value of having a mentor. Second, you will have an automatic career advocate (your mentor), and you need an advocate to help you achieve your career goals. Third, it allows you to learn people management, corporate culture, and your organization from the top down. If you're a parent, how did you learn to be one? Perhaps from observing your parents. I recommend you learn from multiple managers to see different ways of managing people and decide for yourself on the best combination of techniques. Learn from someone who is not necessarily in your chain of command.

The remainder of this chapter provides some general advice that works for most technology positions, not limited to system administration. While the information here is somewhat generic, I believe you'll find value in it because it will help you enjoy a more productive, peaceful, and forward-moving career.

Changing with the Job Market

I once had a job recruiter tell me that open Linux system administrator jobs are rare and undervalued in the market. That was undoubtedly his experience in the city where we both lived at the time, but it isn't true for the national job market. Linux system administrators enjoy a good job market and have for many years. For sysadmins with at least five years of experience, you can find your choice of positions with excellent salaries.

According to the Bureau of Labor Statistics, the national job market in the US changes from year to year, but the outlook is still solid. The projection for Network and Computer Systems Administrators (the closest match I could find) is 5% growth over the coming ten years, with a median salary of just under $85,000 per year. This information is outdated, although the reported date is May 2020. The COVID-19 pandemic has changed the job market for technology professionals. One thing that has come from the pandemic is remote work. Before March 2020, most companies required employees to work in a physical office. This is no longer the case. Remote work is the new normal. And because it's the new normal, you must discipline yourself, make the most of conference calls and instant messaging, and excel at your job. In the following sections, you learn how to navigate online job boards, maintain focus during the workday, and work appropriately using conferencing and collaboration tools.

Searching Online Job Boards

Finding a job online is nothing new, but job boards have evolved dramatically in the last few decades. Job boards provide job seekers with listings by keyword search and include interviewing tips, résumé writing tips, job skills tests, and other educational opportunities for subscribers. I use four sites when looking for jobs for myself or helping other technology professionals find a job: LinkedIn, FlexJobs, Monster, and Indeed. Mentioning these sites here is not an endorsement, nor is the omission of other services a negative review of them. These are the sites I use.

Professional networking via LinkedIn

Finding a job that fits your skills and aspirations on LinkedIn (*https://oreil.ly/jn0Zs*) can be easier than on other job-only sites because LinkedIn uses your professional profile and résumé to build job search results and recommended job lists. LinkedIn is a social networking site where you can create your personal profile, connect with others, join groups, post information, search for job postings, and chat in real time with your connections.

LinkedIn includes several career tools:

- Job alerts
- Salary surveys
- Skill assessments
- Interview preparation
- Résumé builder

It has a learning platform that you can subscribe to in order to gain knowledge or enhance your current skills through online training. You can also subscribe to LinkedIn's premium service, which offers more tools and services for job seekers. If you want your job search to remain private, you can enable recruiters to see that you're available without announcing to the world that you're looking for a new job. I've personally had great success with LinkedIn, and I highly recommend that you develop your profile and start making connections.

Finding a better way to work with FlexJobs

I've held a FlexJobs (*https://oreil.ly/aKRdQ*) membership for several years (since 2014), primarily to search for freelance writing positions. But FlexJobs is more than a simple job search platform. It has some compelling features that I like:

- Job alerts
- A learning center
- Career advice
- Articles
- Seminars and web events
- Low cost ($50 per year)

For job seekers, the low cost and high value of FlexJobs get you a lot for a little. There are thousands of jobs available for all types of work. If you're looking for freelance or part-time employment, it's there. There are many high-paying remote and flexible location jobs on this site. It runs the entire range of positions from entry-level and unskilled to C-level executive positions.

Finding the right fit with Monster

Monster (*https://oreil.ly/v3DrX*) is the oldest online job search tool that I remember using. Many people use it and readily find jobs through it. Daily, I receive emails for open positions based on my résumé on Monster. In many ways, it's a bit behind the times because it doesn't have the richness of design and the number of tools that other sites do. It does have the following features:

- Job search
- Salary tools
- Career advice
- Articles and links to other resources

If you upload your résumé on Monster, you will immediately receive listings for jobs related to your career. Doing so can be helpful if you'd rather have some of the work done by recruiting agencies. The jobs I receive through Monster are mostly contract and contract-to-hire types, which I'm not interested in receiving. I need to turn off those notifications because I'm only interested in full-time, long-term employment outside my freelance work. Sign up on Monster, upload your résumé, and allow job notifications to hit your inbox, but don't use Monster exclusively.

Searching for jobs at Indeed

Indeed (*https://oreil.ly/kyHou*) bills itself as the #1 job site in the world. It's more than a simple job search engine. Like the other sites listed here, Indeed has career guides and information available. Although most features serve employers, that's not a bad thing. When you post your résumé and personal data on a site, you want potential employers to find you with as little hassle as possible.

A simple search for "Linux administrator" yields 841 job matches today. What I like most about Indeed are its speed and its transparency. You see everything known about the job as soon as the service displays a job match. For example, on the company's website, you know the job title, company name, salary, location, job description, and link to apply. No signing up, hassle, third parties, or other barriers exist. And when you're looking for a job, you don't want or need barriers, lengthy processes, or runarounds.

Searching for a job requires patience, trial and error, and wading through a lot of job "fluff," as I refer to it—meaning that some jobs sound good on the surface, but once you click on the description, you realize that you've wasted your time. It's part of the process. But once you've found your new position, you must master working remotely. It sounds easy, but it isn't always. The following section explores working remotely in detail.

Working Remotely

At first glance, working from home seems like the perfect situation, and it can be. Still, as one former coworker described, it can be a "less than optimal" experience. He meant that the lack of a commute to and from a traditional workplace can compel coworkers, managers, and executives to expect your availability every day, at all hours. He and I spent many 14- and 16-hour days working, on the phone, and at all hours of the night supporting customers to the detriment of our own home life and well-being.

Upper management expected us to work eight hours per day, handle maintenance during "off hours," and show up ready to work at the usual time the following day. The promise of "comp" time never came to fruition, nor did any bonuses or other perks. That was my experience, though I knew others who did receive comp time, bonuses, and further compensation for their efforts.

Maintaining focus throughout your workday

You have to be vigilant about how many hours you spend at your desk. You must remember to take your breaks, take lunch away from your work desk, and limit your workday to normal and reasonable hours. Don't feel compelled to work 12-hour days because you can work from home. You need your own time with your family, friends, and yourself.

The other issue that some people have is a lack of focus at home. They'll do laundry, walk their dogs, go grocery shopping, take long lunches, and abuse the privilege so that everyone becomes the subject of micromanagement. Some of those activities are normal even if you go into an office but don't overdo them. Stay at your desk. Do your work. When you're away from your desk, take your phone with you so that your coworkers may contact you in case of outages, questions, or other business-related reasons. There's no harm in taking a short walk or bike ride rather than multiple short breaks during a day, but be courteous about the time you take, let your coworkers know, and keep your phone handy.

Multiple short breaks or one long one can refresh you during the day. If you recall your activities in the office, you probably had some interactions with coworkers, lunches away from the office, and maybe even had access to an on-campus gym. You're entitled to these when you work from home as well. Remember that abusing the system hurts everyone. Focus when required and refresh when necessary.

The following section covers details to make remote collaboration with coworkers, managers, and those outside your organization the best experience.

Learning How to Communicate

Almost every job description lists "excellent written and verbal communication" as one of the job's requirements. Not everyone has to be a professional writer or a great public speaker. Still, you should strive to communicate clearly and professionally with your colleagues, clients, and management. Clear communications elevate your position and will enhance your career options. Using sarcasm, anger, too much humor, or a flippant conversational style makes you look unprofessional and unpromotable. It's not always easy to maintain a professional demeanor, but you must strive to do so.

The following sections focus on communicating using the various tools at your disposal. In electronic communications, meanings can be lost or twisted, so you must learn to share professionally by email, instant messaging/text, and video conference calls.

Working via video conference and instant messaging

If you've never worked remotely before, you should ready yourself and your computer for conference calls. That means you need a camera if you don't have one connected or installed on your computer. Most newer laptop computers have built-in cameras, but you'll have to purchase a USB camera if you use a desktop computer. You can use your mobile phone, but the quality and size are not optimal.

 You'll need to purchase, set up, and test your camera when looking for new positions because interviews now take place via conference calls.

You can purchase a USB camera for as little as $20 US from online sources. In the following section, I discuss video conferencing as a communication method for job interviews and your job and some guidelines for remote communications etiquette.

Video conference calling. Zoom (and other conference call software) calls have been commonplace since the onset of the COVID-19 pandemic. I don't expect that to change soon, because now many technology-oriented employees feel comfortable working remotely. There are a few dos and don'ts associated with video conferencing calls, and you should know them before interviewing or starting a new job:

- Be on time for the call.
- Dress appropriately.
- Mute when not speaking.
- Look into the camera when speaking.

- Avoid distractions.
- Speak clearly.

The old saying, "If you're not early, you're late," certainly holds true for conference calls. Joining calls just before they go live is not only courteous but also shows your enthusiasm for your position and lets the call organizer know that you value their time too. Dress and groom appropriately for your call. Pretend you're in the office and your meetings are "in person." You don't have to look like you're going to a posh affair, but you must look presentable and professional. Remember to mute your microphone when you're not speaking. It's distracting to others to have your microphone pick up random noises. You'd be surprised how well even distant sounds come through the call.

Look into the camera rather than at the people you're talking to on the screen. I know it's hard to do, but the person looking at you while speaking would rather see you looking back at them rather than peering to one side. You should avoid distractions while you're on a business call. Perhaps you've seen the video of the news anchor broadcasting from home when his children break into his room. The video is funny, and most people are forgiving, but it does have the effect of presenting you as less than professional. You must also focus on the call, avoiding being distracted by email, instant messages, or shopping. Attentiveness is professional and expected.

Speak clearly but don't shout into the microphone. Others can hear you better when you face the microphone and fully engage in the conversation. If you need to do something else during a call or if you're interrupted for some reason, be sure that you mute your microphone and turn off your video. You can still listen to the call without distracting others.

Instant messaging.   When you need to send a message, ask a question or set up a meeting, email seems too slow when you can simply send an instant message. Instant messaging can be handy, but it can also annoy your coworkers. Be polite and ask if the other person has time to chat with you. Instant messaging is the virtual equivalent of walking up and speaking to someone in their cubicle. Remember that during the workday, your coworkers are busy. Respect their time. Once you've engaged the other person, state your purpose or ask your question. Be friendly and concise with your conversations. And remember, instant messaging isn't private, so be careful what you write in text-based conversations.

Communicating via email

Email is a primary communication method between colleagues, friends, business associates, and family members and has been so for more than 40 years. Most of us couldn't carry on our daily lives without it, yet some still don't know the rules. Yes, there are rules for email, and we all should learn them. These ten rules will ensure that your email communications are professional and safe for all audiences:

- Be professional in all business communications.
- Be polite.
- Remember that email communications are court-admissible.
- Email can be forwarded and blind copied to others.
- Sarcasm and colloquialisms don't translate well electronically.
- Be careful about opening attachments.
- Email is a popular scam tool.
- Email can be spoofed.
- Do not Reply All.
- Check your spelling.

Maintaining a professional "tone" in business communications is an essential practice. Get to the point of your conversation early, don't ramble, and end the email with a professional signoff. Keep your email signatures professional too. Include your name, phone, company name, department, and title. Quotations and witty signoffs are generally unnecessary and often looked at as unprofessional. It is appropriate to include your gender pronouns in your signatures, such as He/Him, She/Her, or They/Them, and please be respectful of other people's gender pronouns in your communications.

A recipient may print, forward, or blind copy your message, and you have no control over what happens after it leaves your computer. Emails are court-admissible and may be used as evidence to incriminate and show a pattern of behavior. Sarcasm, jokes, and colloquialisms don't always have the same effect in email as in spoken conversation because the recipient can't read facial expressions or hear voice inflections that clue them into alternative meanings. You should avoid colloquialisms when using email to communicate with anyone from a different culture. The possibility of insult or misunderstanding is too great.

Being a system administrator or IT professional, you know (or should know) that email is a popular medium for phishing and scams. No, you haven't won a contest/lottery/raffle that you never entered. No one will deposit any money into your account to help them launder money from another country. Delete these attempts when they pass through your spam filters. Don't forward them to anyone. Ransomware, Trojan horse malware, and viruses are too common and costly to take any chances. Email can be spoofed. An email can look as if it came from a legitimate sender but turn out to be deceptive and is often dangerous to open.

Please check your spelling in email communications. Emails, especially business emails, look completely unprofessional with misspelled or incorrect words. Written communications are more formal than spoken ones. You should read your messages aloud before sending them to ensure they carry the correct meaning and that no one can misinterpret your message.

Leaving Your Current Position

When you leave your current position for another, there are specific rules or standards of conduct that you should adhere to. Not doing so will give you a bad reputation in the business and may limit future opportunities for career moves. You want each position to be a stepping stone for the next. You also want a credible work history. It's far more impressive to a potential employer that your former manager gives you a recommendation as compared to one from a former colleague. Accolades from former customers are also highly regarded if you feel comfortable soliciting them. In the following sections, I cover your resignation letter, your post-resignation behavior, and how to handle coworkers, managers, and customers after your announcement.

Writing the Resignation Letter

Writing letters of resignation is often one of the hardest things you'll do in your career. My emotions have run the gamut when writing resignation letters, and I've experienced joy, anger, depression, and fear. It's often hard to leave a job you love, and it's also hard to leave one where you've gained friends and comfort. You must take extra precautions when resigning from a position you don't like, and restraint is vital.

Giving notice of your intent to leave

The first item of business in your resignation letter is to state your intention to leave your position. Giving your resignation letter to your immediate supervisor or manager is typical. Address them in the letter as you would in a conversation with *Dear Ms. Alvarez* or *Dear Octavia*. Don't use "To Whom It May Concern" or other generic greetings, as it is rude.

Provide the date of your intended last day of work. It's customary in the United States to give a two-week notice of your intent to leave, although not required.

Describing your goals

Don't complain, deny, degrade, or state negative reasons for leaving. Instead, communicate your goals and reasons for going but don't write "to get a better job" or something similar. State your goals as "I've found a position that offers me the growth and opportunity I'm seeking in my career" or "My new position offers me advancement into management." It's also appropriate to state something like "I've decided to reprioritize my goals, and I'm pursuing a new opportunity that allows me to <state the opportunity>."

This letter is not the appropriate place to air your grievances. Be professional and concise. You don't need to write more than one or two sentences that define your goals in seeking a new job.

Offering to help during the transition

State in your letter that you are willing and eager to help transition your duties and responsibilities to a new person. If you have someone in mind who could take over your role or cross-train with you, state, "I believe Anna is a good choice to transfer my duties to as she and I have worked together, and she has expressed an interest in expanding her role." Don't go into lengthy detail. It's your management's decision to choose Anna or a different person.

Leaving your options open

State that you're open to discussing your resignation with your manager. This statement leaves the option open with your management that there could be an opportunity for negotiation.

Sometimes a company values your work to the point that they will give you a counteroffer to stay. The decision to keep your job comes with some caveats, but staying is reasonable. A so-called "buy-back" is not uncommon, and any offer should be listened to and seriously considered.

I've heard both sides of the argument for staying versus leaving after being given a counteroffer. I don't have any particular advice on the matter except that if you're currently unhappy, you'll probably be unhappy again after you decide to stay. If you're not unhappy but are genuinely looking for opportunities that your current position doesn't offer, you now have a chance to discuss and negotiate them.

Delivering the letter

Delivering your resignation letter isn't easy, even if you hate your job. It's stressful and fear-inducing. I always print the letter, put it into an envelope with my manager's name, and place it on their desk when they're not in their office. That's just my nonconfrontational style. I don't know if it's correct or incorrect, but that's how I do it.

Your manager has the time to read your letter in private, discuss it with their manager, and craft a response. Often, an in-person resignation leads to spontaneous complaints or worse by both parties. This method obviously won't work if you're remote from your management.

Leaving Your Job

In some cases, your current employer may cut your notification time short. Some employers dismiss you after submitting your resignation letter with no discussion, negotiation, or exit interview. You have to prepare yourself for any outcome and response. Leaving a job can be as emotionally challenging as getting laid off or fired, and it's not easy for your employer or for you. These sections deal with working during your notification period and how to proceed with dignity and respect.

Transitioning your duties

Most of us feel some ownership of our systems, scripts, documentation, and accomplishments during our tenure at a job. It's normal to feel like you're letting go of something you own. Remember that you're taking on new challenges and leaving old ones behind. Transition your duties to your coworkers with kindness and respect. They're taking on new responsibilities and probably feeling overwhelmed because you're going, and they won't have your experience to rely on in a few days.

Completing unfinished tasks

Complete or transition any unfinished tasks before your last day, if possible. Don't leave a project half done if it's possible to finish. Your level of motivation will be low but remember that you have a responsibility to your coworkers to make this transition easy and comfortable for them.

Writing documentation

If you haven't done so during your tenure at your job, it's time to document what you do. Document your daily tasks. Identify quirks, scripts, and anything that might help a new person take over after you leave. Documentation isn't easy, but you must help your coworkers compensate for your absence. Do the right thing and provide plenty of instruction for them. Even if you hate your current employer, you'll feel better if you don't leave them in an unfavorable position. Doing your best at this point will mean that you don't have to make excuses, feel ashamed, or hide your face at a restaurant should you have a chance meeting with a former employer.

Handling your exit interview

If you have unresolved grievances, make them known during your exit interview. The exit interview is when you can help your former coworkers and clear the air with your employer. Remember to maintain a professional attitude. State facts, not emotional baggage, and then feel satisfied that you've told your employer how you think and why you're leaving.

Sometimes exit interviews have a significant impact on current and future employees. Some employers want to retain good people and attempt to improve a chronic or undesirable situation.

Summary

The last thing I want to tell you is when it comes to your career, don't listen to the naysayers. You will hear that job markets for whatever you're doing are poor, and you're in a dead-end career. Linux system administration is a good career choice. There's growth potential as a system administrator and plenty of jobs available. As more companies move to the cloud, you will have to shift your focus from managing local systems to managing cloud-based ones.

Work on getting your Linux certifications and supplement those with other technology certifications, such as networking and security. No matter where computing goes, security will always be a concern and an opportunity. Good luck to you in your searches and your career.

Index

W

warm rebooting, 164
wget utility, 72
Windows
    capabilities of Windows computers with
        Samba on Linux servers, 146
    drive letters, 4
    interoperability with Linux and Unix, 145
        (see also Samba)
    monitoring Windows-compatible filesystem
        statistics with cifsiostat, 134
    providing services to Windows clients,
        150-156
        browsing for shared directories, 154
        mounting Windows system shares, 155
        serving network storage to desktop cli-
           ents, 150-152
work and research, documenting, 200
working remotely, 208
    via video conference and instant messaging,
        209
world group, 18
    (see also other permissions)
world readable files, 18
write (w) permissions, 15

X

x (see execute permissions)
XFS, 78
    creating for new disk partition, 85
    using filesystem with quota system, 103
xfs_growfs command, 91
xorg-x11-server-common package, 175
xorg-x11-server-utils package, 175

Y

yum-utils package, 60
YUM/DNF utility, 58
    default behavior for updates, 106
    dnf groupinstall command, 70
    dnf install aide command, 187
    using yum to patch Red Hat Enterprise
        Linux–based system, 105
    yum remove command, 175
    yum update command, 58

Z

ZFS, 78
zones (SSH), 52

About the Author

Kenneth Hess has been a Linux system administrator for more than 25 years and a technology writer and journalist for the past 20 years. Kenneth has written hundreds of articles covering desktop Linux, virtualization, databases, and the general topic of system administration.

Colophon

The stately animal on the cover of *Practical Linux System Administration* is a Breton horse.

Although their ancestral origins are disputed, Breton horses were bred in the Brittany region of France as early as the Middle Ages, when they were sought for their strength, stamina, and comfortable riding gait. Today, two subtypes of Breton horse are widely recognized: the lighter, more agile Postier Breton and the heavier Trait Breton. The latter is regarded as more suitable for agricultural work, though both types are principally raised as a source of food.

Relatively small for draft horses, Bretons are typically around 15 hands in height at the shoulder and weigh 1,250 to 1,700 pounds. They are most commonly a rich chestnut or roan color, with flaxen manes and tails, and occasionally some limited white markings.

Due in part to their perceived quality and versatility, Bretons remain quite common as draft horses in France and are exported worldwide. From a conservation standpoint, they are not considered to be at risk. Many of the animals on O'Reilly covers are endangered; all of them are important to the world.

The cover illustration is by Karen Montgomery, based on an antique line engraving from *Histoire Naturelle*. The cover fonts are Gilroy Semibold and Guardian Sans. The text font is Adobe Minion Pro; the heading font is Adobe Myriad Condensed; and the code font is Dalton Maag's Ubuntu Mono.

Printed in the USA
CPSIA information can be obtained
at www.ICGtesting.com
LVHW081949271223
767554LV00011B/187